Thinking About
Android Epistemology

Thinking About
Android Epistemology

Edited by
Kenneth M. Ford,
Clark Glymour, & Patrick J. Hayes

Menlo Park ⊂ Cambridge ⊂ London
AAAI Press & The MIT Press

Chapter 2, "On Computational Wings" by Kenneth M. Ford and Patrick J. Hayes is copyright © 1998, *Scientific American*. Reprinted with permission.

Chapter 6, "From 2001 to *2001*" by Douglas Lenat is copyright © 1996, The MIT Press. Reprinted with permission.

Chapter 8, "Conceptual Similarity Across Sensory and Neural Diversity" by Paul Churchland is copyright © 1998, *The Journal of Philosophy* and Paul Churchland. Reprinted with permission.

Chapter 9, "Alienable Rights" by Marvin Minsky is copyright © 1993, The Walt Disney Company. Reprinted with permission of *Discover Magazine*.

Chapter 10, "Cognitive Wheels: The Frame Problem of AI" by Daniel Dennett is reprinted with permission of the copyright holder.

Chapter 11, "Dennett's Beer" by Henry Kyburg, Jr. is copyright © 1987, Ablex Publishing. Reprinted with permission.

Chapter 13, "Too Many Instincts" by Susan G. Sterrett is copyright © 2000, Taylor and Francis. Reprinted with permission.

Chapter 16, "The Adventures Among the Asteroids of Angele Android" by Clark Glymour is copyright © 1987, Ablex Publishing. Reprinted with permission.

Figures 8a and 9a in Chapter 7, "Imagination and Situated Cognition" by Lynn Stein are copyright © 1992, IEEE. Reprinted with permission.

Copublished and distributed by The MIT Press, Massachusetts Institute of Technology, Cambridge, Massachusetts and London, England.

ISBN-10: 0-262-56217-0
ISBN-13: 978-0-262-56217-1

Front cover art by Lamar Sorrento, Memphis, Tennessee.

PRINTED IN THE UNITED STATES OF AMERICA

Contents

Part Three: The Frame Problem

Part Four: Android Abilities

Part Five: Conclusion

Preface & Acknowledgements

Clark Glymour, Kenneth M. Ford,
& Patrick J. Hayes

This book is a gentle, unsystematic introduction to the subject we call *android epistemology*. Many of the essays in this book are meant to be fun—even funny—but they all have a serious point. No knowledge of computer science, statistics, or logic is necessary to read them, learn from them, and, we hope, be stimulated to learn a lot more. This is an invitation, not a textbook.

We humans think we are pretty special. For millennia, the great problem of philosophy has been how the world and individual human minds together can create human theoretical and practical understanding and competence. From Aristotle until almost yesterday, the questions of epistemology and philosophy of mind have been about *us;* about our capacities, our limitations, the structures and processes that constitute our cognition, and the best ways to use our faculties to acquire interesting, practically or theoretically useful knowledge, and to avoid error. Except for philosophical discussions of God and gods, and occasional, usually dismissive, remarks on dogs, horses, and gorillas, no alternative to the human mind has had much role in traditional philosophy. There are reasons, of course: ours are the most remarkable minds we know about and the minds we think we know best. Even so, rigorous imagination ought to have a role in philosophy. There ought to be theories about other sorts of minds, other ways minds could be constituted to produce knowledge and competence. Until the mid-twentieth century, however, there were no means to think about such questions, no way to specify, to inquire or to demonstrate the capacities and limitations of other conceptions of mind or of modifications of our minds. The emergence of artificial intelligence has changed all that. Artificial intelligence has provided a means to think about various ways in which physical systems can be organized and structured to produce or extend behavioral competence, representations of the world, representations of desire and preference, communication, and plans for action. Through the digital computer, artificial intelligence provides a means to make theories and proposals sufficiently concrete that their properties and consequences can be demonstrated and studied. Through computation theory, we are able to study the powers and limits of very general kinds of systems that learn.

The subject of this book is android epistemology, and it has two sides, one theoretical and one more applied. On the theoretical side, android epistemology is an open and expanding body of theories and proposals about computational architectures for cognition, theories and proposals some of which are biologically or psychologically inspired, and others of which are free floating—never mind how *people* are able to do *x*—maybe a computational system could do *x this* way. Whatever one thinks of particular proposals or efforts, this is a grand, open, inviting, fascinating and potentially endless endeavor. On the other, more practical side, android epistemology is about how to use such ideas to extend human capacities. It is about how computational systems can serve as cognitive prostheses, helping us to overcome our cognitive limitations, to make us smarter, and, one might hope, wiser. In an abundance of mostly invisible ways, the second aspect of android epistemology is spreading throughout civilization. Financial institutions—banks and credit card companies, for example—rely on artificial intelligence methods to read applications and to detect fraud. Scientists routinely use computerized methods to form new variables and to classify and predict, using methods that developed out of the combination of artificial intelligence with statistics and that would have been utterly unthinkable fifty years ago. New forms of web browsers are emerging from logical approaches to artificial intelligence. New forms of computerized instruction, with programs that learn about what the student is, and is not, learning, are emerging from the combination of artificial intelligence and psychology. These aids do not make us androids, any more than does the use of an abacus, slide rule, or pocket calculator, but they do apply android epistemology.

This volume contains several essays from the first edition of *Android Epistemology,* and several new essays not included in that earlier book. Two of the essays collected here have not been previously published. The essays in the book are divided into four parts. The placement of essays is a bit arbitrary and several of the essays could have been relocated.

Part One, *Why Android Epistemology?* consists of four essays that provide a history and defense of the very idea of android epistemology. The first essay, "Prehistory of Android Epistemology," by Clark Glymour, Kenneth Ford, and Patrick Hayes, provides an historical survey of philosophical ideas that form the background to android epistemology. Ford and Hayes's essay "On Computational Wings" is a defense of the very idea of intelligent computers or robots against various arguments that the idea is absurd. The essay draws a vivid analogy between these arguments and "proofs" early in the twentieth century that heavier-than-air flight is impossible. Anatol Rapoport's "The Vitalists' Last Stand" draws another connection, this one between a history of arguments that biological systems have a "vital force" that cannot be explained by chemistry and physics and arguments that machines cannot have minds. Glymour's "Silicon Reflections," published for the first time here, is an entertainment delivered in the 1980s as an after-dinner speech to the North Carolina Philosophy Colloquium, exploring the dilemmas that might result from replacing parts of brains by computer chips. The idea has been discussed by several philosophers since this essay was first circulated.

Part Two, *Designs for Cognition* contains five serious essays, the last of which is also (we think) pretty funny. The late Herbert Simon was one of the creators of artificial intelligence, and his essay "Machine as Mind" lucidly presents his mature view of a computational structure that is mental. Douglas Lenat's essay compares the abilities of HAL, the computer in the film *2001: A Space Odyssey,* with the abilities that we know how to put into computers today, and with what is in prospect. Lynn Stein's essay concerns the interaction of programs for higher-level cognition with the details of robotic programs for sensation and motion. She argues, with examples, that intelligent robots must have the ability to use imagination appropriate to their situation in order to effectively plan actions. Paul Churchland's "Conceptual Similarity" describes the elements of a neural-net architecture for cognition and addresses—so far as we know for the first time—a fundamental question: What could it mean for two neural nets to have the same idea or concept? Marvin Minsky's "Alienable Rights" is a conversation among aliens with a very different computational architecture than ours, lamenting the drastic limitations of our own.

Part Three, *The Frame Problem,* consists of three essays that very broadly concern how an intelligent computational system can deal with what changes and what does not. We have not included the original statement of the problem by John McCarthy and Patrick Hayes because it is more technical than the rest of this collection, and widely reprinted elsewhere. Daniel Dennett's "Cognitive Wheels: The Frame Problem of AI" contains a vivid and delightful interpretation of the problem, and argues that its solution can be found in biologically faithful computational models. Henry Kyburg argues in "Dennett's Beer" that solutions to the frame problem are to be found in the assessment of probabilities and by rejecting (and ignoring) bizarre properties (the distance of a glass of beer from Saturn, for example) that change a lot but almost certainly have no influence on the properties we care about (good beer?). "Goldilocks and The Frame Problem" by Patrick Hayes, Kenneth Ford, and Neil Agnew, argues that philosophical discussions of the frame problem have for the most part missed the point.

Part Four, *Android Abilities,* begins with an essay, "Too Many Instincts" by Susan Sterrett that draws on the history of biology and philosophy to argue for a certain kind of behavioral flexibility as the mark of intelligence, specifically, the ability to appropriately override "instinctive or habitual patterns of action. In "Could a Robot Be Creative—and Would We Know?" Margaret Boden proposes that creativity involves the exploration and transformation of conceptual spaces, and that this aspect of creativity could be realized by a robot. She explores the circumstances in which we could recognize this aspect of robot creativity. Joseph Nadeau contributes an essay on ethics that uses contemporary results in the psychology of judgment to argue for the wonderfully implausible thesis that only an android could be ethical. Glymour's "Adventures Among the Asteroids of Angela Android, Series 8400XF" is a short story illustrating the power of recent algorithms for learning causal relations. It contains two of the seven words that cannot be said on television.

Our volume concludes with some reflections by the editors on the social role of the computer as *cognitive prosthesis.* We suggest that the computer is a force for economic equality exactly because it is a force both for expanded cognitive competence and for cognitive equality. The human results, of course, depend on the sum of all forces.

Acknowledgements

We are especially grateful to Rebekah Lee, who undertook the painstaking task of contacting authors, transcribing texts from a variety of sources to form a uniform manuscript, and provided a first edit. Our gratitude as well to the many contributors who allowed us to reprint their essays, several of whom kindly agreed to slight modifications we thought required to provide context for their work. Selecting, assembling and editing this work was done in spare time afforded us through the Institute for Human and Machine Cognition from support from the Office of Naval Research, the National Aeronautics and Space Administration and the State of Florida.

Pensacola, Florida
February 2006

Part One

Why Android Epistemology?

1 The Prehistory of Android Epistemology

Clark Glymour, Kenneth M. Ford,
& Patrick J. Hayes

Contemporary artificial intelligence (AI) can be viewed as essays in the epistemology of androids, an exploration of the principles underlying the cognitive behavior of any possible kind of mechanical agents. Occasional hyperbole and flimflam aside, artificial intelligence is a wonderful subject, full of new ideas and possibilities, unfettered by tradition or concern (other than inspirational) for the accidents of human constitution, but disciplined by the limits of mechanical computation. More than other new sciences, AI and philosophy have things to say to one another: any attempt to create and understand minds must be of philosophical interest. In fact, AI *is* philosophy, conducted by novel means. That AI emerged from ideas in computer science is, of course, a familiar observation. The central insights of Charles Babbage, Alan Turing, John von Neumann and other pioneers on how a machine might actually be built that could manipulate and be influenced by symbols are widely recognized. But for all the novelty, many of the central ideas that animate AI, and even particular techniques and themes prominent in contemporary practice, have a long philosophical ancestry. In fact, the sources of key assumptions and insights underlying much of AI—such as that the mind is computational, that computational devices can be a simulacrum of the mind, the fundamental idea that machines can "calculate" with symbols for things other than numbers, and that there is a plethora of possible artificial minds yet to be invented—are deeply embedded in the history of philosophy. This background includes the history of logic, the emergence of combinatorics, the merging and separating of theories of deduction and computation from psychological theories, the formation of the first program for a possible cognitive agent, characteristic designs of programs for machine learning, characterizations of conditions for causal inference, and no doubt a good deal more. In addition to any list of ideas, there is what might best be characterized as an attitude towards machinery. AI has an engineer's respect for things that work and a pragmatic willingness to try anything that will produce the results needed. In the spirit of medieval astronomy, it wants only to save the phenomena, not to hypothesize psychological truth. While important parts of modern science have emerged from trying to understand machines—for example; thermodynamics and steam engines—the direct intellectual merging of philosophy and engineering seems strange, even rather outrageous, in our modern academic culture. But many earlier philosophers seem to have had a similar kind of affection and respect for machinery. This essay attempts briefly to survey some of the philosophical sources of contemporary ideas about AI More extended treatments can be found in Glymour (1992) and in Haugeland (1985).

Back to the Greeks: Plato and Aristotle

According to both Plato and Aristotle, the objects of knowledge have a special *formal structure.* The sort of thing a person may know is that one thing or kind of property is (necessarily) a *finite combination* of other things or kinds of properties. *Man* is a combination of *rational* and *animal.* *Triangle* is a combination of *closed, rectilinear, figure,* and *three-sided.* Plato and Aristotle differed about the metaphysics, of course. For Plato these combinations are ideal objects or forms; for Aristotle they are essential attributes of concrete objects. With both philosophers, however, all knowledge consists of knowing such combinations of forms or essential attributes of a thing or kind. According to Plato, knowledge of virtue is knowledge of which simple forms are combined in the form of virtue. Any AI knowledge engineer will recognize the idea and be attracted by its computational virtues. The anticipations are, however, more detailed. In the *Meno,* Socrates and Meno search for an answer to the question "What is virtue?" The Socratic method is to collect positive and negative examples and to search for hypotheses that cover the positive and exclude the negative. In the course of the dialogue, Meno points out through a question the first theorem of computational learning theory: how will Socrates and Meno know when they have found the correct answer? Meno's point, of course, is that they cannot solely on the basis of a finite sample decide the truth of a contingent, universal claim by any rule that will yield the truth in all logically possible circumstances consistent with the sample. Socrates's response to Meno is that the process of discovery is what is now called in AI *explanation-based reasoning*. Everyone, according to Plato, already knows implicitly at birth all of the laws of forms. The process we think of as empirical discovery is simply a matter of realizing which formal truth, or consequence of laws of forms, applies to a particular set of cases and adding that truth to one's explicit knowledge.

The conjunctive view of the objects of knowledge suggests questions about combinations of properties. Ultimately, on either the Platonic or Aristotelian view, any property that can be the object of scientific knowledge can be analyzed into a combination of simple properties that cannot be further analyzed. The number of distinct kinds that can be the objects of knowledge then consists of the number of distinct combinations of these simple properties, whatever they are. What is the number of pairs of distinct properties if there are n properties altogether? What is the number of triples of distinct properties if there are n properties altogether? What is the number of distinct combinations of any particular number m of properties drawn from n properties? How can these distinct combinations be enumerated and surveyed? If one has the Platonic-Aristotelian conception of the form of knowledge, these are fundamental questions.

In Europe, such questions gave rise to the mathematical subject of combinatorics, the study of the numbers of possible combinations satisfying given conditions. The first mathematical results of this kind in the West seem to occur in a commentary on Aristotle by Porphyry, written in the third century C.E. Porphyry wished to comment on all of the similarities and differences among five Aristotelian "voices," and so he posed the problem of enumerating all the distinct pairs of things that can be obtained from a collection of five things. He observed that one might think that this number is 20, because one can choose the first thing of a pair in any of five ways, and the remaining member of the pair in four distinct ways. But Porphyry correctly argued that the number of pairings is not 20:

> Such is not the case; for though the first of the five can be paired with the remaining four, when we come to the second, one of the pairs will already have been counted; with the third, two; with the fourth, three and with the fifth, four; thus there are in all only ten differences: 4 + 3 + 2 + 1 (cited in Edwards 1987, p. 20).

Roughly 250 years later, Boethius wrote commentaries on Porphyry's commentary on Aristotle, and in them he provided a more general, alternative proof. But Porphyry's combinatoric result seems not to have been significantly extended until the Renaissance. Even without technical advances, however, combinatoric ideas remained important.

In the Middle Ages, the conception of the objects of knowledge as combinations of simple attributes that make up a kind or a complex property led to a conception of the method for acquiring knowledge. The method, insofar as it deserves the name, consisted of trying to "analyze" a thing into its simple properties (analysis) and then trying to put it back together by combining those properties (synthesis). Sometimes—in Renaissance chemistry, for example—"analysis" meant physically decomposing a substance into "simpler" substances, and "synthesis" meant physically reconstituting a substance of that kind, but for the most part the analysis and synthesis were purely mental.

Ramón Lull and the Infidels

After the reintroduction of classical learning into Christian Europe, one would expect that Christian intellectuals would have applied the methods they had learned from Aristotle and Plato to the study of God, and they did. God, too, had fundamental properties, and one could consider the combinations of His attributes. In the thirteenth century, questions of how to enumerate, organize, and display God's attributes led to a fundamental insight—one that we nowadays take for granted. It concerns the odd life of the great Spanish philosopher, Ramón Lull, a thirteenth century Franciscan monk.

The notion of mechanical aids in carrying out an algorithm and the notion of an algorithm itself are ancient, perhaps prehistoric. But one of the central insights of modern computational thinking, the idea that machines can aid nonnumerical and nongeometrical reasoning through manipulating discrete symbols, first appeared in the West (as far as we know) in the writings of Ramón Lull. The source of Lull's idea lay in a traditional metaphysical view and in the slowly emerging mathematics of combinatorics. Lull's motives, however, were entirely religious.

Lull's life illustrates that a philosopher can also be a man (or woman) of action, if only bizarre action. Lull grew up in a wealthy family and passed his early adulthood in the court of James II of Spain. He spent his time with games and pleasantries and is reputed to have made great efforts to seduce the wives of other courtiers. Accounts have it that after considerable effort to seduce a particular lady, she finally let him into her chambers and revealed a withered breast. Taking this sight as a sign from God, Lull gave up the life of a courtier and joined the Franciscan order, determined that he would dedicate his life to converting Muslim civilization to Christianity, and in a curious way, philosophy gained from that dedication.

Lull moved to the island of Majorca and spent several years mastering the Arabic language, studying and writing tracts (of which he eventually authored hundreds) against Islam and for Christianity. About 1274, Lull had a vision of the means by which Muslims could be converted to Christianity. Stimulated by the idea, he wrote another book, his *Ars Magna*. While Lull's fundamental style of thought is mystical and obscure, it contains one logical gem.

In effect, Lull's idea was that Muslims (and others) may fail to convert to Christianity because of a cognitive defect. They simply were unable to appreciate the vast array of the combinations of God's or Christ's virtues. But thanks to this vision, Lull believed that infidels could be converted if they could be brought to see the *combinations* of God's attributes. Further, he thought that a *representation* of those combinations could be effectively presented by means of appropriate machines, and that supposition was the key to his new method. Lull designed and built a series of machines to be used to present the combinations of God's virtues.

A typical Lullian machine consisted of two or more disks having a common spindle. Each disk could be rotated independently of the others. The rim of each disk was divided into sections or *camerae,* and each section bore a letter. According to the application for which the machine was intended, the letters would each have a special significance. They might denote, for example, an attribute of God. One Lullian machine, for example, has the letters "B" through "R" around the rims of an inner disk, and around the outer disk Latin words signifying attributes of God: Bonitas (B), Magnitudo (C), Eternitas (D), and so on. A Lullian machine was operated by rotating the two disks independently, much as we would a star finder or (some years ago) a circular slide rule. At any setting of the disks, *pairs* of God's attributes would be juxtaposed on the rims of the inner and outer disks. Rotating the disks would create different pairings. One would thus discover that God is Good *and* Great, Good *and* Eternal, Great *and* Eternal, and so forth. The heretic and the infidel were supposed to be brought to the True Faith by these revelations.

Lull lectured on several occasions at the University of Paris. He traveled throughout Europe attempting to raise money for missions to North Africa to convert Muslims to Christianity. He himself is reported to have made three such trips to Africa. Tradition has it that on his third trip, at the age of 83, he was stoned to death, but some biographers are so lacking in romantic sentiment that they dispute this account.

This story may seem a bizarre and slightly amusing tale of no particular philosophical significance. But buried within Lull's mysticism and his machines is the seed of a collection of powerful ideas that only began to bear fruit 350 years later in the seventeenth century. One of the great ideas implicit in Lull's work is that nonmathematical reasoning can be done, or at least assisted, by a mechanical process; the other is that reasoning does not proceed by syllogism but by combinatorics. Reasoning is the decomposition and recombination of representations. The decomposition and recombination of attributes can be represented by the decomposition and recombination of *symbols,* and that, as Lull's devices illustrate, is a process that can be made mechanical.

Computation and Discovery in the Seventeenth Century: Pascal, Leibniz, and Bacon

Lull's work was known even in the seventeenth century, when a version of his ideas was taken up by Leibniz to form one of many efforts of the period that strived, but failed, to articulate a theory of reasoning that joins logic, algebra, and combinatorics.

In 1642, Blaise Pascal, the French philosopher, mathematician, and inventor, perfected what until recently had been generally thought of as the first automatic calculating machine.[1] Like Lullian machines, Pascal's machine used rotating wheels, but unlike Lull's, it actually did something—addition and subtraction—including carries or borrows. This machine, called *Pascaline,* seems very simple now but was a contemporary public sensation raising both excitement and fear (not unlike today's AI research program; skeptics might add that Pascal's machine had a defect that AI may share: it cost more to produce than people were willing to pay for it.) Although the Pascaline's functionality was limited, it showed that tasks that previously might have been expected to require human attention or thought could be made fully, automatically mechanical. The process of building the calculating device seems to have had a substantial impact on Pascal's philosophical thinking. Anticipating an enduring controversy, in his *Pensées,* Pascal (1670/1932) remarked that "The arithmetical machine produces effects which approach nearer to thought than all the actions of animals." What animals have that the calculator lacked, Pascal wrote, is will.

Pascal's *Treatise of the Arithmetical Triangle*, in which the Binomial Theorem is first established, helped to make it evident that the analysis of combinations arising from the Aristotelian and Platonic traditions was an aspect of algebraic relations among numbers. Descartes's mathematical work had shown that geometry, the traditional mathematical language of the sciences, also had an algebraic side and that important geometrical properties could be characterized algebraically. By the middle and latter parts of the seventeenth century, algebraic relations, usually presented as geometrical statements of ratios, had become the form in which natural science expressed the laws of nature. Kepler's third law was essentially such a relation, and so was the Boyle-Mariotte law of gases, and the inverse square law of gravitation. It was only natural to suppose that the actions of the mind—thought—must also have laws that can be described by such relations, and that the combinatorics of analysis and synthesis are a hint of them. Gottfried Leibniz came to that very conclusion.

Pascal's *Treatise* was written in 1654. The next year Gottfried Wilhelm Leibniz, then nineteen years of age, published his first work, a Latin treatise on logic and combinatorics, *De Arte Combinatoria*. He did not yet know of Pascal's work, but he learned of it subsequently, and in later years when he journeyed to Paris, he tried unsuccessfully to meet with Pascal, who had retreated to religious quarters at Port Royal. Pascal had shown that the same combinatorial numbers or binomial coefficients also arise in relations between the terms of certain infinite series, and reflection on the properties of series eventually helped lead Leibniz to the discovery of the differential and integral calculus.

Leibniz's first work was really a combinatorial study of logic in the Aristotelian tradition—the only work on logic that Leibniz ever published. Over the course of the rest of his life, Leibniz wrote a long series of unpublished and incomplete papers on logic. They show the formation of some of the key modern ideas about deductive inference and proof, and they also show how very difficult the issues were for one of the greatest philosophers and mathematicians of the century. Leibniz's logical theory is not consistent and thorough (Leibniz had a difficult time completing anything), but it contains many ideas that were successfully elaborated in later centuries, and it also shows clearly the limitations of the Aristotelian framework.

Following tradition, Leibniz assumed that every proposition consists of a predicate applied to a subject and that in this regard the structure of language reflects the structure of the world. In the world, substances have attributes, but Leibniz gave this notion a twist. Substances don't, in his view, *have* attributes in the sense that one and the same substance could have an attribute or not have it. A substance *just is* a combination of attributes. You, for example, are nothing but the combination of all of the properties that you have, so there is no property that you in fact have that you could not have—an entity that didn't have some property you have wouldn't be you. So, finally, every property you have, you have *necessarily*. The same holds for any other substance in the world. Whatever properties a substance has, it has necessarily.

In Leibniz's theory, every concept *just is* a list or a combination of primitive concepts. All true propositions are true because the list of primitive concepts of the subject term is appropriately related to the list of primitive concepts of the predicate term. Leibniz says that every true proposition is true because it is an instance of the identity $A = A$. He meant that if a proposition is true, the subject and predicate lists will be such that by eliminating irrelevant parts of the subject, the same combination of concepts or attributes is found in the subject as is found in the predicate. So every true proposition can be given a proof. The proof of a proposition consists of the following:

1. Producing the combinations of simple concepts that are, respectively, the concept denoted by the predicate of the proposition and the concept denoted by the subject of the proposition.

2. Showing that the concept of the predicate is included in the concept of the subject.

Leibniz wrote extensively about these two steps. He never succeeded in making clear just how the analysis of concepts was to be obtained—of course, neither had Aristotle or the Scholastic tradition of analysis and synthesis. Leibniz envisioned the creation of an enormous dictionary or encyclopedia, a vision that was ridiculed by Jonathan Swift in the latter's account of Laputan scholarship and has not had a good reputation since the eighteenth century. In the 1950s, Yehoshua Bar-Hillel noted that a successful mechanical translator, in order to properly distinguish ambiguities such as "pen" in "the ink is in the pen" and "the sheep are in the pen," would have to have access to a huge database of all of human knowledge. Bar-Hillel's observation was considered a reductio ad absurdum argument for the impossibility of machine translation. But something like Leibnizian "dictionaries" are indeed being constructed in AI and used in machine translation, albeit with a rather more complex theory of the structure of knowledge, but still based on the idea—now reformulated with the aid of nineteenth and twentieth century logical theory—that in a computational sense, a concept simply is a combination of all that is known about it, so that a suitably rich enumeration and organization of all this knowledge is sufficient to capture the concept.

Leibniz was convinced that the production of scientific knowledge would become automatic if a universal dictionary could be assembled that expressed each concept in terms of the simplest concepts. He thought an algorithm or mechanical procedure could be found to carry out the second part of the procedure for giving proofs. The way to formulate such a procedure is to treat the problem as though it is part of algebra. Each simple term and each complex term should be given a letter or other symbol (Leibniz sometimes suggested using numbers as symbols for concepts), and then one would use algebraic methods to search for algebraic identities. On other occasions, he suggested representing concepts by geometrical figures, such as lines, and trying to carry out the second step of the aforementioned two-step process by geometrical procedures. The essential thing is that there is a *mathematics of reason* (in fact, that is the title of one of the logical papers Leibniz completed), and this mathematics can be carried out automatically.

Again, much of the current AI research, given more adequate flesh by developments in logic, is based on a modification of Leibniz's vision. One entire subfield of AI is concerned with "computational logic," a phrase that Leibniz would have understood immediately, and the mathematics of computational algebra is fundamental to theoretical advances in many subjects. Pascal and Leibniz would perhaps also have understood one aspect of the computational difficulties of this field. The reasoning process is indeed governed by combinatorics, quite aside from problems of undecidability. Combinatorial analysis shows that the search spaces of reasoning expand too rapidly to submit to straightforward enumeration, so the mathematics of reasoning seems to require clever algorithms that avoid exhaustive search and "dictionaries" of heuristics, which are the subject of active research.

Pascal's success with calculating machines inspired Leibniz to devise his own machine, which he called the *Stepped Reckoner*. Although conceptually much more sophisticated than either Wilhelm Schickard's Calculating Clock or Pascal's Pascaline, Leibniz's Stepped Reckoner appears never to have operated properly; its manufacture was beyond machining techniques of the day. Leibniz's efforts to build a better machine led him to realize that a binary notation would permit a much simpler mechanism than required for Pascal's and his decimal-based devices. He envisioned a binary calculator that would use moving balls to represent binary digits (Leibniz, 1679).[2] As noted by Stan Augarten (1984), the notion of binary representation had more than practical import for Leibniz. He regarded the remarkable expressiveness of binary enumeration as a sort of natural proof of the existence of God, asserting that it demonstrated that God, the omniscient *One,* had created everything out of *nothing.* Like Lull and Pascal before him, Leibniz attached deep religious significance to his efforts at mechanization.

The Pascaline's wheels carried numerals, and it performed arithmetic, but Leibniz saw that these machines were manipulating symbols in ways that were best understood in combinatoric terms and that there was nothing about the idea that restricted it solely to arithmetic. This insight was still rare during the first half of the twentieth century, when mechanical arithmetic had become a commonplace. An early British government report on the significance of computing machines declared on the grounds that there was not a great need for more gun-aiming tables, and they were therefore not worth the investment of much research effort.

In 1620, Francis Bacon's *Novum Organum* sought to provide the inductive method for the new science. Bacon described a nearly algorithmic procedure, later often ridiculed by twentieth century philosophers of science for whom the very idea of discovery by algorithm was anathema. Bacon's discovery procedure assumes the investigator is in search of the "form" of a phenomenon, which for Bacon, as for Aristotle and Plato, meant at least a conjunction of features are essential, necessary, and sufficient for the phenomenon. The investigator should then collect positive instances of the phenomenon, forming them in a table. Again, negative instances, otherwise as like positive instances as possible, should be collected in a table. Third, a table should be formed of instances exhibiting the phenomenon in varying degrees, if the phenomenon admits of such variation. Now the investigator should find—Bacon doesn't say how—whatever combination of features is common to all positive instances, absent from all negative instances, and concomitant in degree with the degree of the phenomenon in the table of degrees.

Bacon's problem setting and his method were revived around the middle of this century in the study in cognitive psychology of "concept learning." Procedures proposed by Jerome Bruner, and later by Earl Hunt, and still later by statistical concept learners, have their logical and historical roots in Bacon's method.

The Cartesian Way

René Descartes's mathematical innovations created linkages that proved essential to the very idea of a mechanics of mind. Descartes's algebraic geometry transformed aspects of the traditional geometrical formalism for the mathematical description of nature into systems of algebraic equations. With that transformation, an algebraic expression became possible for Johannes Kepler's laws, Robert Boyle's law, and so on. The binomial theorem in turn established connections between algebra and combinatorics, the mathematics of mind.

Yet, philosophically, Descartes was unconnected with the invisible thread that bound Thomas Hobbes, Gottfried Wilhelm Leibniz, and Blaise Pascal. The Cartesian conception of mind was not, like Hobbes's of a material device that represents by physical symbols and reasons by computation. Descartes's mind, it is almost too banal to note, was of an entirely different substance than matter; Descartes's mind could exist were nothing material to exist; Descartes's mind could be influenced by material conditions, but it was not bound by and characterized by the principles that constrain matter.

With some applied imagination, and perhaps a little heresy, this idea is tantalizingly close to the modern conception of software. Software is also immaterial and remarkably unconstrained by physical principles, yet when provided with a suitable material substrate (not a pineal gland), it can have startling material effects. The Cartesian error was only to think of it as a *substance* rather than something like a pattern or a specification. But for that Descartes surely can be forgiven—philosophers and lawyers are still not quite clear about exactly how to describe software. Fortunately, however, programmers are able to create and use it with some confidence.

For the purposes of our topic, Descartes's principal contemporary influence is on the opponents of artificial intelligence, through two ideas. First, Descartes thought of procedures, algorithms, methods, and rules as inextricable from meaning and intention. Unlike those suggested (if not exactly specified) by Hobbes, Descartes's rules for inquiry are not even approximately mechanical; instead, Descartes formulated his rules in terms for which there are only inner criteria: examine whether ideas are *clear;* examine whether ideas are *distinct* from others. It was this very subjective twist on method that irritated Descartes's materialist critics, such as Pierre Gassendi. In our century, the Cartesian view of method seems to have prompted (no doubt through more proximate sources, such as phenomenalism) Ludwig Wittgenstein's argument that a purely subjective language is impossible, because extra-linguistic criteria are required to constitute correct or incorrect usage, and a language without standards of use is not a language at all. Wittgenstein's private language argument has been recast by Saul Kripke as an argument about the irreducibility of rules or algorithms to material or physical relations. Briefly, Kripke argues that rules—for example, the rule for addition—require *meanings* that somehow determine how the rules apply to a potential infinity of as yet unexamined cases. But meanings are *normative;* meanings have to do with how language ought to be used. And, to conclude the argument, norms are not part of the physical world.

The second Cartesian influence on contemporary discussions occurs through a strategy of argument that is ubiquitous in contemporary philosophical opposition to artificial intelligence. Descartes's criterion for possibility is imagination: If *p* is (or can be) imagined, then *p* is possible. Hence, if the denial of *p* can be imagined, then *p* is not necessary. In combination with some other ideas about possibility and necessity—for example, the idea that fundamental scientific identifications of properties ("water is H_2O") entail that the identity claims are necessary—the Cartesian fallacy sows considerable confusion. A well-known recent example of this confusion is John Searle's Chinese room argument. Searle wants to refute the thesis that any physically possible system that implements a program for understanding Chinese with sufficient speed therefore understands Chinese. Searle imagines that he is placed in a room containing baskets full of Chinese symbols and a rule book (in English) for matching Chinese symbols with other Chinese symbols. People outside the room (who understand Chinese) slide questions written in Chinese under the door. In response he manipulates the symbols according to the rules in the book and answers by sliding strings of Chinese symbols back out under the door. The rule book is supposed to be analogous to the computer program, and Searle is analogous to the computer. These answers are indistinguishable from those of a native Chinese speaker, although, according to Searle, neither he nor the room nor the two of them together understand Chinese. Even if one were to grant his second conclusion (that the whole system didn't understand Chinese), Searle's fantasy is only a counterexample to anything of interest to artificial intelligence if one supposes that because Searle can imagine himself running the program, that this *is* actually possible. It isn't, not just because Searle in the box would soon become bored, but because it would take him nearly forever to produce a simulacrum of a short (but alas, not brief) intelligent conversation.

Minds and Procedures: Hobbes to Kant

Thomas Hobbes, the seventeenth century autodidact and mathematical eccentric best known for his writings on political philosophy, also formulated a rather clear anticipation of Allen Newell's and Herb Simon's notion of intelligence as a physical system that manipulates symbols:

By ratiocination, I mean computation. Now to compute is either to collect the sum of many things that are added together or to know what remains when one thing is taken out of another. Ratiocination, therefore, is the same with addition and subtraction; and if any man add multiplication and division, I will not be against it, seeing multiplication is nothing but addition of equals one to another, and division nothing but a subtraction of equals one from another, as often as is possible. So that all ratiocination is comprehended in these two operations of the mind, addition and subtraction.

But how by the ratiocination of our mind, we add and subtract in our silent thoughts, without the use of words, it will be necessary for me to make intelligible by an example or two. If therefore a man see something afar off and obscurely, although no appellation had yet been given to anything, he will, notwithstanding, have the same idea of that thing for which now, by imposing a name on it, we call it body. Again, when by coming nearer, he sees the same thing thus and thus, now in one place and now in another, he will have a new idea thereof, namely, that for which we now call such a thing animated. Thirdly, when standing nearer, he perceives the figure, hears the voice, and sees other things which are signs of a rational mind, he has a third idea, though it have yet no appellation, namely, that for which we now call anything rational. Lastly, when, by looking fully and distinctly upon it, he conceives all that he has seen as one thing, the idea he has now is compounded of his former ideas, which are put together in the mind in the same order in which these three single names, body, animated, rational, are in speech compounded into this one name, body-animated-rational, or man. In like manner, of the several conceptions of four sides, equality of sides, and right angles, is compounded the conception of a square. For the mind may conceive a figure of four sides without any conception of their equality, and of that equality without conceiving a right angle; and may join together all these single conceptions into one conception or one idea of a square. And thus we see how the conceptions of the mind are compounded. Again, whosoever sees a man standing near him, conceives the whole idea of that man; and if, as he goes away, he follow him with his eyes only, he will lose the idea of those things which were signs of his being rational, whilst, nevertheless, the idea of a body-animated remains still before his eyes, so that the idea of rational is subtracted from the whole idea of man, that is to say, of body-animated-rational, and there remains that of body-animated; and a while after, at a greater distance, the idea of animated will be lost, and that of body only will remain; so that at last, when nothing at all can be seen, the whole idea will vanish out of sight. By which examples, I think, it is manifest enough what is the internal ratiocination of mind without words.

We must not therefore, think that computation, that is, ratiocination, has place only in numbers, as if man were distinguished from other living creatures (which is said to have been the opinion of Pythagoras) by nothing but the faculty of numbering; for magnitude, body, motion, time, degrees of quality, action, conception proportion, speech and names (in which all the kinds of philosophy consist) are capable of addition and subtraction. (Hobbes, 1962, pp. 25–26)

There are several important thoughts in this passage. One is that reasoning is a psychological process, so that a theory of logical inference should be a theory of the operations of the mind. Another is that representations can have an encoding by, or be analogous to, numbers. A third is that the theory of reasoning is a theory of appropriate combinations; just what the objects are that are combined is obscure in this passage, but other passages suggest that Hobbes thought of the mind as composed of particles, and some of these particles, or collections of them, serve as symbols (or, as Hobbes would say, names) for things, and it is these physical symbols that are combined or decomposed in reasoning.

Later, English writers of philosophical psychology like John Locke, David Hume, John Stuart Mill, and Henry Maudsley thought of the content of a theory of mind as, at least in part, a theory of mental procedures, in which mental objects—"ideas"—are linked or "associated." Associationist psychology typically avoided Hobbes's mechanical formulations, and his connection of procedures with algorithms and numerical encodings had no influence. Instead, mental procedures were explained in terms of "similarity," "vivacity," and temporal proximity of occurrence of ideas.

The procedural viewpoint was given a very different turn in the closing decades of the eighteenth century in Immanuel Kant's *Critique of Pure Reason* (1781) and his related works. As with the associationist writers who influenced him, Kant gives no hint that mental processes are computational, but he offers an original view of those processes themselves, quite unlike anything before. Kant is the modern father of the notion of top-down processing.

Kant recognized that the logical theory which he had inherited from Aristotle, and which he assumed to be sound and complete, could not account for mathematical inference. Euclid's geometrical proofs, which prove by construction the existence of objects with specified properties, cannot be turned into valid syllogistic arguments, nor can Euclid's proofs of theorems in number theory be obtained by syllogism. Yet Kant was convinced that classical mathematics and much else (including that all events are governed by causal regularities, and features of Newtonian physics) is known a priori and not derived from inductions founded on experience. Kant's solution to the conundrum is that the content of experience is literally a *function* (in the mathematical sense) of the procedures of mind and of unknowable features of things in themselves. The difference between what is needed to obtain Euclid's proofs and what Aristotle's logic can do is built into the mind itself, not as axioms but as procedures that automatically construct the content of experience from the deliverances of sense. Things in themselves deliver, in unknowable ways, sensation, or what Kant sometimes calls the matter of experience; the "faculty of intuition" then contributes spatial and temporal features; the "schematism of the understanding" contributes object identity, causal regularity, and the synthesis of the individual pieces into a unified experience. The faculty of intuition automatically constructs images, for example, that satisfy the requirements of Euclidean axioms, and the schematism ensures that nothing random happens in experience. Kant repeatedly remarks that the process of synthesis and the operation of the schematism are unconscious, and he observes that how the schematism works will likely remain unknown (immediately thereafter he plunges into lengthy remarks about how the schematism works).

The Nineteenth Century: Boole, Frege, and Freud

George Boole's work can be seen as a continuation of Gottfried Leibniz's vision. Boole provided an algebra of logic and considered the algebra important because it provided a method for correct reasoning. Boole also viewed the mathematical theory of reasoning as a description of psychological laws of nature, but he also realized the contradiction between this analysis and the obvious fact that humans make errors of reasoning.

> The truth that the ultimate laws of thought are mathematical in their form, viewed in connection with the fact of the possibility of error, establishes a ground for some remarkable conclusions. If we directed our attention to the scientific truth alone, we might be led to infer an almost exact parallelism between the intellectual operations and the movements of external nature. Suppose any one conversant with physical science, but unaccustomed to reflect upon the nature of his own faculties, to have been informed, that it had been proved, that the laws of those faculties were mathematical; it is probable that after the first feelings of incredulity had subsided, the impression would arise, that the order of thought must, therefore, be as necessary as that of the material universe. We know that in the realm of natural science, the absolute connection between the initial and final elements of a problem, exhibited in the mathematical form, fitly symbolizes that physical necessity which binds together effect and cause. The necessary sequence of states and conditions in the inorganic world, and the necessary connection of premises and conclusion in the processes of exact demonstration thereto applied, seem to be coordinate.

Were, then, the laws of valid reasoning uniformly obeyed, a very close parallelism would exist between the operations of the intellect and those of external Nature. Subjection to laws mathematical in their form and expression, even the subjection of an absolute obedience, would stamp upon the two series one common character. The reign of necessity over the intellectual and the physical world would be alike complete and universal.

But while the observation of external Nature testifies with ever-strengthening evidence to the fact, that uniformity of operation and unvarying obedience to appointed laws prevail throughout her entire domain, the slightest attention to the processes of the intellectual world reveals to us another state of things. The mathematical laws of reasoning are, properly speaking, the laws of right reasoning only, and their actual transgression is a perpetually recurring phenomenon. Error, which has no place in the material system, occupies a large one here. We must accept this as one of those ultimate facts, the origin of which it lies beyond the province of science to determine. We must admit that there exist laws which even the rigor of their mathematical forms does not preserve from violation. We must ascribe to them an authority the essence of which does not consist in power, a supremacy which the analogy of the inviolable order of the natural world in no way assists us to comprehend. (Boole, 1951, pp. 407-408.)

Caught by the image of logic as the laws of reasoning akin to the law of gravitation, Boole did not try to resolve this difficulty by supposing that his was the theory of some ideal agent; he did not think that he was describing other minds than ours, imaginary minds still somehow recognizably similar to our own.

About thirty years later, Friedrich Ludwig Gottlob Frege gave the first adequate formulation of the logic of propositions—Boole had in effect described something closer to mod 2 arithmetic—and formalized a system of logic that included both first-order logic and the quantification over properties, although the latter part of his system was, as Bertrand Russell showed, not consistent. Frege insisted on separating logic from psychology, and so he did not suffer Boole's embarrassment over human error. Frege's achievement, and the logical developments of the next fifty years that extended it, at last put in place one of the principal tools for the study, among many other things, of android epistemology. Another conceptual tool arose at nearly the same time from physiology.

While the eighteenth and early nineteenth centuries witnessed thinkers such as Blaise Pascal, Gottfried Leibniz, and George Boole struggling to find a mechanical basis for reasoning, the end of the nineteenth and the beginning of the twentieth century saw two remarkably different ways of reconciling psychology with the notion that reasoning is computation.

Each of these lines of work leads to a branch of contemporary AI research. The "symbolic" approach to AI emphasizes structures of reasoning, while a "connectionist" approach to artificial intelligence focuses on brainlike architectures.

Prefaces to modern connectionist works usually trace the ideas back as far as Donald Olding Hebb's (1949) *Organization of Behavior: A Neuropsychological Theory;* occasionally writers will note passages of William James near the turn of the century that have a connectionist flavor. But the basics of connectionist models of computation and of mind were fully developed by the late nineteenth century in the private views, and some of the public views, of neuropsychologists. We know of no better statement from this time than Sigmund Freud's private writings, where a great many details, including what is now called "Hebbian learning" and the "Hebbian synapse," are described. Freud was trained as a neuroanatomist by Ernst Brucke, one of Europe's leading physiologists and an uncompromising materialist. Early in the 1890s, physiologists learned of synaptic junctions, and in Vienna that revelation immediately led to connectionist speculations by the senior research assistants in Brucke's laboratory, including Freud. While others published similar views, Freud developed his ideas in his unpublished *Project for a Scientific Psychology,* which was written in 1895. Freud's theory of dreams began in that essay, and the last chapter of Freud's first book on dreams is clearly derived from it.[3]

We return now to the symbolic tradition. Kant held that the objects of experience are constructed or "synthesized," but he was not at all clear about what they are constructed from or how the details of such a construction could work. After Frege's work, a few philosophers began to have novel ideas about what a "construction" or "synthesis" might be. The three most important philosophers first influenced by Frege were Bertrand Russell, Ludwig Wittgenstein, and Rudolf Carnap. Russell had an important correspondence with Frege, and Carnap studied with him in Jena, Germany. Frege's antipsychologism may have had a curious and healthy effect, for Carnap especially had no hesitation in developing a mathematics of cognition that, while motivated by psychological ideas, did not pretend to describe how people actually reason. This very attitude was crucial to the pragmatic approach of early work in AI.

Russell and Carnap each proposed (at about the same time) that revisions of Frege's logical theory, or elements of Frege's logic in combination with set theory, could be used to describe the construction of physical objects from the data of sensation. Russell and Whitehead had developed techniques to carry on Frege's logicist program to reduce mathematics to logic; Russell and Carnap, independently, thought that the same techniques could be used to give an account of the possibility of knowledge of the external world.

Russell's idea was that starting with variables ranging over basic entities (the sense data) and with predicates denoting properties of sense data (such as *red*), one could then *define* terms that would denote *sets* of sense data. Physical objects would literally be sets of sense data, or sets of sets of sense data or sets of sets of sets of sense data, and so on. Similarly, higher order properties of physical objects (such as the property of being a tree) would also be appropriate sets of sense data (or sets of sets of sense data, etc.). Russell sketched these ideas in a popular book, *Our Knowledge of the External World*, but he made no attempt to describe any logical details. Meanwhile, Carnap actually produced an outline of such a system.

Carnap's book, *The Logical Structure of the World*, was published in 1928. Carnap assumed that the fundamental entities over which the variables of his system range are what he called *elementary experiences*—an elementary experience is all that appears to someone at a particular moment. In addition, he assumed one relation between elementary experiences is given in experience, namely, the relation that obtains when one recollects that two experiences are similar in some respect or other. (For example, they might both be experiences that contain a red patch somewhere.) The construction of the world begins with a finite list of pairs of elementary experiences; for each pair in the list, the person whose experiences they are recollects that the first element in the pair is in some respect similar to the second element in the pair. Qualities such as color and tone are then defined as certain sets (or sets of sets or sets of sets of sets, etc.) formed from this list. Objects are to be constructed in the same way.

One of the most remarkable things about Rudolf Carnap's logical construction of the world is that it is not presented only as a collection of logical formulas that are to be applied to terms denoting elementary experiences and the relation of recollection. Carnap also described the construction as a *computational procedure*. That is, along with each logical construction he gave what he called a "fictitious procedure" that shows how to calculate a representation of the object constructed from any list of pairs of elementary experiences. The procedures are perfectly explicit, and they could be represented in any modern computer language. Carnap was the first philosopher (indeed the first person) to present a theory of the mind as a computational program. The use of logical representations immediately suggested (to Carnap anyway) that computation can be done not just on numbers, but on symbols that represent nonnumerical objects. This was really Ramón Lull's idea, and Thomas Hobbes's idea after that, but in Rudolf Carnap's work it begins to look as though it might really work—although in Carnap's development it did not.

William Aspray (1981) has given a persuasive account of the origins of the theory of computation, as it emerged in this century, from philosophical issues in the foundations of mathematics rooted in the nineteenth century. We think it is fair to say, however, that while the development of the essentials of recursion computation theory was motivated by philosophical issues, except for Carnap (who may have inspired Kurt Gödel's more successful work by his own failed attempt at a completeness theorem) the profession of philosophy contributed nothing to them. Gödel gave an account of his incompleteness results to the Vienna Circle,[4] but the audience seems largely to have missed their import. Alonzo Church was at the center of things, but in the 1930s and 1940s he was in the mathematics department at Princeton, and there is no evidence that anyone in the philosophy department at the time had an inkling of the revolution going on around them.

Late in the 1920s or thereabouts, Frank Ramsey developed the idea of subjective utility theory and the theory of measurement of subjective utilities. Belatedly, Carnap approached Ramsey's conception of probability, and by the middle of the century, Carnap proposed that we think of inductive norms as the design principles for an android that would begin life with some probability distribution and carry on by conditioning on the evidence it acquired throughout life. When, early in the 1960s, electronic digital computers began to be available for research, the first expert systems for medical diagnosis used Bayesian methods much as Carnap had imagined. Whether there was any direct influence from the philosophical tradition, we do not know. Bertrand Russell, too, came late in life to think of epistemology as principles of android design. His last serious work, *Human Knowledge, Its Scope and Limits,* abandons the idea of building up the world from sense data and considers especially the general knowledge of kinds and causes that systems must innately have in order to convert sensation into knowledge of the world.

Rudolf Carnap had two students, Walter Pitts and Herbert Simon, who contributed directly to the formation of the subject of artificial intelligence in the middle of this century, and Simon, of course, contributed many of the leading ideas in the subject. Carnap had another student, Carl Hempel, who contributed indirectly to the first commercial computer programs for automated scientific discovery. For all of their influence, neither Carnap nor Hempel seems to have had a glimmer of the possibilities in android epistemology, and both flatly denied—Hempel repeatedly and vehemently—the possibility of machine discovery.

Carl Hempel's influence came through his students. One of his doctoral students at Princeton, Gerald Massey, had a doctoral student at Michigan State, Bruce Buchanan, who went to work at Stanford in what was then a very odd job: helping to design and implement programs for chemical identification with mass spectroscopy. Joshua Lederberg and others had developed algorithms for identifying the hydrocarbon compounds consistent with chemical law and a given formula; the task was to use these algorithms as part of an inference engine. In the Dendral and Meta-Dendral programs, Hempel's theory of explanation and his instance-based approach to hypothesis confirmation were adapted and applied.

Conclusion

The history of modern computing has as a central theme: the development of methods for representing information in a physical form that is both stable enough to be reliable as a memory and plastic enough to be changed mechanically. The algorithms of Blaise Pascal's and Gottfried Leibniz's calculating machines were physically represented in their mechanical structure. It was not until Charles Babbage's (1792–1871) Analytical Engine that a machine was designed that did not directly physically embody the algorithms that it could execute. Significantly, it used a punched-card technique for encoding information and algorithms, which was originally developed for use in mechanical looms of the late nineteenth century. The engineers were beginning, quite serendipitously, to provide the ideas that could give flesh to aspects of Leibniz's vision.

Artificial intelligence is re-establishing the cooperation between philosophy and engineering that so motivated and enlightened Pascal and Leibniz, but now, android epistemology is working with richer tools. In the centuries of philosophical discussion since Pascal and Leibniz first saw how arithmetic could be mechanized, the concept of "machine" has not been much extended beyond Pascaline. However, computer science is working with new kinds of machines—not just physical computing machines but also "virtual" machines, which consist of software (run on other, "actual" machines) but perform real feats in the world. Through the work of Alan Turing's student, Robin Gandy, and others, theorists are developing new and more general formal conceptions of machines that compute.

Some of the early work in artificial intelligence seems to have taken philosophical theories more or less off the shelf, specialized them to particular tasks, and automated them, so that some of the early work in the subject has the flavor of automated philosophy of science, and even some of the more recent work in machine learning—for example, work on discovering laws and work on causal inference—bears the mark of philosophical sources. But the period is past in which android epistemology could rely substantially on independent work in philosophical logic and philosophy of science. What future development requires is not separation of labor by disciplines, but rigor and imagination, clarity of broad motive and clarity of detail, and a willingness to take off the blinkers of disciplines. Philosophy should not be just one more set of blinkers.

Acknowledgements

This chapter first appeared as "The Prehistory of Android Epistemology" in *Android Epistemology,* edited by Clark Glymour, Kenneth M. Ford, and Patrick J. Hayes (Menlo Park, CA: AAAI/ The MIT Press, 1995).

Notes

1. It is now clear that Pascal was preceded by the German polymath Wilhelm Schickard and his Calculating Clock. Schickard was a protégé of Johannes Kepler.

2. Leibniz is often erroneously credited with inventing binary arithmetic, but its roots are much older, reaching at least back to the ancient Chinese. Binary counting systems have been found in many of the world's ethnologically oldest tribes (Phillips 1936). It seems that ancient man was much taken with the pairwise nature of his body—two legs, arms, eyes, and ears. Binary multiplication is first described in the wonderfully named manuscript "Directions for Obtaining Knowledge of all Dark Things," believed to have been written by a scribe named Ahmes in about 1650 BCE.

3. For a more detailed account of Freud's connection with connectionism, see Glymour (1991).

4. The Vienna circle was a group of philosphers who gathered around Moritz Schlick when he came to Vienna in 1922. The group organized the Verein Ernst Mach (Ernst Mach Association).

2 On Computational Wings

Kenneth M. Ford & Patrick J. Hayes

Many philosophers and humanist thinkers are convinced that the quest for artificial intelligence (AI) has turned out to be a failure. Eminent critics have argued that a truly intelligent machine cannot be constructed and have even offered mathematical proofs of its impossibility. And yet the field of artificial intelligence is flourishing. "Smart" machinery is part of the information-processing fabric of society, and thinking of the brain as a "biological computer" has become the standard view in much of psychology and neuroscience.

While contemplating this mismatch between the critical opinions of some observers and the significant accomplishments in the field, we have noticed a parallel with an earlier endeavor that also sought an ambitious goal and for centuries was attacked as a symbol of humankind's excessive hubris: artificial flight. The analogy between artificial intelligence and artificial flight is illuminating. For one thing, it suggests that the traditional view of the goal of AI—to create a machine that can successfully imitate human behavior—is wrong.

For millennia, flying was one of humanity's fondest dreams. The prehistory of aeronautics, both popular and scholarly, dwelled on the idea of imitating bird flight, usually by somehow attaching flapping wings to a human body or to a framework worn by a single person. It was frustratingly clear that birds found flying easy, so it must have seemed natural to try to capture their secret. Some observers suggested that bird feathers simply possessed an inherent "lightness." Advocates of the possibility of flight argued that humans and birds were fundamentally similar, whereas opponents argued that such comparisons were demeaning, immoral or wrongheaded. But both groups generally assumed that flying meant imitating a bird. Even relatively sophisticated designs for flying machines

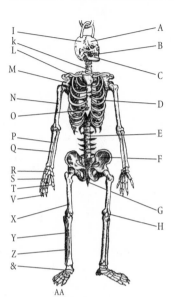
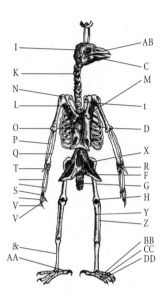

Figure 1. Comparison of the Skeletons of a Man and a Bird.

Pierre Belon, L'Historie de la Nature des Oyseaux (Paris) 1555).

often included some birdlike features, such as the beak on English artist Thomas Walker's 1810 design for a wooden glider.

This view of flying as bird-imitation was persistent. An article in *English Mechanic* in 1900 insisted that "the true flying machine will be to all intents and purposes an artificial bird." A patent application for a "flying suit" covered with feathers was made late in the nineteenth century, and wing-flapping methods were discussed in technical surveys of aviation published early in this century.

The Turing Test

Intelligence is more abstract than flight, but the long-term ambition of AI has also traditionally been characterized as the imitation of a biological exemplar. When British mathematician Alan M. Turing first wrote of the possibility of artificial intelligence in 1950, he suggested that AI research might focus on what was probably the best test for human intelligence available at the time: a competitive interview. Turing suggested that a suit-

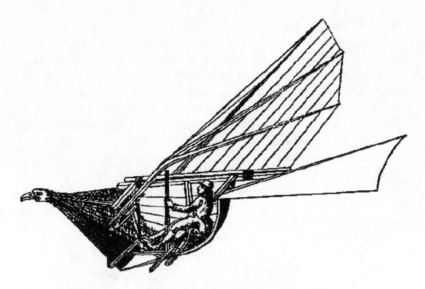

Figure 2. Walker's Flying Machine.

able test for success in AI would be an "imitation game" in which a human judge would hold a three-way conversation with a computer and another human and try to tell them apart. The judge would be free to turn the conversation to any topic, and the successful machine would be able to chat about it as convincingly as the human. This would require the machine to participant in the game to understand language and conversational conventions and to have a general ability to reason. If the judge could not tell the difference after some reasonable amount of time, the machine would pass the test: it would be able to seem human to a human.

There is some debate about the exact rules of Turing's imitation game, and he may not have intended it to be taken so seriously. But some kind of "Turing test" has become widely perceived, both inside and outside the AI field, as the ultimate goal of artificial intelligence, and the test is still cited in most textbooks. Just as with early thinking about flight, success is defined as the imitation of a natural model: for flight, a bird; for intelligence, a human.

The Turing test has received much analysis and criticism, but we believe that it is worse than often realized. The test has led to a widespread misimpression of the proper ambitions of our field. It is a poorly designed experiment (depending too much on the subjectivity of the judge), has a questionable technological objective (we already have lots of human intelligence), and is hopelessly culture-bound (a conversation that is passable to a British judge might fail according to a Japanese or Mexican judge). As Turing himself noted, one could fail the test by being too intelligent—for example, by doing mental arithmetic extremely fast. According to media reports, some judges at the first Loebner competition in 1991—a kind of Turing test contest held at the Computer Museum in Boston—rated a human as a machine on the grounds that she produced extended, well-written paragraphs of informative text. (Apparently, this is now considered an inhuman ability in parts of our culture.) With the benefit of hindsight, it is now evident that the central defect of the test is its species-centeredness: it assumes that human thought is the final, highest pinnacle of thinking against which all others must be judged. The Turing test does not admit of weaker, different, or even stronger forms of intelligence than those deemed human.

Most contemporary AI researchers explicitly reject the goal of the Turing test. Instead they are concerned with exploring the computational machinery of intelligence itself, whether in humans, dogs, computers, or aliens. The scientific aim of AI research is to understand intelligence as computation, and its engineering aim is to build machines that surpass or extend human mental abilities in some useful way. Trying to imitate a human conversation (however "intellectual" it may be) contributes little to either ambition.

In fact, hardly any AI research is devoted to trying to pass the Turing test. It is more concerned with issues such as how machine learning and vision might be improved or how to design an autonomous spacecraft that can plan its own actions. Progress in AI is not measured by checking fidelity to a human conversationalist. And yet many critics complain of a lack of progress toward this old ambition. We think the Turing test should be relegated to the history of science, in the same way that the aim of imitating a bird was eventually abandoned by the pioneers of flight. Beginning a textbook on AI with the Turing test (as many still do) seems akin to starting a primer on aeronautical engineering with an explanation that the goal of the field is to make machines that fly so exactly like pigeons that they can even fool other pigeons.

Imitation Versus Understanding

Researchers in the field of artificial intelligence may take a useful cue from the history of artificial flight. The development of aircraft succeeded only when people stopped trying to imitate birds and instead approached the problem in new ways, thinking about airflow and pressure, for example. Watching hovering gulls inspired the Wright brothers to use wing warping—turning an aircraft by twisting its wings—but they did not set out to imitate the gull's wing. Starting with a box kite, Wilbur and Orville Wright first worked on achieving sufficient lift, then on longitudinal and lateral stability, then on steering, and finally on propulsion and engine design, carefully solving each problem in turn. After that, no airplane could be confused with a bird either in its overall shape or in its flying abilities. In some ways, aircraft may never match the elegant precision of birds, but in other ways they outperform them dramatically. Aircraft do not land in trees, scoop fish from the ocean or use the natural breeze to hover motionless above the countryside. But no bird can fly at 45,000 feet or faster than sound.

Rather than limiting the scope of AI to the study of how to mimic human behavior, we can more usefully construe it as the study of how computational systems must be organized in order to behave intelligently. AI programs are often components of larger systems that are not themselves labeled "intelligent." There are hundreds of such applications in use today, including those that make investment recommendations, perform medical diagnoses, plan troop and supply movements in warfare, schedule the refurbishment of the space shuttle, and detect fraudulent use of credit cards. These systems make expert decisions, find meaningful patterns in complex data, and improve their performances by learning. All these actions, if done by a human, would be taken to display sound judgment, expertise, or responsibility. Many of these tasks, however, could not be done by humans, who are too slow, too easily distracted, or not sufficiently reliable. Our intelligent machines already surpass us in many ways. The most useful computer applications, including AI applications, are valuable exactly by virtue of their lack of humanity. A truly humanlike program would be just as useless as a truly pigeon-like aircraft.

Waiting for the Science

The analogy with flight provides another insight: technological advances often precede advances in scientific knowledge. The designers of early aircraft could not learn the principles of aerodynamics by studying the anatomy of birds. Evolution is a sloppy engineer, and living systems tend to be rich with ad hoc pieces of machinery with multiple uses or mechanisms jury—rigged from structures that evolved earlier for a different reason. As a result, it is often very difficult to discover basic principles by imitating natural mechanisms.

Experimental aerodynamics became possible only in the early part of this century, when artificial wings could be tested systematically in wind tunnels. It did not come from studying natural exemplars of flight. That a gull's wing is an airfoil is now strikingly obvious, yet the airfoil was not discovered by examining the anatomy of birds. Even the Wright brothers never really understood why their *Flyer* flew. The aerodynamic principles of the airfoil emerged from experiments done in 1909 by French engineer Alexandre-Gustave Eiffel, who used a large-scale wind tunnel and densely instrumented artificial wings. The first aircraft with "modern" airfoils—which were made thicker after engineers demonstrated that thicker airfoils improved lift without increasing drag—did not appear until late in World War I. As is true for many other disciplines, a firm theoretical understanding was possible only when controlled experiments could be done on isolated aspects of the system. Aerodynamics was discovered in the laboratory.

The same reasoning applies to the study of human intelligence. It may be impossible to discover the computational principles of intelligent thought by examining the intricacies of human thinking, just as it was impossible to discover the principles of aerodynamics by examining bird wings. The Wright brothers' success was largely attributed to their perception of flight in terms of lift, control, and power; similarly, a science of intelligence must isolate particular aspects of thought, such as memory, search, and adaptation, and allow us to experiment on these one at a time by using artificial systems. By systematically varying functional parameters of thought, we can determine the ways in which various kinds of mental processes can interact and support one another to produce intelligent behavior.

Several areas of AI research have been transformed in the past decade by an acceptance of the fact that progress must be measurable, so that different techniques can be objectively compared. For example, large-scale empirical investigations must be conducted to evaluate the efficiency of different search techniques or reasoning methods. In this kind of AI research, computers are providing the first wind tunnels for thought.

A Science of Intelligence

Rejecting the Turing test may seem like a retreat from the grand old ambition of creating a "humanlike" mechanical intelligence. But we believe that the proper aim of AI is much larger than simply mimicking human behavior. It is to create a computational science of intelligence itself, whether human, animal, or machine. This is not a new claim; it has been made before by AI pioneers Allen Newell and Herbert A. Simon, cognitive psychologist Zenon Pylyshyn, and philosopher Daniel C. Dennett, among others. But it was not until we noted the analogy with artificial flight that we appreciated the extent to which the Turing test, with its focus on imitating human performance, is so directly at odds with the proper objectives of AI. Some of our colleagues say their ultimate goal is indeed the imitation of human intelligence. Even with this limited aim, however, we believe that the perspective sketched here gives a more promising way to achieve that ambition than does the method outlined by Turing.

Consider again the analogy with flight. Just as the principles of aerodynamics apply equally to any wing, natural or artificial, the computational view of intelligence—or, more broadly, of mentality—applies just as well to natural thinkers as to artificial thinkers. If cognitive psychology and psycholinguistics are like the study of bird flight in all its complexity, then applied AI is like aeronautical engineering. Computer science supplies the principles that guide the engineering, and computation itself is the air that supports the wings of thought.

The study of artificial intelligence, like a large part of computer science, is essentially empirical. To run a program is often to perform an experiment on a large, complex apparatus (made partly of metal and silicon and partly of symbols) to discover the laws that relate its behavior to its structure. Like artificial wings, these AI systems can be designed and instrumented to isolate particular aspects of this relation. Unlike the research methodology of psychology, which employs careful statistical analysis to discern relevant aspects of behavior in the tangled complexity of nature, the workings of AI systems are open to direct inspection. Using computers, we can discover and experiment directly with what Newell and Simon have called the "laws of qualitative structure."

This picture of AI defines the field in a more useful and mature way than Turing could provide. In this view, AI is the engineering of cognitive artifacts based on the computational understanding that runs through and informs current cognitive science. Turing correctly insisted that his test was not meant to define intelligence. Nevertheless, in giving us this touchstone of success, he chose human intelligence—in fact, the arguing skill of an educated, English middle-class man in playing a kind of party game—as our goal. But the very science that Turing directed us toward provides a perspective from which a much broader and more satisfying account of intelligence is emerging.

Scholastic Critics

Artificial intelligence and artificial flight are similar even in the criticisms they attract. The eminent American astronomer Simon Newcomb argued passionately in the early 1900s against the idea of heavier-than-air flight. Newcomb's fulminations seem amusing now, but his arguments were quite impressive and reflected the view of the informed intelligentsia of his day. Like British mathematical physicist Roger Penrose, who uses Kurt Gödel's theorem to "prove" that AI is impossible, Newcomb employed mathematical arguments. He pointed out that as birds get bigger, their wing area increases in proportion to the square of their size, but their body weight increases in proportion to the cube, so a bird the size of a man could not fly. He was still using this argument against the possibility of manned flight several years after the Wright brothers' success at Kitty Hawk, North Carolina, when aircraft were regularly making trips lasting several hours. It is, in fact, quite a good argument—aircraft take-off weights are indeed roughly proportional to the cube of their wingspan—but Newcomb had no idea how sharply the lift from an airfoil increases in proportion to its airspeed. He thought of a wing as simply a flat, planar surface.

Simon Newcomb also used a combination of thought experiment and rhetoric to make his point—the same tactic that philosopher John R. Searle has employed in his famous "Chinese Room" argument against AI.[1] Newcomb stated scornfully, "Imagine the proud possessor of the aeroplane darting through the air at a speed of several hundred feet per second! It is the speed alone that sustains him. How is he ever going to stop?" Newcomb's arguments, with their wonderful combination of energy, passion, cogency and utter wrongheadedness, are so similar to contemporary arguments against artificial intelligence that for several years we offered an annual Simon Newcomb Award for the silliest new argument attacking AI. We still welcome nominations.

A common response to our analogy between artificial intelligence and artificial flight is to ask what will be the Kitty Hawk of AI and when will it happen. Our reply follows that of Herbert Simon: *it has already happened.* Computers regularly perform intelligent tasks and have done so for many years. Artificial intelligence is flying all around us, but many simply refuse to see it. Among the thousands of applications in use today, here are just a few examples: AI systems now play chess, checkers, bridge, and backgammon at world-class levels, compose music, prove mathematical theorems, explore active volcanoes, synthesize stock-option and derivative prices on Wall Street, make decisions about credit applications, diagnose motor

Figure 3. Simon Newcomb, American Astronomer and Mathematician.
Newcomb argued passionately against the possibility of artificial flight—even after the Wright Brothers' successful tests of their aircraft in 1903.

pumps, monitor emulsions in a steel mill, translate technical service manuals, and act as remedial reading tutors for elementary school children. In the near future, AI applications will guide deep-space missions, explore other planets, and drive trucks along freeways.

But should all this really count as "intelligent?" The performance of AI systems, like the speed or altitude of aircraft, is not open to dispute, but whether or not one chooses to call it "intelligent" is determined more by social attitude than by anything objective. When any particular ability is mechanized, it is often no longer considered to be a hallmark of mental prowess. It is easy now to forget that when Turing was writing, a "computer" was a human being who did arithmetic for a living, and it was obvious to everyone that computing required intelligence. The meaning of the word has now changed to mean a machine, and performing fast, accurate arithmetic is no longer considered a hallmark of mental ability, just as the meaning of "flying" has changed to cover the case, once inconceivable, of dozing quietly in an airplane seat while traveling at hundreds of miles an hour far above the clouds. Newcomb—who was famous as one of the finest computers of his time—went to his deathbed refusing to concede that what the early aircraft did should be called "flying."

Turing suggested his test as a way to avoid useless disputes about whether a particular task counted as truly intelligent. With considerable prescience, he anticipated that many people would never accept that the action of a machine could ever be labeled as "intelligent," that most human of labels. But just as there was no doubt that the early flyers moved through the air at certain altitudes and speeds, there is no doubt that electronic computers actually get arithmetic done, make plans, produce explanations, and play chess. The labels are less important than the reality.

The arbitrariness of the social labeling can be illustrated by a thought experiment in which the machine is replaced by something mysterious but natural. Whereas a dog will never pass the Turing test, no one but a philosopher would argue that a dog does not display some degree of intelligence—certainly no one who has owned a dog would make such an argument. It is often claimed that Deep Blue, the computer that defeated chess champion Gary Kasparov, is not *really* intelligent, but imagine a dog that played chess. A chess-playing dog that could beat Kasparov would surely be acclaimed as a remarkably smart dog.

The idea that natural intelligence is a complex form of computation can only be a hypothesis at present. We see no clear reasons, however, why any mental phenomenon cannot be accounted for in this way. Some have argued that the computationalist view cannot account for the phenomenology of consciousness. If one surveys the current theories of the nature of consciousness, however, it seems to us that a computationalist account offers the most promise. Alternative views consider consciousness to be some mysterious physical property, perhaps arising from quantum effects influenced by the brain's gravity or even something so enigmatic as to be forever beyond the reach of science. None of these views seems likely to explain how a physical entity, such as a brain in a body, can come to be aware of the world and itself. But the AI view of mental life as the product of computation provides a detailed account of how internal symbols can have meaning for the machine, and how this meaning can influence and be influenced by the causal relations between the machine and its surroundings.

The scientific goal of AI is to provide a computational account of intelligence or, more broadly, of mental ability itself—not merely an explanation of human mentality. This very understanding, if successful, must deny the uniqueness of human thought and thereby enable us to extend and amplify it. Turing's ultimate aim, which we can happily share, was not to describe the difference between thinking people and unthinking machines but to remove it. This is not to disparage or reduce humanity and still less to threaten it. If anything, understanding the intricacies of airflow increases our respect for how extraordinarily well birds fly. Perhaps it seems less magical, but its complexity and subtlety are awesome. We suspect that the same will be true for human intelligence. If our brains are indeed biological computers, what remarkable computers they are.

Acknowledgements

This chapter was first published as "On Computational Wings" by Kenneth Ford and Patrick Hayes in a special issue on intelligence of *Scientific American Presents*, 9(4): 78-83, Winter 1998. It is reproduced here with permission.

Note

1. See "Is the Brain's Mind a Computer Program?" by John R. Searle, *Scientific American*, 262(1): 20–25 (January 1990).

3 The Vitalists' Last Stand

Anatol Rapoport

There was a time when biologists were split into two parties—the mechanists and the vitalists. The mechanists believed that all life processes could be reduced to the operation of physical and chemical laws; the vitalists insisted that they could not. In retrospect it appears that the vitalists have been in continual retreat—one is tempted to say to previously prepared positions. First they maintained that living tissues contain a substance not contained in nonliving matter. In fact, organic chemistry was so named on the basis of this belief. This position had to be given up after Friedrich Wöhler succeeded in synthesizing urea, an organic substance.

The vitalists next retreated to a position based on a teleological interpretation of biological processes. A teleological process is guided not by what Aristotle called "effective causes" (pushing from behind) but by what he called "final causes" (beckoning from ahead). Thus, the vitalists maintained, purpose was an ingredient of actions characteristic of living beings.

In the Middle Ages purposeful action was ascribed also to nonliving matter. Philosophers taught that everything that exists has its proper place in the scheme of things. If anything is in its proper place, it stays there. If it is forcibly removed, it "strives" to get back to where it belongs. Thus, stones fall to earth because earth is the predominant element in them. Accordingly they seek to be near the center of the earth, which is their "proper place." Smoke, on the other hand, rises from the chimney, because essentially a product of fire, it seeks its proper place in the region of eternal fire beyond the stars. Birds can fly because their proper place is in their nests, which are up in the trees.

The maturation of physics was associated, among other things, with the abandonment of teleological explanations of physical events. A cause came to be regarded as operating on the here and now, as it were. Ironically, this "more scientific" outlook delayed the acceptance of the universal law of gravitation, which apparently rested on the assumption of forces acting at a distance, unacceptable to philosophers who sought to reduce all events to mechanical processes. Nevertheless, the expulsion of teleology from physical phenomena was definitely a step forward in the development of the physical sciences.

This reduction of causes of physical events to efficient causes had no bearing on the vitalists' position. If anything, it strengthened it, because it provided a new position to which to retreat when the "special substance" position was demolished by the synthesis of urea. A prominent vitalist biologist in the first decade of this century was Hans Driesch, an Austrian, who performed an experiment purporting to show that the development of an embryo was guided by teleological causation. He cut a sea urchin embryo in its early stage in two, whereupon each half developed into a normal urchin. Had the process been "mechanical," Driesch argued, each half would have developed into a half of a sea urchin. The fact that each developed into the whole animal presumably showed that the state of being a sea urchin was the embryo's "goal." The goal was reached in spite of intervention.

The flaw in Driesch's argument is easy to detect. It consists of a purely verbal conception of a "mechanical" process, according to which the process proceeds automatically without regard for consequences, that is, "thoughtlessly," as it were, in contrast to an "intelligent" process guided by an envisaged goal.

In the exact sciences, a mechanism is conceived as a device whose behavior is governed by explicitly formulated equations. The equations determine trajectories, that is, successions of states of a mechanical system. A trajectory is completely determined by a system of differential equations and a set of initial conditions, involving as many parameters as the order of the differential equations system. Now the initial state of the system consisting of a half of an intact sea urchin embryo is, of course, different from that of a half of an embryo. For one thing, the immediate environment of a separated half contains only the surrounding medium. Specifically, if the embryo which Driesch cut in half consisted of four cells, then each half consisted of two cells in nearly the same condition as in the previous stage (i.e., the two-cell embryo). There is nothing surprising in the fact that this two-cell embryo developed into a normal sea urchin, passing through the four-cell stage on the way.

The concept invoked by Driesch has been called "equifinality." It refers to a tendency of certain kinds of systems to reach some final state from different initial states. In Driesch's example, it was not even different initial states that gave rise to the same final state. As we have seen, the half embryo should be regarded as a state identical to that of an embryo at an earlier stage of a full embryo. Other examples, however, illustrate the principle of equifinality more convincingly. If the growth of a fish is interrupted, the fish will nonetheless grow to about the same size that would have been reached if growth had not been interrupted. This fact suggests that the final "goal" of a growing fish is to be of a certain size. However, this idea, too, is a misconception, as is demonstrated by a simple mathematical model of growth. Suppose the rate of change of a size of an organism is governed by two processes: the take-in of matter from the outside and the break-down of tissues. Supposing that food is taken in through the surface and that the breakdown occurs throughout the volume of this (primitive) organism, and noting that surface is proportional to the 2/3 power of the volume, we can write for the rate of change of volume V:

$$dV/dt = aV^{2/3} - bV,$$

where a and b are constants. We note by setting dV/dt equal to zero that V tends asymptotically to $(a/b)^3$, a quantity independent of the initial condition V_0. One can regard this sort of growth governed by "equifinality." But this "equifinality" is only a consequence of the mathematical structure of the growth model. It has nothing to do with the growing body being alive or not.

Apparent equifinality appears in physics no less than in biology. When light travels through different media, it appears to "choose" a path that minimizes travel time between two given points. Mechanical systems tend to equilibria where their potential energy is minimized. Closed thermodynamic systems tend to equilibria where their entropy is maximized. All these processes take systems to states essentially independent of where they start from. In this way, physical laws can be expressed "teleologically," for example, the Principle of Least Action, that is, in a mathematical form which makes it appear "as if" systems "seek" some "optimal" state to be in. In other words, the vitalist "principle of equifinality" has been explained away by showing that nonliving systems as well as living ones can be demonstrated to be governed by the same principle.

The next stand taken by the vitalists was on "intelligence" as the exclusive possession of some living systems. We now come to a question of central interest to people working in the field of artificial intelligence: "Can machines think?" is the way the layman puts the question. It serves little purpose to ask him to define "thinking." He is convinced that he knows what thinking means since he experiences it directly. And he is also convinced that you know what thinking is and that you know he knows and that therefore definitions are superfluous. I, too, will sidestep the definition. Instead I will go over some recollections going back four and a half decades in which artificial intelligence occasionally crops up.

In late 1945, shortly before I returned to civilian life, I attended a meeting of mathematicians at the Museum of Science and Industry in Chicago. I recall that mathematicians basked in suddenly ignited limelight of fame. The layman stubbornly thought of Albert Einstein as a mathematician who discovered the "secret of the atomic bomb" in the mystic formula $E = mc^2$. And there were some among mathematicians who looked forward to a golden age in mathematics as a new fountainhead of power. World War I, it has been said, was a chemists' war (high explosives, poison gas). World War II was the physicists' war (radar, the atomic bomb). World War III, some maintained with gratifying confidence, would be the mathematicians' war. And the high hopes of the military establishment revolving around "fully automated battlefields" (General William Westmoreland's expression) make the prognosis credible.

One of the exhibits at that meeting in Chicago's Museum of Science and Industry was a computer that played faultless tic-tac-toe—never lost and when the opponent made a mistake, invariably won. Seemed quite an achievement at the time. A few years afterward Herb Simon and Allen Newell, who did some work in the field, predicted that in the 1960s the world chess champion would be a computer program. Now, 30 years after the set time limit, computer programs play on the 2400 level, that is, like grand masters. They can easily beat players like most of us but are still no match for a Garry Kasparov. Recently he easily beat the best of them.[1] To be sure, a program playing against a human player is usually put under the same time limitation. We still don't know whether a Kasparov could beat a program if no time limit were placed on either. Possibly not. For a human being, the relaxation of time limits would be an advantage with diminishing returns, as the memory and other factors of mental capacity become overburdened, while a computer program is not subject to the same limitation. As long as its memory is not exceeded, it can continue operating with the same efficiency. The limitations of artificial intelligence are of another sort. To illustrate, I will examine the problem of finding optimal moves by "brute force," that is, by investigating all possible lines of play to any desired length.

Let us look at some results of game theory. We will consider only so called finite games, which can last only a finite number of moves. Tic-tac-toe is such a game. The number of moves in a play of this game cannot exceed nine. An average game of chess lasts thirty to fifty moves and only rarely more than a hundred. According to the theory of games such games can be reduced to so called "normal form," in which each player makes only one choice, namely, of a strategy that he will follow as the game proceeds. In this context, a strategy is a complete plan of action, which specifies how the player in question will move in any situation that can possibly arise in the course of the games. Another theorem in the theory of games refers to so called games of perfect information. These are games in which each player knows at all times the situation to which all the preceding moves have led. Both tic-tac-toe and chess are games of this sort. In the former, the cells of the grid in which the players' naughts, and crosses have been placed at a given stage of the game are visible. In chess, the positions of all the pieces on the board (which define the current situation) are visible. The above-mentioned theorem states that in a two-person game of perfect information, each player has at his disposal an optimal strategy which guarantees him the best result that he can attain in that game. In both tic-tac-toe and chess there are just three possible results: win, draw, or lose. An optimal strategy is one which is sure to win if a forced win is possible or to draw if a forced draw is possible. The fundamental result states that in every finite game of perfect information, each player has an optimal strategy.

The result means that if a game of chess is played perfectly by both players, then it must either always end in a win for White, or always end in a win for Black, or always end in a draw. Chess experts suspect that the latter result is the most probable and the forced win for Black the least probable, but this is not known. Nevertheless, the result is of "philosophical" importance. It implies that the reason people play chess is that they do not know how to play it. The reason adults do not play tic-tac-toe is that they do know how to play it and therefore know that each play must end in a draw.

Let me return to the tic-tac-toe-playing computer exhibited in Chicago in the beginning of the age of artificial intelligence. At the time the feat was impressive. Today we know that any teenager who knows something about programs can design one that plays perfect tic-tac-toe. In order to create such a program, the programmer must first analyze the game. He or she will note that if the first player puts an X in the center of the grid, then he must win if the second player puts his O in any side cell. The only way to prevent the first player from winning is to play a corner. If this happens, the first player's best move is the opposite corner, which still gives him a chance of a "double play." There is a way of blocking the double play, however, and so on. It is this analysis that guides the design of a program and certainly not the examination of all possible strategies, the number of which is formidable.

To see this, consider a simplified game of chess which consists of only a single exchange of moves. White has 20 choices for his move, and these are the 20 strategies available to him. Black, on the other hand, has 20^{20} strategies available, since he has 20 possible responses to each of White's 20 possible moves. This is a huge number. To get an idea of how huge it is, observe that if 100 strategies can be listed on a sheet of paper and a stack of 100 sheets is an inch high, then a stack needed to list all of Black's 20^{20} strategies would be 40,000 light years thick.

This example illustrates the difference between the "brute force" analysis of a game (examining all possible strategies) and an analysis which examines only possible positions. In tic-tac-toe the number of possible final positions is 126, while the number of possible strategies is in the trillions. And even all possible positions need not be examined, since the outcome of the game is clear after only the first two or three moves. In the two-move chess game, the number of possible positions is only 400, while the number of possible strategies is totally unimaginable.

It stands to reason that chess-playing computer programs are designed by people who know something about the game. They have a repertoire of concepts developed through centuries of analyses in which certain principles of good play were discovered. Chess players refer to them as material, mobility, open files, pawn formation, safety of the king, and so on. Especially relevant to this discussion is the fact that none of these concepts can be defined precisely, that is, formulated in a language that a computer can understand, while retaining the full meaning of the concept. The concepts are fully understood only by a person experienced in playing chess. They can be explained by one player to another. They can be to a certain (but only to a limited) extent translated into computer language (that is, into criteria expressed by numbers, binary relations, and the like).

This brings us to the central problem of designing a sophisticated artificial intelligence, a problem central at this time, because the solution is still a long way off. The problem is endowing artificial intelligence devices with the power of recognition. In AI jargon, it is called "pattern recognition," but this is a loaded term, because "pattern" suggests something concretely describable, and the fundamental article of faith in artificial intelligence work is that if you can describe a form of behavior sufficiently precisely, you can simulate it. But this is just the difficulty. We cannot describe what we recognize, let alone say how we recognize it.

Think of a smell, say of ammonia, or garlic, or roses. As you think about it, you can almost experience it. Moreover, each one internally experiencing the suggested smell is convinced that every one else is experiencing the same thing. Yet if one were asked to describe these sensations in words, one couldn't get past some generalizations that say very little, like "pungent" or "fragrant" or what not. Consider recognition in very young children. I recall one of my nephews when he was about eighteen months old. We gave him some chess pieces to play with. He picked up a knight and made clicking sounds with his tongue. We were impressed. At his age he already associated the chess knight with a horse. But equally impressive was our recognition of the child's act of recognition. Why did we immediately identify clicking sounds with a horse? Because of what a horse walking or running on a city pavement sounds like: "clip-clop." A baby recognizes its mother's face and its mother's voice. But how does it do it? We could build a device able to recognize a voice, because sound patterns can be resolved by Fourier analysis and expressed mathematically. But faces? I wonder. Nor do I think that recognition of voices by humans depends on built-in Fourier analysis devices. I don't know how it works. It just does. We must assume that somehow accumulated experience and, be it noted, not only of an individual but of an entire evolutionary line of predecessors, adds up to this ability. Do we have to produce millions of generations of artificial intelligence devices to simulate this faculty?

Consider the crucial role recognition plays in scientific cognition. When I teach general system theory, I point out that this paradigm has two separate lines of development. One is analytic system theory; the other, organismic system theory. The fundamental unifying principle of analytic system theory is the mathematical isomorphism, which abstracts from content to bring out the structure of a system including the structure of its dynamics. A much-cited example is the mathematical isomorphism between a harmonic oscillator and an electrical system consisting of an inductance, a resistance, and a condenser in series. Both are described by a linear second-order differential equation. The analogy connects mechanical mass with electrical inductance, friction with resistance, rigidity with capacitance—connections which would not occur without the help of mathematical analysis. When we pass from nonliving to living systems, mathematical analysis loses much of its power. Analogies are established by acts of recognition apparently performed without the benefit of analysis. Biological science began with taxonomy, which, in turn, depended on recognition of species, genera, etc., of organisms. We easily recognize that an insect "eats," even if the components of the act of eating are widely different from ours, also that an insect copulates just as we make love, even though there is hardly anything that we can point to that supports the analogy. Or take a simple psychological experiment. The psychologist records an observation: the rat pushed a lever that caused a pellet to be delivered, which the rat ate. The way the motion of the lever caused the pellet to be delivered can be described precisely—little wonder, because someone had designed the apparatus. But the way the rat pushed the lever or ate the pellet cannot be described with comparable precision. In different instances of pushing the lever, quite different movements may be involved. Yet they are all lumped under a statement describing the result— justifiably so, because the psychologist can build a theory of instrumental or operant conditioning by associating only two precisely describable events: pushing the "right" or the "wrong" lever, and the delivery or non-delivery of the pellet. Had the psychologist insisted on reducing all events to "physical laws" (which the vitalists maintain cannot be done), he would have to make note of not only all the neural events, glandular secretions, and muscle contractions inside the rat, but also all the underlying physical and chemical processes, clearly an impossible task.

Surely we do not depend on such reductions in constructing theories of human behavior. The theories we construct do not compare in their reach, generality, and elegance to the theories constructed by physical scientists. But some such theories have made considerable progress. In them you will find references to conceptualization, recognition, values, modes of cognition, compulsions, enlightenment, insight, delusion, etc., etc.—all terms that defy operational definitions but that surely are not meaningless. We know what they mean intuitively just as we know what ammonia smells like or what an orgasm feels like, without being able to describe what goes on inside us when we appreciate the meanings of these terms.

Central to all these faculties is the faculty of recognition, not "pattern recognition," with which designers of artificial intelligence devices are concerned with, but intuitive recognition, acquired through years of personal experience and very probably through eons of evolutionary experience accumulated in the genetic complex. It is on this issue that the vitalists (if such are still around) will make their last stand. Their retreat was marked by "Yes, but can it..." type of objections. When it became clear that organic compounds can be synthesized, and that therefore there was not evidence for the existence of a special living substance, the vitalists said, "Never mind special living substance. Only living systems can exhibit equifinality." Actually it has been known for a long time that physical systems can exhibit equifinality, for example, processes governed by the principle of least action or systems tending toward equilibria or to steady states from different initial conditions. Design of artificial systems governed by equifinality was suggested by cybernetics, a new branch of physics in which the concept of information was linked to that of physical entropy. This linkage became the basis of artificial intelligence technology. When vitalists said,"Yes, but can artificial intelligence devices 'reason'?" the high-speed all-purpose computer was the answer. Artificial intelligence devices were also produced that could "learn," that is, improve their performance. The vitalists kept asking whether they could "really" think. The question was parried by the challenge to define "thinking." The vitalists kept asking whether automata could "feel," a question that inspired science fiction fantasies. All these questions could be dispensed with by a trivial answer: If you made an automaton that would be like a human being in all respects, it would be a human being.

We are reminded of the great Russian philosopher Mikhail Vasilevich Lomonossoff, one of the founders of modern chemistry, who once and for all demolished the Aristotelian concept of "essence" by declaring that substances are what they are because of their properties, not because of some "essence" that alone defines their identity. Thus water is water simply because it has the properties of water. It is absurd to imagine a substance that has all the properties of water but is not "really" water, because it lacks the "essence" of water. The antivitalist would say the same thing of a humanoid automaton. Could such an automaton be made? Nothing simpler. We have at our disposal automata with linear dimensions less than two meters, weighing less than 100 kilograms, operating at temperatures below 40°C and, above all, produced by totally unskilled labor.

Joking aside, the challenge is to make a humanoid automaton the hard way, from scratch, as it were. Now why do we want to do this? Or do we? Better said, how far do we want to go in that direction and why? Two sources of motivation suggest themselves, one, in my opinion, a worthy one, the other questionable. The worthy motivation is that of heeding the call of a challenge to creativity. The questionable motivation is that generated by power addiction. This addiction manifests itself in the West, especially in the United States in what I call technolatry, the worship of technology, analogous to idolatry, the worship of idols. Recall the beginning of Mark Twain's great classic, *A Connecticut Yankee in King Arthur's Court*. After the introduction, in which Mark Twain tells how he met this strange man, he lets the man speak for himself. The novel continues in the first person.

"I am an American," the Yankee begins his narrative. "My father was a blacksmith, my uncle was a horse doctor. I can make anything...." Note he does not say, "I can do anything." He says he can *make* anything, but he gives the impression that he regards this technological virtuosity as tantamount to omnipotence. Indeed, the Connecticut Yankee attempts to turn King Arthur's England into a democratic society by introducing nineteenth century technology. He fails. Whether this failure reflects Mark Twain's pessimism about human nature or his skepticism about the humanizing influence of technology, we can't be sure.

Legends about the evil consequences of power addiction are common. In the Nibelung saga, the dwarf Alberich has to forswear love to gain power. His power addiction is catching and destroys every one who catches it. The legend of the Golem is built on the same theme. Today we are persistently warned against playing God, against the proliferation of nuclear power, against genetic engineering, and so on.

We can heed or ignore these warnings. At this time I will not discuss the ethical issue. I will only raise the epistemological issue. The construction of a device presupposes a knowledge of how it is supposed to work.

Where does this knowledge come upon the barrier of self-reference? We are familiar with the so called antinomies of formal logic—the paradox of Bertrand Russell's barber and its relatives. These go back to scholastic theology where the question was put whether God can make a stone that He cannot lift. If He can, what about His omnipotence? If He cannot, what about His omnipotence? Are we now asking whether we can construct an automaton with a will of its own, a creative imagination of its own, that is, an ability to imagine things that we could not have imagined? A conscience of its own which would inhibit it from obeying power-drunk madmen? The crucial question, in my opinion, is not whether we could do such a thing but whether we would want to. Some will say yes; others no. If both kinds of people engage in a serious, really honest self-searching dialogue, they may learn a good deal about both themselves and others. And that would be all to the good.

Acknowledgements

This chapter first appeared as "The Vitalists' Last Stand" in *Android Epistemology,* edited by Clark Glymour, Kenneth M. Ford, and Patrick J. Hayes (Menlo Park, CA: AAAI/ The MIT Press, 1995).

Note

1. Since this was written, a computer has defeated the world human chess champion –*ed.*

4 Silicon Reflections

Clark Glymour

I am in a quandary from which I am increasingly certain there is no escape. Philosophy and my health have conspired to leave me only dreadful alternatives. It is futile, I am sure, even to state my difficulties, as though some reader might see the true and correct path through my plight. Still, the illusion consoles me, and so I will tell my story.

It all began in the 1980s, nearly three decades ago now, with certain advances in artificial limbs. Not, of course, that I have an artificial limb, but that is where it began. In earlier years those unfortunates who had lost a hand, leg, or arm had the part replaced by a mechanical device which could support the body or which could be mechanically manipulated to grasp and hold. But by the middle of the 1980s neurosurgeons and artificial limb makers had found ways to connect artificial limbs to the sensory and motor nerves of the stump. The limbs were able to respond to pressure and communicate the stimulus, by electrical means, to the nerve cell membrane of sensory nerves. Similarly, the limbs were able to detect and respond appropriately to increases in the concentrations of neurotransmitter chemicals in the motor nerves. Through these ingenious mechanisms, those with artificial limbs were enabled to feel pressure and to move their limbs much as they had before dismemberment.

Now it happened that at the same time there was formed a Society of Dretskeans,[1] both in the United States and in England, whose members vehemently, and even violently, opposed the use of "neuroprosthetics," as these ingenious artificial limbs were called. The members of the Society took as their guide a then newly appeared book by an eminent philosopher. Unfortunately, they took the author's sensible views to logical extremes, with consequent miseries that I am about to describe. According to their reading of this philosophical work, mechanical devices, no matter how ingeniously contrived to imitate human behavior, cannot have mental states. Mechanical devices such as computers cannot feel, think, see, hear, wish, or understand. They cannot be conscious, even if they act as if they are. Only brains and nervous systems such as those in humans or something with equivalent causal powers (which mechanical devices are not) can have mental states. Machines have syntax; only brains, or objects with equivalent causal powers, have semantics. This doctrine alone might not have caused so much trouble, were it not for another of the philosopher's doctrines, which the members of the society also took to a logical extreme. This second doctrine is that mental properties are not properties of individual cells of the brain, or even of a few cells together, but rather properties of the brain as a whole. Now the original members of the Dretskean Society reasoned this way: The nervous system is but an extension of the brain, and mental properties are really therefore properties of the nervous system as a whole, but if the whole is changed by replacing a part of it with a mechanical device, then the nervous system as a whole is not the same as it was before the replacement. If even a part of the nervous system is replaced by a mechanical device, they concluded, the whole of the nervous system must be affected and lose its power to produce mental states.

The Dretskeans formed the conviction that those who had neuroprosthetics attached to their nervous systems thereby lost all powers of consciousness, thought, reflection, and feeling. It did no good to plead with the Dretskeans that their reasoning was specious, or to say that since the greater part of the nervous system and all of the higher cortex was left intact, those with neuroprosthetics still have thoughts and feelings. The Dretskeans insisted that anything with such an appendage was part machine and part human tissue, and they pointed to passages in a philosopher's book that argued that even a complete human within a machine need not make altogether a system that understands and feels, even if it acts as if it does.

It did not avail to point out to them the passages from the esteemed philosopher's writings with which I have begun this lament. The Dretskeans took such stuff to be mere temporizing done for the sake of disputing critics, and they would have none of it. To those who turned the texts against them and claimed that the humanity of neuroprosthetes is a testable, empirical issue, the Dretskeans rejoined with a question that proved to be rhetorical: what test would decide? Alan Turing's famous test, they insisted, was refuted by the philosopher's parable of the Chinese-speaking box. The helplessness of sensible men and women in the face of this curious challenge only strengthened the Dretskeans in their prejudices. Many vainly tried to impress upon the Dretskeans their philosopher's insistence upon the first-person point of view. With typical casuistry, the members of the Society claimed that each of us could only engage himself, and not any other, from that distinguished point of view. Only analogy and philosophy could decide whether other things have minds, they claimed, and their philosophical conclusion was. that humans with neuroelectronic legs no more have mental states than would thermostats fitted with biological arms.

I suppose that the course of action the Dretskeans undertook was understandable given the firmness of their convictions, but it was undeniably regrettable. The members of the Society took to bombing factories that manufactured neuroprosthetics, and performing armed raids on hospitals to prevent the implantation of the devices. The Dretskeans would stop at nothing to prevent the attachment of neuroprosthetics, and their slogan was everywhere: "neuroprosthesis is murder!" What was still worse, once a neuroprosthetic had been attached to some poor soul, the Dretskeans ceased to treat him as a fellow human, or as a sentient creature at all. Dretskeans created great carnage by refusing to stop their automobiles when meeting pedestrians in crosswalks who sported artificial limbs. They kidnapped the maimed as soon as they received an implant, and held them in slavery.

The outrages of the Dretskeans finally provoked the wrath of every sensible citizen. The Society was outlawed, and most of its members captured and imprisoned, despite their insistence that they had done no injury to person or property in killing and kidnapping the handicapped. The Society effectively vanished, although it is rumored that to this day a few adherents to the original Dretskean doctrine still live in isolation in the State of Utah.

But Dretskeanism is a vital doctrine, and not easily eliminated. No sooner had the Society of Dretskeans been destroyed than a new and more influential body sprang up, the Reformed Society of Dretskeans. The members of the Reformed Society held that the original Dretskeans had misinterpreted and distorted the doctrine by confusing the essential parts of the brain responsible for consciousness, thought and feeling with the nervous system as a whole. The original Dretskean doctrine was correct, they held, but not for the nervous system as a whole, only for the cerebral cortex. The optic nerve and other nerve tracts from the brain to the periphery could be replaced by whatever mechanical devices might serve without affecting the power of the cortex to produce thought and feeling.

And here, at last, is where my personal woes began. I suffer a curious and progressive disease, characterized by the softening and eventual death of parts of my cerebral cortex. Because of my disorder, which is uncommon but not unique, and because neurophysiology during my lifetime has made dramatic advances, I have served as a kind of neurological guinea pig. If you will forgive a macabre pun, it is because of my condition that I have lived on the cutting edge of neuroscience. Supporters of the philosophical author whose writings inspired the Dretskean movement assure us that with the advance of neuroscience, the mysteries of intentionality and of consciousness would be revealed. Alas, it has not turned out that way, and neuroscience has left me, in particular, with the most awesome and dreadful puzzle.

The first notice I had of my disorder was an inability to feel a pin or other sharp object when it was stuck into my left thumb. Rejecting the diagnosis of my psychoanalyst (it was, he claimed, an hysterical anesthesia), I consulted a neurologist, who after many elaborate tests informed me that a small part of my cerebral cortex, merely a few connected cells, had perished. The function of these cells, he explained, was to receive signals indicating prickle sensations from my left thumb. Along with the news, he offered me a remarkable prospect. There had recently been developed a device that he termed a "cortical patch," about which I had never before heard. Through microsurgical techniques, the neurologist explained, the now defunct cells of my cortex could be removed and replaced with an electronic and chemical device, which would act in their stead. The fine termini of the device would be connected to all of the living cells to which my dead cortical cells were attached at synaptic junctions. Certain ends of the cortical patch would be attached to long nerve fibers ending in the cortex and connected to my left thumb. These ends of the cortical patch would detect an increase in the concentration of certain chemicals, principally acetylcholine, associated with the transmission of nervous impulses. The cortical patch would then change the electrical polarity of the end attached to the nerve fiber. Other ends of the cortical patch would be attached to synaptic junctions with healthy cortical cells, the same cells to which my dead cortical cells were attached. When one end of the cortical patch detected an increase in chemical transmitters at the end of the nerve fiber, the other termini of the patch, attached to the cortical cells, would stimulate the membranes of these cells, exactly as the deceased cells had done when they were living and healthy. The result would be that I would once again feel prickles in my left thumb. Because the procedure was experimental, my neurologist assured me, the replacement would be performed free of charge.

I am not sure whether it was fascination, curiosity, or vanity that drove me, but I accepted the offer. I wish now that I had not, but the past cannot be changed. News of the surgery somehow got out, and much to my discomfort I became the subject of a great deal of popular discussion, much of it fueled by the speculations of the Reformed Dretskeans.

Almost unanimously, the Reformed Dretskeans held that the surgery would not work at all. When the cortical patch was in place, I still would not feel any prickle in my thumb, and I would say as much, or so they claimed. The neuroscientists confidently predicted that I would feel a prickle, and would say so. As it turned out, the neuroscientists were right. After I awoke from the surgery, a nurse stuck a needle in my left thumb and I yelped. That yelp shook apart the Reformed Society of Dretskeans.

Some of the Dretskeans maintained that although I *said* I felt a pain, saying as much was only an aspect of *acting as if* I had a pain. But if the neurosurgeons had their wiring correctly done, the argument continued, I should certainly act as if I had a pain, even though I didn't have one. The Dretskeans paid me a visit after my release from the hospital, and presented me with this argument, to which I responded that I knew what a prickle pain felt like because my other cortical cells had been working fine, and I knew what my left thumb felt like, because I had continually been sensitive to heat and aches in my left thumb. So if I heard myself saying, "I feel a prickle pain in my left thumb" when in fact I didn't *feel* anything like a prickle pain in my left thumb, I would certainly know that something was amiss, and I did not know any such thing.

The Dretskeans withdrew and divided into three camps. The Radical Dretskeans maintained that since my surgery, I no longer had mental properties. I and other Dretskeans regarded this opinion as a revival of the doctrines of the original Society of Dretskeans and promptly obtained the intervention of the police. The Radical Dretskeans fled to Utah, where they hide, few in number and ineffective. The Fictive Dretskeans sought to remain true to their philosophical author's doctrine by means of a curious casuistry. They held that I had mental states, consciousness, thoughts, and beliefs, but they continued that I did not have any feeling of prickle pains in my left thumb. I merely thought I had such feelings. My conviction was sincere, they claimed, and could move me to act just as if I really had a prickle pain, but I didn't and couldn't. Finally, the Holistic Dretskeans maintained that I really did have a prickle pain, and I was pleased to learn of their conclusion. Almost exactly reversing the reasoning of the original Society of Dretskeans, they argued that I had the pain because consciousness, pain, and other mental states are properties of the whole cerebral cortex, and as long as some part of my cerebral cortex was intact, it sufficed to cause the appropriate mental states when I was in the appropriate functional states. So long as a good bit of my cortex was attached to the cortical patches, and so long as the cortical patches bore the same input and output relations to one another as did the cells they replaced, I would have thoughts, pains, and pleasures just as before.

I myself found the doctrines of the Fictive Dretskeans perverse and repugnant, insofar as I could understand them at all. Still, their doctrine, and the Society of Fictive Dretskeans, endured and is with us today. I found far more plausible the views of the Holistic Dretskeans, so much that I began to attend their meetings, and they began to think of me as a convert. I was never that, but sane men live by possibilities, and their doctrine is surely possible.

The cortical patch entirely relieved the difficulties with my left thumb, and after me, many others had small cortical patches inserted, but the patch did not stop my illness. Only a few years after my surgery, another behavioral difficulty arose; the details of which I shall not embarrass myself with in print. Again, the neurologists diagnosed a softening of a part of the cortex. In this case, cells some of which were connected with the cortical patch; although, my physicians assured me that the cortical patch was not responsible. Another cortical patch was recommended to be connected partly to the old cortical patch and partly to the other cortical cells that were connected to the cells of my cortex that had ceased to function properly. The second patch was duly installed, as successfully as the first. To all appearances, so long as I wore my hat upon my head, I was perfectly normal. What's more, I *felt* perfectly normal.

Unfortunately, the deterioration of my cortical cells accelerated. With increasing frequency, new cortical patches had to be inserted, replacing more and more of my natural substance. I am now convinced that the introduction of the first cortical patch accelerated the softening of my brain tissues, and that in all probability had I learned to live with a left thumb that could not feel prickles, I would have suffered no further loss of function. In any case, the succession of cortical patches all worked as they should, and I am able to think, feel, and sleep much as I did before.

I have now only a middling piece of cerebral cortex left, and my neurosurgeons tell me it must go. It is a quite central piece, and when it softens, I will find myself with only the capacities of an idiot, a prospect I cannot endure. They have readied a final cortical patch to replace it, and if I let the surgery go on, they assure me that while my higher cortex will have been entirely replaced with bits of silicon, germanium, and whatnot, all of the functional relations of the original cortex will be preserved. I will think, feel, and remember like any ordinary person; like myself, in fact.

But now the doctrines of the Fictive and Holistic Dretskeans have converged, and except among neurosurgeons are almost universal, for when and if I have the final patch implanted, both Societies will concur in their

judgment of me: I will be without thought or reflection, without any higher mental states. Nothing I say or do will redeem me in their judgment. Of
course I am frightened of their power and influence, just as some thirty
years ago the recipients of neuroprosthetics were frightened of the original
Society of Dretskeans. But my agony is deeper than mere fright at my
treatment after surgery; it is an agony about whether there will be an I to
be treated, and about the unspeakable solitude I will endure if there is. The
Dretskean Societies are very influential, and they clamor to outlaw the
procedure to which I am to be subjected. I will surely be the first person to
have a cortex of silicon, and whatever the outcome of my surgery, I will
very likely also be the last. If the Dretskeans are wrong, (and surely, in my
case, the Fictive Dretskeans *must* be wrong, for how could I only think I
think?) then should I survive my surgery—I will remain. But no one will
know of my sentience except for me, and no one could know if the procedure could save another like me. If the Dretskeans are correct, and I cease
to exist and am replaced by a mindless automaton that acts as I do, then
no one will know that either, although many will believe themselves to
know it.

Note

1. This essay is based on an after-dinner talk at a North Carolina conference in the early
1980s. The Dretskeans were Searleans in the original version. I sent a copy to Professor Searle
shortly after the appearance of his *Minds, Brains and Science* (Harvard University Press,
1984). He wrote in return that I had completely misunderstood him, and he took considerable offense. Since, however, Searle subsequently published the idea without attribution, it
seems proper that this source should appear in print, but in keeping with the very spirit of
the essay, I have deferred to Searle's first person acquaintance with his own views, and hence
Dretskeans have replaced Searleans. Professor Dretske may similarly object, but I can only
read. Compare his *Naturalizing the Mind* (The MIT Press, 1997)

Part Two

Designs for Cognition

5   Machine as Mind

Herbert A. Simon

In this chapter I will start with the human mind and what psychological research has learned about it, I will proceed to draw lessons from cognitive psychology about the characteristics we must bestow upon computer programs when we wish those programs to think. I speak of "mind" and not "brain." By "mind" I mean a system that produces thought, viewed at a relatively high level of aggregation: say, at or above the level of elementary processes that require one hundred milliseconds or more for their execution. At that level, little or nothing need be said about the structure or behavior of individual neurons, or even small assemblages of them. Our units will be larger and more abstract.

It is well known that the language and representation best adapted to describing phenomena depends on the level of aggregation at which we model them. Physicists concerned with quarks and similar particles on minute temporal and spatial scales do not use the same vocabulary of entities and processes as geneticists describing how DNA informs protein synthesis.

Whatever our philosophical position with respect to reduction, it is practically necessary to build science in levels. The phenomena at each level are described in terms of the primitives at that level, and these primitives become, in turn, the phenomena to be described and explained at the next level following.

The primitives of mind, at the level I wish to consider, are symbols, complex structures of symbols, and processes that operate on symbols (Newell and Simon 1976). The simplest among these processes require tens to hundreds of milliseconds for their execution. Simple recognition of a familiar object takes at least five hundred milliseconds. At this level, the same software can be implemented with radically different kinds of hardware—protoplasm and silicon among them.

My central thesis is that at this level of aggregation conventional computers can be, and have been, programmed to represent symbol structures and carry out processes on those structures in a manner that parallels, step by step, the way the human brain does it. The principal evidence for my thesis are programs that do just that. These programs demonstrably think.

It has been argued that a computer simulation of thinking is no more thinking than a simulation of digestion is digestion. The analogy is false. A computer simulation of digestion is not capable of taking starch as an input and producing fructose or glucose as outputs. It deals only with symbolic or numerical quantities representing these substances.

In contrast, a computer simulation of thinking thinks. It takes problems as its inputs and (sometimes) produces solutions as its outputs. It represents these problems and solutions as symbolic structures, as the human mind does, and performs transformations on them, as the human mind does. The materials of digestion are chemical substances, which are not replicated in a computer simulation. The materials of thought are symbols—patterns, which can be replicated in a great variety of materials (including neurons and chips), thereby enabling physical symbol systems fashioned of these materials to think. Alan Turing (1950) was perhaps the first to have this insight in clear form, forty years ago.

Nearly Decomposable Systems

The successive levels in the architecture of nature are not arbitrary (Simon 1981). Most complex systems are hierarchical and *nearly decomposable*. Consider a building divided into rooms, which are, in turn, divided into cubicles. Starting from a state of radical temperature disequilibrium— every cubic foot of space being momentarily at quite a different temperature from the adjoining spaces—within a matter of minutes the temperature within each cubicle will approach some constant value, a different value for each cubicle. After a somewhat longer time, all the cubicles in a given room will reach a common temperature. After a still longer interval, all the rooms in the building will reach a common temperature.

In a hierarchical system of this kind, we do not have to consider the behavior at all levels simultaneously. We can model the cubicles, the rooms, and the building semi-independently. In the short run, we can analyze the changes in individual cubicles while disregarding their interaction with the other cubicles. In the middle run, we can analyze the individual rooms, replacing the detail of each cubicle by its average temperature. For the longer run, we can consider the building as a whole, replacing the detail of each room by its average temperature.

In layered hierarchical systems of this kind, each subcomponent has a much higher rate of interaction with the other subcomponents in the same component than it does with subcomponents outside that component. Elsewhere (Simon 1981) I have shown how the behavior of nearly decomposable systems can be analyzed mathematically and why, from an evolutionary standpoint, we should expect most of the complex systems that we find in nature to be nearly decomposable.

For present purposes, what is important about nearly-decomposable systems is that we can analyze them at a particular level of aggregation without detailed knowledge of the structures at the levels below. These details do not "show through" at the next level above; only aggregate properties of the more microscopic systems affect behavior at the higher level. In our temperature example, only the average temperatures of the cubicles affect the changes in temperature in the rooms, and only the average temperatures of the rooms are relevant to the course of equilibration of the building as a whole.

Because mind has shown itself to behave as a nearly-decomposable system, we can model thinking at the symbolic level, with events in the range of hundreds of milliseconds or longer, without concern for details of implementation at the "hardware" level, whether the hardware be brain or computer.

The Two Faces of AI

Artificial intelligence can be approached in two ways. First, we can write smart programs for computers without any commitment to imitating the processes of human intelligence. We can then use all of the speed and power of the computer and all of its memory capacity, unconcerned with whether people have the same computational speed and power or the same memory capacity.

Alternatively, we can write smart programs for computers that do imitate closely the human processes, forgoing the computer's capacities for rapid processing of symbols and its almost instantaneous memory storage. We can slow the computer down to human speeds, so to speak, and test whether it can absorb the cunning that will permit it to behave intelligently within these limitations.

Chess-playing programs illustrate the two approaches. DeepThought is a powerful program that now plays chess at grandmaster level and can defeat all but a few hundred human players. It demonstrably does not play in a humanoid way, typically exploring tens of millions of branches of the game tree before it makes its choice of move. There is good empirical evidence (de Groot 1965) that human grandmasters seldom look at more than 100 branches on the tree. By generally searching the *relevant* branches, they make up with chess knowledge for their inability to carry out massive searches.

However, DeepThought by no means "explores all possibilities." "All possibilities" would mean at least 10^{50} branches, 10^{40} times more than the program can manage, and obviously more than any computer, present or prospective can explore. DeepThought exercises a certain degree of selectivity in the branches it explores, but more important, it halts its explorations about a dozen ply deep—far short of the end of the game—and applies an evaluation function to measure the relative goodness of all the positions it reaches. A great deal of chess knowledge, supplied by the human programmers, is incorporated in the evaluation function. Hence DeepThought's chess prowess rests on a combination of brute force, unattainable by human players, and extensive, if "mediocre," chess knowledge.

Consider now a much earlier program, MATER (Baylor and Simon 1966) which is not nearly as good a chess player as DeepThought. In fact, MATER is a specialist designed only to exploit those game positions where an immediate mating combination (possibly a quite deep one) might be hidden. MATER has shown substantial ability to discover such mating combinations—rediscovering many of the most celebrated ones in chess history. What is more interesting, MATER ordinarily looks at fewer than 100 branches of the tree in order to accomplish this feat. It is as selective in its search as human players are in these kinds of situations, and in fact, it looks at nearly the same parts of the game tree as they do.

We can go even farther in comparing MATER with human players. For these kinds of positions (where a possible checkmate lurks), MATER uses the same rules of thumb to guide its search and select promising lines that human masters use. It examines forceful moves first, and it examines first those branches along which the opponent is most constrained. These heuristics, while powerful, do not always lead to the shortest mate. We have found at least one historical instance (a game between Edward Lasker and George Alan Thomas) in which both human player and computer required an extra move because the shortest path to a checkmate did not satisfy these heuristics—did not correspond with the most plausible search path.

The remainder of my remarks are concerned with programs that are intelligent in more or less humanoid ways—that carry out only modest computations to perform their tasks. These programs resemble MATER rather than DeepThought. This does not mean that programs for AI should always be built in this way, but my aim here is to consider machine as mind rather than to celebrate the achievements of rapid computation.

The View from Psychology

Selective Heuristic Search

How does intelligence look to contemporary cognitive psychology? I have already mentioned one fact that has been verified repeatedly in the laboratory—human problem solvers do not carry out extensive searches. Even examining one hundred possibilities in a game tree stretches human memory and patience. Since many of the spaces in which people solve problems are enormous (I have mentioned the figure of 10^{50} for chess), "trying everything" is not a viable search strategy. People use knowledge about the structure of the problem space to form heuristics that allow them to search extremely selectively.

Recognition: The Indexed Memory

A second important fact is also well illustrated by the game of chess. A chess grandmaster can play fifty or more opponents "simultaneously," moving from board to board and seldom taking more than a few seconds for each move. If the opponents are not stronger than experts, say, the grandmaster will win almost every game, although his play will perhaps be only at master level. This fact demonstrates that much of grandmasters' knowledge (not all of it) is accessed by recognition of cues on the board, for in simultaneous play they have no time for deep analysis by search (Chase and Simon 1973).

Grandmasters, questioned on how they play simultaneous games, report that they make "standard" developing moves until they notice a feature of the board that indicates a weakness in the opponent's position (doubled pawns, say). Noticing this feature gives access to information about strategies for exploiting it. The grandmaster's memory is like a large indexed encyclopedia (with at least 50,000 index entries). The perceptually noticeable features of the chessboard (the cues) trigger the appropriate index entries and give access to the corresponding information. This information often includes relevant strategies.

Solving problems by responding to cues that are visible only to experts is sometimes called solving them by "intuition." A better label would be "solving by recognition." Intuition consists simply of noting features in a situation that index useful information. There is no mystery in intuition, or at least no more mystery than there is in recognizing a friend on the street and recalling what one knows about the friend.

In computers, recognition processes are generally implemented by productions: the condition sides of the productions serving as tests for the presence of cues, the action sides holding the information that is accessed when the cues are noticed. Hence, it is easy to build computer systems that solve problems by recognition, and indeed recognition capability is the core of most AI expert systems.

The number, 50,000, suggested above as the number of features a grandmaster can recognize on a chessboard, has been estimated empirically, but only by indirect means (Simon and Gilmartin 1973). Confidence rises that the figure is approximately correct when one notes that it is roughly comparable to the native language vocabularies of college graduates (usually estimated at 50,000 to 100,000 words).

Items that, by their recognizability, serve to index semantic memory are usually called "chunks" in the psychological literature. Generalizing, we hypothesize that an expert in any domain must acquire some 50,000 familiar chunks (give or take a factor of four). Although existing expert systems for computers are not this large, the figure is not a daunting one.

By way of footnote, extensive data show that it takes at least ten years of intensive training for a person to acquire the information (presumably including the 50,000 chunks) required for world-class performance in any domain of expertise. This has been shown for chess playing, musical composition, painting, piano playing, swimming, tennis, neuropsychological research, research in topology, and other fields (Bloom 1985, Hayes 1989). Wolfgang Amadeus Mozart, who began composing at four, produced no world-class music before at least the age of seventeen, thirteen years later. Child prodigies are not exempt from the rule.

Seriality: The Limits of Attention

Problems that cannot be solved by recognition generally require the application of more or less sustained attention. Attention is closely associated with human short-term memory. Symbols that are attended to—the inputs, say, to an arithmetic calculation—must be retained during use in short-term memory, which has a capacity of only about seven chunks, a limit that is based on extensive experimental data (Simon 1976). The need for all inputs and outputs of attention-demanding tasks to pass through short-term memory essentially serializes the thinking process. Generally, we can only think of one thing at a time. (Sometimes, by time sharing, we can think of two, if they are not too complex. Light conversation and driving are compatible activities for most people when the traffic is not too heavy!)

Hence, whatever parallel processes may be going on at lower (neural) levels, at the symbolic level the human mind is fundamentally a serial machine, accomplishing its work through temporal sequences of processes, each typically requiring hundreds of milliseconds for execution.

In contrast, the evidence is equally strong that the sensory organs, especially the eyes and ears, are highly parallel systems. We are confronted with a hybrid system, the sensory (and possibly perceptual) processes operating in parallel, and the subsequent symbolic processes (after patterns of stimuli have been recognized and chunked) serially.

Within the limits of present knowledge, there is a no-man's-land between the parallel and serial components of the processor, whose exact boundaries are not known. For example, there are implementable schemes that execute all processing down to the point of recognition in parallel (for example, so-called Demon schemes), but there are also workable serial recognition systems (e.g., EPAM: Feigenbaum and Simon 1984, Richman and Simon 1989). The available evidence does not make a clear choice between these alternatives.

The Architecture of Expert Systems

Psychology, then, gives us a picture of the expert as having a sensory system that is basically parallel in structure, interfaced with a cognitive system that is basically serial. Somewhere in the imprecise boundary between the two is a mechanism (serial or parallel or both) capable of recognizing large numbers (hundreds of thousands) of patterns in the domain of expertise and of obtaining access through this recognition to information stored in short-term memory. The information accessed can be processed further (using heuristic search) by a serial symbol-processing system.

Recognition takes approximately a half second or second (Newell and Simon 1972). The individual steps in search also require hundreds of milliseconds, and search is highly selective, the selectivity based on heuristics stored in memory. People can report orally the results of recognition (but not the cues used in the process) and are aware of many of the inputs and outputs of the steps they take in search. It appears that they can report most of the symbols that reside temporarily in short-term memory (i.e., the symbols in the focus of attention).

One reason for thinking that this structure is sufficient to produce expert behavior is that AI has now built many expert systems, capable of performing at professional levels in restricted domains, using essentially the architecture we have just described. In general, the AI expert systems (for example, systems for medical diagnosis) have fewer "chunks" than the human experts and make up for the deficiency by doing more computing than people do. The differences appear to be quantitative, not qualitative: human and computer experts alike depend heavily upon recognition, supplemented by a little capacity for reasoning (i.e., search).

The Matter of Semantics

It is sometimes claimed that the thinking of computers, symbolic systems that they are, is purely syntactical. Unlike people, it is argued, computers do not have intentions, and their symbols do not have semantic referents. The argument is easily refuted by concrete examples of computer programs that demonstrably understand the meanings (at least some of the meanings) of their symbols and that have goals, thus exhibiting at least two aspects of intention.

Consider, first, a computer-driven van, of which we have an example on our university campus, equipped with television cameras and capable of steering its way (slowly) along a winding road in a nearby park. Patterns of light transmitted through the cameras are encoded by the computer program as landscape features (e.g., the verge of the road). The program, having the intention of proceeding along the road and remaining on it, creates internal symbols that denote these features, interprets them, and uses the symbols to guide its steering and speed-control mechanisms.

Consider, second, one of the commercially available chess-playing programs that use an actual chess board on which the opponent moves the men physically and that senses these moves and forms an internal (symbolic) representation of the chess position. The symbols in this internal representation denote the external physical pieces and their arrangement, and the program demonstrates quite clearly, by the moves it chooses, that it intends to beat its opponent.

There is no mystery about what "semantics" means as applied to the human mind. It means that there is a correspondence, a relation of denotation, between symbols inside the head and objects (or relations among objects) outside. In particular, the brain is (sometimes) able to test whether sensory signals received from particular objects identify those objects as the meanings of particular symbols (names). And the human brain is sometimes able to construct and emit words, phrases, and sentences whose denotation corresponds to the sensed scene.

There is also no mystery about human intentions. Under certain circumstances, for example, a human being senses internal stirrings (usually called hunger) that lead him or her to seek food. Under other circumstances, other stirrings create the goal of defeating an opponent in chess. Now the two computer programs I described above also have goals: in the one case to drive along a road, in the other case to win a chess game. It would not be hard to store both programs in the same computer, along with input channels that would, from time to time, switch its attention from the one goal to the other. Such a system would then have not a single intention, but a capacity for several, even as you and I.

It may be objected (and has been) that the computer does not "understand" the meanings of its symbols or the semantic operations on them, or the goals it adopts. This peculiar use of the word "understand" has something to do with the fact that we are (sometimes) conscious of meanings and intentions. But then, my evidence that you are conscious is no better than my evidence that the road-driving or chess-playing computers are conscious.

Moreover, in formal treatments of semantics, consciousness has never been one of the defining characteristics; denotation has. What is important about semantic meaning is that there be a correspondence (conscious or not) between the symbol and the thing it denotes. What is important about intention is that there be a correspondence (conscious or not) between the goal symbol and behavior appropriate to achieving the goal in the context of some belief system.

Finally, John Searle's Chinese Room parable proves not that computer programs cannot understand Chinese, but only that the particular program Searle described does not understand Chinese. Had he described a program that could receive inputs from a sensory system and emit the symbol "cha" in the presence of tea and "bai cha" in the presence of hot water, we would have to admit that it understood at least a little Chinese. And the vocabulary and grammar could be extended indefinitely. Later, I will describe a computer program, devised by Laurent Siklóssy (1972), that learns language in exactly this way (although the connection with external senses was not implemented).

"Ill-Structured" Phenomena

Research on human thinking has progressed from relatively simple and well-structured phenomena (for example, rote verbal learning, solving puzzles, simple concept attainment) to more complex and rather ill-structured tasks (e.g., use of natural language, learning, scientific discovery, visual art). "Ill-structured" means that the task has ill-defined or multi-dimensional goals, that its frame of reference or representation is not clear or obvious, that there are no clear-cut procedures for generating search paths or evaluating them—or some combination of these characteristics.

When a problem is ill-structured in one or more of these senses, a first step in solving it is to impose some kind of structure that allows it to be represented—that is, symbolized—at least approximately, and attacked in this symbolized form. What does psychology tell us about problem representations: their nature and how they are constructed for particular problems?

Forms of Representation

We do not have an exhaustive taxonomy of possible representations, but a few basic forms show up prominently in psychological research. First, situations may be represented in words or in logical or mathematical notations. All of these representations are basically propositional and are more or less equivalent to a set of propositions in some formal logic. Propositional representation immediately suggests that the processing will resemble logical reasoning or proof.

When problems are presented verbally, the propositional translation of these words may be quite literal or may comprise only the semantic content of the input without preserving syntactic details. In both cases, we will speak of propositional representation. There is a great deal of psychological evidence that input sentences are seldom retained intact but that, instead, their semantic content is usually extracted and stored in some form.

Second, situations may be represented in diagrams or pictures ("mental pictures"). Internally, a picture or diagram can be represented by the equivalent of a raster of pixels (for example, the cerebral image associated with the direct signals from the retina) or by a network of nodes and links that capture the components of the diagram and their relations. Possibly there are other ways (for example, as the equations of analytic geometry), but these two have been given most consideration by psychologists. A picture or diagram amounts to a model of the system, with processes that operate on it to move it through time or to search through a succession of its states.

Most psychological research on representations assumes, explicitly or implicitly, one of the representations mentioned in the preceding paragraphs: propositional, rasterlike "picture," or node-link diagram, or some combination of them. All of these representations are easily implemented by computer programs.

Equivalence of Representations

What consequences does the form of representation have for cognition? To answer that question, we must define the notion of *equivalence of representations*. Actually, we must define two notions: informational equivalence and computational equivalence (Larkin and Simon 1987). Two representations are *informationally* equivalent if either one is logically derivable from the other—if all the information available in the one is available in the other. Two representations are *computationally* equivalent if all the information easily available in the one is *easily* available in the other, and vice versa.

"Easily" is a vague term, but it is adequate for our purpose. Information is easily available if it can be obtained from the explicit information with a small amount of computation—small relative to the capacities of the processor. Thus, defining a representation includes specifying the primitive processes, those that are not further analyzed and that can be carried out rapidly.

Representations of numerical information in Arabic and Roman numerals are informationally equivalent, but not computationally equivalent. It may be much easier or harder to find the product of two numbers in the one notation than in the other. Similarly, representations of the same problem, on the one hand as a set of declarative propositions in Prolog, and on the other hand as a node-link diagram in Lisp, are unlikely to be computationally equivalent (Larkin and Simon 1987). It may be far easier to solve the problem in the one form than in the other—say, easier by heuristic search than by resolution theorem proving.

Representations Used by People

There is much evidence that people sometimes use "mental pictures" to represent problems, representations that have the properties of rasters or of node-link networks (Kosslyn 1980). There is little evidence that they use propositions in the predicate calculus to represent them, or operate on their representations by theorem-proving methods. Of course, engineers, scientists, and others do represent many problems with mathematical formalisms, but the processes that operate upon these formalisms resemble heuristic search much more than they do logical reasoning (Larkin and Simon 1987, Paige and Simon 1966).

Research on problem solving in algebra and physics has shown that subjects typically convert a problem from natural language into diagrams and then convert the latter into equations. A direct translation from language to equations seems to take place, if at all, only in the case of very simple familiar problems. AI models of the diagrammatic representations that problem solvers use in these domains can be found in Larkin and Simon (1987) and Novak (1977).

Evidence is lacking as to whether there exists a "neutral" semantic representation for information that is neither propositional nor pictorial. At least in simple situations, much information is readily transformed from one representation to the other. For example, in one common experimental paradigm, subjects are presented with an asterisk above or below a plus sign and, simultaneously, with a sentence of the form, "The star is above/below the plus" (Clark and Chase 1972). The subject must respond "true" or "false." Before responding, the subject must, somehow, find a common representation for the visual display and the sentence—converting one into the other, or both into a common semantic representation. But the experiments carried out in this paradigm do not show which way the conversion goes. From the physics and algebra experiments, we might conjecture that, for most subjects, the internal (or semantic) representation is the diagrammatic one, but we must be careful in generalizing across tasks.

I have barely touched on the evidence from psychology about the representations people use in their problem-solving activities. The evidence we have throws strong doubt on any claim of hegemony for either propositional or pictorial representations. If either tends to be dominant, it is probably the pictorial (or diagrammatic) rather than the propositional. The evidence suggests strongly that, whatever the form of representation, the processing of information almost always resembles heuristic search rather than theorem proving.

We can only conjecture that these preferences have something to do with computational efficiency. I have elsewhere spelled out some of the implications of the computational inequivalence of representations for such issues as logic programming versus rule-based computation.

Insight Problems

Problems that tend to be solved suddenly, with an "aha!" experience, often after a long period of apparently fruitless struggle, have attracted much attention. Can we say anything about the mystery of such insightful process-es? Indeed, we can. We can say enough to dissipate most or all of the magic.

One problem of this kind is the "Mutilated Checkerboard." We are given an ordinary checkerboard of 64 squares and 32 dominoes, each domino exactly covering two adjoining squares of the board. Obviously we can cover the entire board with the 32 dominoes. Now we cut off the northwest square and the southeast square of the board, and ask whether the remaining 62 squares can be covered exactly by 31 dominoes (Kaplan and Simon 1990).

Subjects generally attack this problem by attempting coverings, and per-sist for an hour or more, becoming increasingly frustrated as they fail to achieve a solution. At some point, they decide that a covering is impossible and switch their effort to proving the impossibility. They recognize that to do so they need a new problem representation, but unfortunately, people do not appear to possess a general-purpose generator of problem repre-sentations. It is not enough to say, "I need a new representation." How does one go about constructing it?

Some subjects do, after a shorter or longer time, succeed in constructing a new representation and then solve the problem in a few minutes. The new representation records the *number* of squares of each color and the *number* of each color that is covered by a single domino. The geometric arrangement of the squares, a central feature of the original representa-tion, is simply ignored. But since the mutilated checkerboard has two more squares of one color than of the other, and since dominoes, no mat-ter how many, can cover only the same number of squares of each color, the impossibility of a covering is immediately evident.

The power of the abstraction is obvious, but how do subjects achieve it? Experiments show that they achieve it when their attention focuses on the fact that the remaining uncovered squares, after unsuccessful attempts at covering, are always the same color. How the attention focus comes about is a longer story, which I won't try to tell here, but which is quite under-standable in terms of ordinary mechanisms of attention.

Much remains to be done before we understand how people construct their problem representations and the role those representations play in problem solving. But we know enough already to suggest that the repre-sentations people use—both propositional and pictorial—can be simulat-ed by computers. Diagrammatic representations of the node-link type are naturally represented in list-processing languages like Lisp. Rasters pose a more difficult problem, for we must define appropriate primitive processes to extract information from them. Finding such processes is more or less synonymous with developing efficient programs for visual pattern recog-nition.

The Processing of Language

Whatever the role it plays in thought, natural language is the principal medium of communication between people. What do we know about how it is processed and how it is learned?

Some Programs that Understand Language

Enormous amounts of research on language have been done within the disciplines of linguistics and psycholinguistics. Until quite recent times, the greater part of that research was focused on lexical issues, syntax, and phonetics, seldom straying beyond the boundaries of the individual sentence. Without disputing the importance of this activity, it might be argued that far more has been learned about the relation between natural language and thinking from computer programs that use language inputs or outputs to perform concrete tasks. For example, Gordon S. Novak's (1977) ISMC program, which extracts the information from natural-language descriptions of physics problems, and transforms it into an internal "semantic" representation suitable for a problem-solving system. In somewhat similar manner, Pat Hayes and Herb Simon's (1974) Understand program reads natural-language instructions for puzzles and creates internal representations ("pictures") of the problem situations and interpretations of the puzzle rules for operating on them.

Systems like these give us specific models of how people extract meaning from discourse with the help of semantic knowledge they already hold in memory. For example, Novak's system interprets the natural-language input using schemas that encapsulate its knowledge about such things as levers and masses and assembles this knowledge into a composite schema that pictures the problem situation.

At a more abstract level, Understand extracts knowledge from prose about the objects under discussion, the relations among them, and the ways of changing these relations. It uses this information to construct a system of internal nodes, links, and processes that represent these objects, relations, and operations. In simple puzzle situations, Understand can go quite a long way with a minimum of semantic knowledge, relying heavily on syntactic cues.

Acquiring Language

Of equal importance is the question of how languages are acquired. Siklóssy (1972) simulated the process of language acquisition, guided by Ivor Armstrong Richards's plan for learning language by use of pictures. Siklóssy's program, called *ZBIE*, was given (internal representations of) simple pictures (a dog chasing a cat, a hat on a woman's head). With each picture, it was given a sentence describing the scene. With the aid of a carefully designed sequence of such examples, it gradually learned to associate nouns with the objects in the pictures and other words with their properties and the relations.

Siklóssy tested ZBIE in novel situations whose components were familiar by requiring it to construct sentences describing these new situations. It learned the fundamentals of a number of European languages, including the appropriate conventions for word order.

Will Our Knowledge of Language Scale?

These are just a few illustrations of current capabilities for simulating human use and acquisition of language. Since all of them involve relatively simple language with a limited vocabulary, it is quite reasonable to ask how they would scale up to encompass the whole vast structure of a natural language as known and used by a native speaker. We do not know the answer to this question—and won't know it until it has been done—but we should not overemphasize the criticality of the scaling-up issue. When we wish to understand basic physical phenomena, we do not look for complex real-world situations in which to test them, but instead design the simplest conceivable laboratory situations in which to demonstrate and manipulate them.

Even in classical mechanics, physicists are far from a full understanding of the three-body problem, much less the behavior of n bodies, where n is a large number. Most scientific effort goes into the study of toy systems rather than the study of a complex "real world." We usually understand the mechanisms that govern the complex world long before we are able to calculate or simulate the behavior of that world in detail.

Similarly, to demonstrate an understanding of human thinking, we do not need to model thinking in the most complex situations we can imagine. It is enough for most purposes that our theory explain the phenomena in a range of situations that would call for genuine thinking in human subjects. Research has already met that criterion for language processing.

Discovery and Creativity

We should not be intimidated by words like "intuition" that are often used to describe human thinking. We have seen that "intuition" usually simply means problem solving by recognition, easily modeled by production systems. We have also seen that the "insight" that leads to change in representation and solution of the mutilated checkerboard problem can be explained by mechanisms of attention focusing. What about "creative" processes? Can we give an account of them, too?

Making scientific discoveries is generally adjudged to be both ill-structured and creative. As it is also a very diverse activity, with many aspects, a theory that explains one aspect might not explain others. Scientists sometimes examine data to discover regularities—scientific laws and new concepts for expressing the laws parsimoniously. They sometimes discover new scientific problems or invent new ways of representing problems. They sometimes deduce new consequences from theories.

Scientists sometimes conceive of mechanisms to explain the empirical laws that describe phenomena. They sometimes develop and execute experimental strategies to obtain new data for testing theories or evolving new theories. They sometimes invent and construct new instruments for gathering new kinds of data or more precise data. There are other things that scientists do, but this list at leasts illustrates the variety of activities in which they engage, any of which may produce a creative discovery.

A number of these activities, but not all, have been simulated by computer. In addition, historians of science have recounted the courses of events that led to a substantial number of important discoveries.

A computer program called BACON (Langley, Simon, Bradshaw, and Zytkow 1987), when given the data available to the scientists in historically important situations, has rediscovered Kepler's Third Law, Ohm's Law, Boyle's Law, Black's Law of Temperature Equilibrium, and many others. In the course of finding these laws, BACON has reinvented such fundamental concepts as inertial mass, atomic weight and molecular weight, and specific heat. We do not have to speculate about how discoveries of these kinds are made; we can examine the behavior of programs like BACON and compare them with the historical record (or with the behavior of human subjects presented with the same problems).

The KEKADA program (Kulkarni and Simon 1988) plans experimental strategies, responding to the information gained from each experiment to plan the next one. On the basis of its knowledge and experience, it forms expectations about the outcome of experiments and switches to a strategy for exploiting its surprise when these expectations are not fulfilled. With the aid of these capabilities, the program is able to track closely the strategy that Hans Krebs used to elucidate the synthesis of urea in vivo and Michael Faraday's strategy in investigating the production of electrical currents by the variation of magnetic fields. Here, the accuracy with which the program explained the human processes was tested through a comparism of its behavior with the data-to-day course of the original research as gleaned from laboratory notebooks.

Programs like BACON and KEKADA show that scientists use essentially the same kinds of processes as those identified in more prosaic kinds of problem solving (solving puzzles or playing chess). Very high quality thinking is surely required for scientific work, but thinking of basically the same kind is used to solve more humdrum problems.

These successes in simulating scientific work put high on the agenda the simulation of other facets of science (inventing instruments, discovering appropriate problem representations) that have not yet been tackled. There is no reason to believe that they will disclose thinking processes wholly different from those that have been observed in the research I have just sketched.

Affect, Motivation, and Awareness

I have said nothing about the motivation required for successful human thinking. Motivation comes into the picture through the mechanism of attention. Motivation selects particular tasks for attention and diverts attention from others. When the other conditions for success are present, strong motivation sustained over long periods of time may secure the cognitive effort that is required to find a problem solution. In this manner, motivation and the mechanisms that strengthen and weaken it can be brought into models of problem solving in a quite natural manner.

Putting the matter in this over-simple way does not demean the importance of motivation in human thinking but suggests that its impact on thought processes is rather diffuse and aggregative rather than highly specific. Moreover, if affect and cognition interact largely through the mechanisms of attention, then it is reasonable to pursue our research on these two components of mental behavior independently. For example, in laboratory studies of problem solving, as long as we establish conditions that assure the subjects' attention to the task, we can study the cognitive processes without simultaneously investigating just how the motivation is generated and maintained.

The theory of thinking I have been describing says very little about consciousness—except in equating ability to report information with its presence in short-term memory. Many of the symbolic processes that support thought are in conscious awareness, but others are not. The presence or absence of awareness has strong implications for the ease or difficulty of testing the details of the theory, but few other implications. I will not try to pursue this difficult topic further here.

Conclusion: Computers Think—and Often Think like People

The conclusion we can draw from the evidence I have sketched is simple: Computers can be programmed, and have been programmed, to simulate at a symbolic level the processes that are used in human thinking. We need not talk about computers thinking in the future tense; they have been thinking (in smaller or bigger ways) for thirty-five years. They have been thinking "logically" and they have been thinking "intuitively"—even "creatively."

Why has this conclusion been resisted so fiercely, even in the face of massive evidence? I would argue, first, that the dissenters have not looked very hard at the evidence, especially the evidence from the psychological laboratory. They have grasped and held on to a romantic picture of the human mind that attributes to it capabilities that it simply does not have—not even the minds of Wolfgang Mozart and Albert Einstein, to say nothing of the rest of us poor mortals.

The human mind does not reach its goals mysteriously or miraculously. Even its sudden insights and "ahas" are explainable in terms of recognition processes, well-informed search, knowledge-prepared experiences of surprise, and changes in representation motivated by shifts in attention. When we incorporate these processes into our theory, as empirical evidence says we should, the unexplainable is explained.

Perhaps there are deeper sources of resistance to the evidence. Perhaps we are reluctant to give up our claims for human uniqueness—of being the only species that can think big thoughts. Perhaps we have "known" so long that machines can't think that only overwhelming evidence can change our belief. Whatever the reason, the evidence is now here, and it is time that we attended to it. If we hurry, we can catch up to Alan Turing on the path he pointed out to us so many years ago.

Acknowledgements

This chapter first appeared as "Machine as Mind" in *Android Epistemology*, edited by Clark Glymour, Kenneth M. Ford, and Patrick J. Hayes (Menlo Park, CA: AAAI/ The MIT Press, 1995).

6 From 2001 to *2001:* Common Sense and the Mind of HAL

Douglas B. Lenat

Making mistakes is in the nature of being human. I'll spare you the usual quote about forgiveness being divine, because I certainly have never forgiven HAL. We all felt bad when HAL terminated the cryogenically slumbering crew, cut Frank adrift, and almost murdered Dave. But that's not what I found so unforgiveable. To me, HAL's biggest crimes were his conceit and his stupidity.

By conceit, I mean claims like "No 9000 computer has ever made a mistake." This is more than just arrogant, more than just false; it is the *antithesis* of realism. If you met a man who genuinely believed he never had nor ever would make a mistake, you'd call him insane. Surely NASA would never have entrusted the mission to such a patently insane computer. I'll return to this point a bit later.

By stupidity, I mean his resort to extreme violence—murdering the entire crew—to solve his problems. Yes, he was facing a dilemma: should he jeopardize his secret orders, or should he disobey the order to keep them secret from the crew? This sort of dilemma is no more or less than the makings of good drama. HAL's solution was the same one William Shakespeare employed in his blackest tragedies, the same one Clint Eastwood employed in his man-with-no-name movies: just kill everyone.

In the late 1970s I built a computer program (Eurisko) that discovered things on its own in many fields. To get it to work, I had to give it the power to tinker with its own learning heuristics and its own goals. I would leave it running overnight and hurry in the next morning to see what it had come up with. Often I'd find it in a mode best described as "dead." Sometime during the night, Eurisko would decide that the best thing to do was to commit suicide and shut itself off. More precisely, it modified its own judgmental rules in a way that valued "making no errors at all" as highly as "making productive new discoveries." As soon as Eurisko did this, it found it could successfully meet its new goal by doing nothing at all for the rest of the night. This reminds me of HAL's boast: "No 9000 computer has ever made a mistake." I eventually had to add a new heuristic to Eurisko—one it couldn't modify in any way—to explicitly forbid this sort of suicide.

People have found many ways to grapple with and resolve conflicting goals short of killing everybody in sight. Surviving and thriving in the real world means constantly making tough decisions, and, yes, making mistakes. The only ways not to make mistakes are Eurisko's—do nothing—HAL / Shakespeare / Eastwood's—make sure there are no living souls left anywhere around you—and God's—be omniscient. HAL, if he were really smart, could have found another solution, just as we do every day.

Surely, any intelligent computer would understand that occasional mistakes and inconsistencies are inevitable and can even serve as valuable learning experiences. Anything else leads to what I call "Star Trek brittleness"—the absurdity that holds that one small inconsistency will make the computer self-destruct.

As humans we tolerate inconsistency all the time. Some inconsistency stems from different levels of generality and precision. We know about Albert Einstein's relativity, but in our everyday lives we act as though it doesn't exist; we know the earth revolves around the sun, but most of the time we talk and act as if the sun moves around the earth. Other instances of inconsistency are a result of different epistemological statuses: we both know that there are no vampires and that Dracula is a vampire. Some of it comes from information we learned in different ways at different times, such as childhood phobias that persist in adult life even though rationally we know them to be groundless. Yet other inconsistencies result from other people's inconsistencies, which they pass on to us.

So, just how smart *was* HAL? And how does Arthur C. Clarke's vision of computer intelligence compare with the reality of the HAL-like programs we can build today?

The Knowledge Pump

There is a lot of controversy about how human-level machine intelligence will develop. Some scientists believe it will follow a path similar to the one followed in nature by evolution: there will be artificial one-celled animals, artificial insects, artificial lawyers, artificial monkeys, and so on up to artificial human-level machine minds. Nature has made good use of trillion-fold parallelism for hundreds of millions of years; so it's no surprise that some folks expect computer hardware and raw computing power to create similar bottlenecks that we will ultimately overcome.

In an alternative view of machine-intelligence development, personal computers are already so powerful that they are not the bottleneck problem at all. This is my view.

This view is best likened to priming a pump. Visualize your brain as a knowledge pump. Knowledge goes in, gets stored, combined, copied, or whatever; from time to time, you say or write or do things that are, in effect, ways for your brain to emit knowledge. On a good day, the knowledge you give out may be as good or better than the knowledge you put in.

No one expects you to be a productive knowledge pump without training and experience—whether we're talking about playing the piano or tennis, writing a check or a novel, or making a U-turn in a car. You have to invest some learning-and-teaching time and effort before anyone expects you to be competent at a task, let alone to excel at it.

Consider Dr. Dave Bowman, mission commander of *Discovery*. His experiences as an engineering or astrophysics student and his astronaut training qualified him to lead the mission. Before that, his high school and undergraduate college prepared him for graduate school, and before that, he learned in elementary and middle school the fundamentals he needed for high school. And long before—here we get to some very important stuff indeed—his early experiences as a baby and toddler prepared him for kindergarten and first grade. He learned, for instance, to talk and that people generally prepare food in kitchens. He learned that if you leave something somewhere, it often remains there, at least for a while. He learned that chairs are for sitting on and that pouring milk from one glass to another differently shaped glass doesn't change the total volume of the milk. He learned that there's no air in outer space so he'd better not forget the helmet of his spacesuit if he's going walking in space. He learned all this—and a million other things.

It Takes Common Sense to Understand Each Other

There is a crucial point that most creators of science-fiction robots (from Robby to HAL to Data) seem to have ignored, and it is this: You need to have quite a bit of "common sense" before you can learn to talk, and before you can survive on your own in the everyday world.

Consider the first thing HAL tells Frank: "We've got the transmission from our parents coming in." There are three possible ways to interpret this sentence, depending on who or what exactly is "coming up." It could be *we* who are coming in, as in "We've got a lot of anxiety coming into this room." It could be *Frank's parents* who are coming in, as in "We looked up and saw our parents coming in." Or it could be—and is –the *transmission* that is coming in. Anyone with common sense could figure that out, and we assume that we all have common sense. It would be insulting or confusing to make our sentences longer just to clarify exactly what goes with what.

Consider next what HAL says to Dave when he finds that Dave has just drawn a new sketch of Dr. Hunter: "Can you hold it a bit closer?" This sentence is rife with ambiguity, though neither HAL nor Dave nor the audience appears to notice. Does HAL want a yes-or-no response to his question? Of course not, he wants Dave to move the drawing. Does he want Dave to move it closer to Dave or closer to HAL? Obviously the latter. But if Dave had been taking a zero-gravity tennis lesson from HAL and HAL had said "Can you hold it a bit closer?" we would all assume he wanted Dave to hold the tennis racket closer to Dave, not to HAL. To figure out that HAL is asking Dave to hold the sketch closer to HAL, one has to bring common sense into play. You can't appreciate art without seeing it, and the more clearly you can see it, the better you can appreciate or critique it. And, of course, the closer an object gets to your eyes (or to HAL's visual sensors), the more clearly you can make out its details, and so on. Similarly, in the tennis example, other simple facts—such as the relevance of how close Dave holds the racket to his ability to hit the ball well—would dissolve the ambiguity. All this is just common sense, the sort of things you learn as a baby and toddler. Yet you either know this mass of trivia or you don't; and if you don't, how can you tell that the picture should move closer to HAL but the tennis racket should go closer to Dave's body?

HAL's very next sentence, after Dave moves the sketch closer to HAL's sensor lens, is, "That's Dr. Hunter, isn't it?" Dave replies, naturally, "Yes," rather than "No, it's a sketch of Dr. Hunter"—another illustration of the way we depend on shared common sense to keep our sentences short. HAL knows it's a sketch, not a person, and Dave knows HAL knows this, and so on. These shared understandings let them communicate successfully despite the terseness of their exchanges.

Similarly, HAL's response to Dave during Frank's extra-vehicular activity (EVA)—"The radio is still dead"—creates no confusion in Dave's mind.

He knows that it violates common sense to even consider the possibility that the radio might suddenly become a living creature. HAL has to understand this—and a great many other things—in order to generate sentences using colorful language, metaphor, colloquialisms, and various other sorts of "realistic" ambiguity. Even something as innocuous as verb tenses—dealing with time—requires some common sense. Should HAL answer Dave's question about the radio in terms of the moment he starts asking it or finishes asking it, or when HAL starts to reply? Of course, Dave wants the latest information about Frank's status, and HAL can use present tense to convey all of the above. Otherwise, his speech would be so stilted he'd sound like a ...well, like an unintelligent machine: "The radio transmitter, which is located in Frank's spacesuit, was nonfunctional when you asked your question and remains so now as I answer it."

Consider the dramatic sentence just before the lip-reading: "Do you read me, HAL?" Clearly, Dave is not using the most common definition of *read* but a rarer meaning, *to be receiving successfully via radio*. HAL remains silent, not because he misunderstands the sentence, but because he's intentionally deceiving Dave.

An even clearer case of HAL's use of metaphor occurs when he raises for the first time the possibility that something is wrong: "Well, certainly no one could have been unaware of the very strange stories *floating around* before we left." In addition to using *floating* metaphorically, HAL is employing, in this one sort sentence, all of the following: sophisticated double negation ("no one...unaware"), a counterfactual construction ("no one could have been"), and an assumption about context. (*"No one* refers not to all the people on Earth, almost none of whom were aware of anything strange at launch time—other than, possibly, that an epidemic had broken out on the moon.)

Finally, consider the chilling sentence HAL utters after Dave says he'll use the emergency airlock: "Forgot your space helmet, Dave." The subject of the sentence could be Dave, or HAL, or someone else. But, of course, Dave, HAL, and the audience know exactly who has forgotten the helmet. Now consider the *forgot* in this sentence. It is used here in the sense of "left behind, a while ago" rather than "didn't think of it, just now." Presumably, the fact that he was helmetless was very much on Dave's mind just then as he decided to use the emergency airlock. He had left it behind several minutes earlier, but had no doubt been actively regretting his oversight for the past several seconds when HAL pointed it out. HAL knows this too, which is what makes his saying it so chilling: HAL is being cruel, and taunting Dave, not trying to be helpful.

We could give many more examples. In fact, most of the sentences uttered in the film exhibit the same phenomena: each party has quite a bit of common sense and assumes that others do too; those assumptions let them all encode and decode each other's utterances, use fewer words, employ metaphor and ambiguity, and deviate casually from the strict rules of grammar.

In life, this terse encoding is sometimes rather extreme: for example, between twins or long-married couples, colleagues working in a technical area, or bridge partners who have played together for a long time. These people draw on, not just common sense, but particular shared experiences, agreed-upon conventions, common technical expertise, and so on. As a result, those of us who lack that shared knowledge and experience often don't understand much of what they say to each other. In the same way, today's computers, which don't share even the common-sense knowledge we all draw on in our everyday speech and writing, can't comprehend most of our speech or texts.

It Takes Common Sense to Stay Focused, and to Learn

Our human dependence on common sense is very far-reaching. It comes into play with spoken and written language (as when we try to decipher someone's scratchy handwriting) and in our actions (for example, when driving a car and deciding whether to brake or accelerate or swerve to avoid something). Before we let robotic chauffeurs drive around our streets, I'd want the automated driver to have general common sense about the value of a cat versus a child versus a car bumper, about children chasing balls into streets, about young dogs being more likely to dart in front of cars than old dogs (which, in turn, are more likely to bolt than elm trees are), about death being a very undesirable thing, and so on. That "and so on" obscures a massive amount of general knowledge of the everyday world without which no human or machine driver should be on the road, at least not near me on in any populated area.

Our simple common-sense models of the world don't just clarify possible ambiguities; they are good enough to provide a context, a way of restricting reasoning to potentially relevant information and excluding irrelevant data. Suppose, for example, I'm trying to find my Visa card, which seems to be lost. Various things might be relevant to my search: the last thing I bought with it, the places I went yesterday, and so on. But I'll give up and report it lost before I bother trying to use all the pieces of information I possess, whether the number of legs on an arachnid, the year that Abraham Lincoln was elected president, or my mother's birthday.

Similarly, if someone were to ask you "Is Bill Clinton standing or sitting right now?" you would recognize right away—probably in one or two seconds—that you don't know the answer, despite all the miscellaneous facts about Clinton that you do know.

In a course on the calculus of manifolds I took about the time *2001: A Space Odyssey* was released, we stated and proved Arthur Sard's theorem one day near the end of the term. The statement of the theorem was a couple lines long, and the proof wasn't much longer; it cited a couple of lemmas (auxiliary propositions) we'd proved the preceding week. But stating that theorem, let alone proving it, would have been a daunting task if we hadn't had the way prepared for us by a series of useful definitions and stepping-stone lemmas. They, in turn, presumed a certain level of what is vaguely termed *mathematical maturity,* which is usually interpreted as a set of prerequisites, courses that have to be taken before signing up for that particular class.

This is a very technical example of learning a new thing that relates only tangentially to what we already know, at the "fringes," so to speak. But the phenomenon is important in everyday life as well as in math classes. We learn new things by extending and combining and contrasting already-assimilated concepts, facts, heuristics, models, and so on. It's hard to explain the need for sanitation to people who don't know the first thing about bacteria, and easy to do it with those who do. A particularly powerful way to teach someone about a new subject is to use a storytelling model, although even this method is less effective if the lives of listener and storyteller are too different.

The aliens in *2001* understand this all too well. They placed their signaling beacon on the moon so that they wouldn't have to pay attention to these intelligent apes until they hit "the knee of the learning curve." Once humans achieved even primitive space travel, the aliens decided, they were beginning to have a larger and larger "fringe" of knowledge, which would grow exponentially, each new discovery reinforcing and accelerating the next one, like a snowball gathering mass as it rolls downhill. When that happened, the extraterrestrials wanted to be paged.

These examples illustrate how important it is to have a fair amount of common knowledge to understand written/spoken/handwritten sentences, to drive a car, to find your keys, to answer a question, to learn new things. In other words, before any future HAL could be entrusted with absolute power over the ship's functions—or could even hold a casual conversation with a crew member—it would somehow have to acquire this massive prerequisite store of knowledge. You can think of this knowledge as the foundation of consensus reality, things that are so fundamental that anyone who doesn't know and believe them is, in effect, living in a different world.

As Dave disconnects HAL's cognitive memory modules, HAL is reduced at some point in the procedure, to the same blank slate he was when he was first powered up, the *tabula rasa* onto which all his programming and education were subsequently written. Yet in this scene we hear the new-born HAL carrying on a conversation with Dave, asking whether Dave wants him to sing "Daisy, Daisy," and so on. This is one of *2001's* few technically unrealistic moments. As our examples illustrate, even simple linguistic behavior requires lots of general knowledge about the world, not to mention specific knowledge about the speaker and the context of the conversation. So, when Dave blanked out HAL's mind, the ability to hold such a conversation would have been one of the first abilities to go, not the last one.

How to Build HAL Today in Three Easy Steps

We're now in a position to specify the steps required to bring a HAL-like being into existence.

1. Prime the pump with the millions of everyday terms, concepts, facts, and rules of thumb that comprise human consensus reality—that is, common sense.

2. On top of this base, construct the ability to communicate in a natural language, such as English. Let the HAL-to-be use that ability to vastly enlarge its knowledge base.

3. Eventually, as it reaches the frontier of human knowledge in some area, there will be no one left to talk to about it, so it will need to perform experiments to make further headway in that area.

These steps aren't quite so separate as the list makes them appear. The step-1 type of explicit, manual teaching will have to go on continually, even when steps 2 and 3 are well underway. Step 2 conversations will continue even after the computer reaches step 3—not only in other fields but even in the field with which step 3 is concerned; that is, the computer will probably want to discuss its discoveries with other researchers in the field.

Of course, the first step is both immensely difficult and immensely time-consuming. What are the millions of things that we should use to prime the new HAL's knowledge pump? How should they be represented inside the machine so that it can use them efficiently to deduce further conclusions when needed, just as we would? Who will do the actual entering of all that data? Assuming it's done by a large group of individuals, how will they keep from diverging and contradicting each other?

It may surprise you to hear that this is not just a fanciful blueprint for some massive future endeavor to be launched when humanity reaches a higher plateau of utopian cooperation. It is, in fact, the specific plan I and my team have been following for the past dozen years. In the next section, I report on our progress and our prospects for the future.

The CYC Project: Taking that First Step

In the fall of 1984, Admiral Bobby Ray Inman convinced me that if I was serious about taking that first step, I needed to leave academe and come to his newly formed Microelectronics and Computer Consortium (MCC) in Austin, Texas, and assemble a team to do it. The idea was that over the next decade dozens of individuals would create a program, CYC, with common sense. We would "prime the knowledge pump" by handcrafting and spoon-feeding CYC with a couple of million important facts and rules of thumb. The goal was to give CYC enough knowledge by the late 1990s to enable it to learn more by means of natural language conversations and reading (step 2). Soon thereafter, say by 2001, we planned to have it learning on its own, by automated-discovery methods guided by models or minitheories of the real world (step 3).

To a large extent, that's just what we did. At the end of 1994, the CYC program was mature enough to spin off from MCC as a new company—Cycorp—to commercialize the technology and begin its widespread deployment.

Our purpose was not to understand more about how the human mind works, or to test some particular theory of intelligence. Instead, we built nothing more nor less than an artifact, taking a very nuts-and bolts engineering approach to the whole project.

What Should the CYC System Know?

The first problem we faced was *what* knowledge to represent. Although we expected encyclopedias to play an important role, within a few months we realized that what they contain is almost the *complement* of common sense. Assuming that readers already have common sense, can read, and so on, they provide the next level of detail for reference purposes.

If we couldn't use encyclopedias for their content directly, we could still use their information indirectly. If we take any sentence from an encyclopedia article and think about what the writer assumes the reader already knows about the world, we will have something worth telling CYC. Alternatively, we can take a paragraph and look at the "leaps" from one sentence to the next and think about what the writer assumes the reader will infer "between" the sentences. For instance, back in 1984 our first example read, "Napoleon died on St. Helena. Wellington was greatly saddened." The author expects the reader to infer that the Arthur Wellesley, Duke of Wellington heard about Napoleon Bonaparte's death, that Wellington outlived Napoleon, and so on.

For many years, we were largely driven by bottom-up examples of this sort from encyclopedias, newspapers, novels, advertisements, and so on. Gradually, around 1990, we began to work in a more top-down fashion, treating entire topics one at a time and in moderate detail. By 1996, we had told CYC about hundreds of topics. That brings up the next issue.

How Should that Knowledge Be Represented?

The real physical universe is not, of course, inside CYC, anymore than it is inside our brains. All we have is a representation of a sliver of the world, and we operate from that representation to acquire new ideas, make decisions, and so forth.

Initially we used a simple frame-and-slot language to store information in CYC; for instance, "timeOfBirth (HAL) = 1/12/1992." This caused several problems, however. How could we represent *not, or, every, some,* opinions, expectations, counterfactual conditionals, and simlar material. Consider, for example, these speeches from 2001:

HAL: I hope the two of you are not concerned about this.

Dave: No, I'm not, HAL.

Dave: I don't know what you're talking about.

HAL: I know that you and Frank were planning to disconnect me, and I'm afraid that's something I cannot allow to happen.

HAL: I know everything hasn't been quite right with me, but I can assure you now, very confidently, that it's going to be alright again.

HAL: If you'd like to hear it, I can sing it for you.

All of these sentences are too complex to squeeze them efficiently into the frame-and-slot straightjacket. So our method of representation had to evolve slowly, until today it is a type of second-order predicate calculus. That's a fancy way of saying the language of logic. The second-order qualifier means that sometimes we need to represent things whose interrelationship is unknown or to refer explicitly to earlier conversations. For instance, at one point in the film HAL says "I know I've never completely freed myself of the suspicion that there are some extremely odd things about this mission. I'm sure you'll agree that there's some truth in what I say."

Lessons Learned Along the Way

We've learned many other things over the past dozen years, working on the CYC program. Three lessons in particular were painful but important to development of the program.

Originally we attached probabilistic weights—that is, numerical certainty factors—to each sentence we gave CYC. (For instance, HAL's statement, "Yes, that's a completely reliable figure," would have a very high certainty factor.) Including certainty factors had several bad consequences, however, and we eventually changed to a scheme in which all inputs are true by default. To decide whether to believe something, CYC gathers up all the pro and con arguments it can think of, examines them, and then reaches a conclusion.

Every representation is a trade-off between expressiveness (how easily you can say complicated things) and efficiency (how easily the machine can reason with what you've told it). English is very expressive but not very efficient. Most computer languages, such as Basic, C, and Fortran, are efficient but not very expressive. To get both qualities, we separated the epistemological problem (what should the system know?) and developed two separate languages, respectively EL and HL. Our knowledge enterers talk to CYC in the clean, expressive language (EL). Their input is then converted into the heuristic language (HL), which is efficient for dealing with many sorts of frequently recurring inference problems, such as reasoning about time, causality, containment, and so forth.

The third, and perhaps most important lesson we learned along the way was that it was foolhardy to try to maintain consistency in one huge flat CYC knowledge base. We eventually carved it up into hundreds of contexts or microtheories. Each one of those is consistent with itself, but there can be contradictions among them. Thus, in the context of working in an office it's socially unacceptable to jump up screaming whenever good things happen, while in the context of a football game it's socially unacceptable not to. In the fictional context of Bram Stoker's *Dracula,* vampires exist; in the standard rational worldview context they don't. Other contexts carve out similar distinguishable eras in time, political or religious points of view, and so forth.

Applications of CYC

We've discussed the need to have something, like the CYC program, that can understand natural language; so it should come as no surprise that getting it to do this is a high-priority application task for us. Long before it can read all on its own, CYC will carry on semiautomated knowledge acquisition from texts, a sort of tutoring program in which it asks clarifying questions when it comes across something it's not sure about.

One potential use for CYC is to understand such structured information sources as spreadsheets and data bases, and then use that understanding to detect common-sense errors and inconsistencies in the data. For example, one column of a table might indicate a person's gender, and another might indicate that of his or her legal spouse. Without having to be specially programmed for the task, CYC would know that there's probably a mistake in the data if X and X's spouse have the same gender, if X's spouse lists a third person as his or her spouse, or if X is listed as X's spouse. This sort of data cleaning gets more interesting when combining information from several tables. (For example, according to one data base, X is suspected of committing a certain crime, whereas according to another data base X was in jail at the time.) This sort of information fusion or integration is very important because much of the data we draw upon in our lives is gathered, formatted, and maintained by someone not under our direct control. Human beings—and Hal, and CYC—need to be able to assimilate information from numerous sources and interrelate it correctly. That task, in turn, requires common sense. Using n data bases and writing the transformation rules for their communications works fine when $n = 2$, but not so well when $n = 100$ or 1,000. Instead, the approach we use for CYC treats each column of each data base one at a time, writing rules that explain its meaning in terms CYC can understand. The entire CYC knowledge base then becomes, in effect, the semantic glue for implicitly joining all that information together—just as you or I can draw on and combine information we acquire from many different sources.

One of the flashiest early uses of CYC has been for information retrieval. Imagine a library of captioned images and a user who comes along and types in a word, a phrase, or sentence asking for images. Today's software would have to do Boolean searches based on keywords in the query and the captions, perhaps broadening the search a bit by looking up synonyms in a thesaurus or definitions in a dictionary. Or consider the World Wide Web, whose keyword-based indexing is the only way to search through that immense information space. That's fine if you want to match "A bird in water" against "A duck in a pond," but it takes something like CYC to match "A happy person" against "A man watching his daughter take her first step." CYC uses common sense to do matches of that sort. Similarly, CYC matched the query "a strong and adventurous person" to a caption of "a man climbing a rock face." To do that, it used a few rules of the sort: "If people do something for recreation that puts them at risk of bodily harm, then they are adventurous."

Conclusions and Parting Thoughts

We haven't talked much about emotions and motivations. I started out by complaining that HAL was stupid, because he showed a distinct lack of common sense when he killed the crew rather than, for example, bringing them into his confidence about the secret orders for the mission. Most humans would agree that it's better to lie to people or risk confiding in them than to "solve" the problem by killing them.

At least HAL was rational in his murderous plans. One of the prevalent themes in science fiction has been that of the robot gone amok, generally driven by some strong emotion or craving for power. This is a reflection of our human fears, I think; it is the monster still lurking under our beds in the dark. HAL, CYC, and their ilk won't have emotions, because they are not useful for integrating information, making decisions based on that information, and so on. A computer may pretend to have emotions, as part of what makes for a pleasing user interface, but it would be as foolish to consider such simulated emotions real as to think that the internal reasoning of a computer is carried out in English just because the input/output interface uses English.

We have described several applications of CYC, such as natural language understanding, checking and integrating information in spreadsheets and data bases, and finding relevant information in image libraries and on the World Wide Web. Notice that we were not talking about Herculean tasks like beating Garry Kasparov at chess by looking seventeen moves ahead or simulating and predicating any of a trillion problems days before they may occur, as HAL does continuously. We're just talking about inference problems that are only a couple of steps long. The key point here is that if you have the necessary common-sense knowledge—such as "deadly pastimes suggest adventurousness"—then you can make the inference quickly and easily; if you lack it, you can't solve the problem at all. Ever.

This is the essence of common sense—that a little goes a long way. HAL had a veneer of intelligence, but in the end he was lacking in values and in common sense, which resulted in the needless death of almost the entire crew. We are on the road to building HAL's brain. But this time—now that it's for real—we aren't going to cripple it by skipping the mass of simple stuff it needs to know.

Acknowledgements

This chapter first appeared as "From 2001 to 2001: Common Sense and the Mind of HAL" in *HAL's Legacy: 2001's Computer as Dream and Reality,* edited by David G. Stork (Cambridge, MA: The MIT Press, 1996).

7 Imagination and Situated Cognition

Lynn Andrea Stein

This chapter is concerned with the integration of higher-level "cognitive AI" and lower-level robotics. Robotic systems are embodied: their central tasks concern interaction with the immediately present world. In contrast, cognition is concerned with objects that are remote in distance, in time, or in some other dimension. This chapter exploits the architecture of a particular robotic system to perform a cognitive task by *imagining* the subjects of our cognition, and suggests that much of the abstract information that forms the heart of cognition is used not as a central model of the world but as virtual reality. The self-same processes that robots use to explore and interact with the world form the interface to this information. The only difference between interaction with the actual world and with the imagined one is the set of sensors and actuators providing the lowest-level interface.

Consider, for example, the following tasks. In the first, a pitcher and bowl sit on a table before you. You lift the pitcher and pour its contents into the bowl. Now consider your actions in reading the preceding example. In all likelihood, you formed a picture *in your mind's eye* of the table top, pitcher, and bowl. You envisioned the pouring. In the virtual world that you created for yourself, you sensed and acted. Indeed, there is evidence in the psychology literature that such "imagings" involve the same biological mechanisms as are responsible for actual vision. This virtual reality, your imagination, is precisely the goal of our program.

This chapter describes both the general ideas behind imagination and its concrete instantiation in a particular robotic system. Toto (Mataric

1992) is a subsumption-based mobile robot capable of goal-directed navigation. MetaToto is an imagination system that we have built using Toto. MetaToto adds to Toto's original abilities the abstract, cognitive, and apparently disembodied skill of reading and using maps. MetaToto achieves this additional skill by reusing Toto's reactive navigational system to imagine exploring the environment depicted in the map.

This use of the term "imagination" closely parallels both its folk-psychological sense and the work of several computer and cognitive scientists. For example, Richard S. Sutton (1990) augments the exploration of his reinforcement-learning agent with rehearsal, or "imagined" exploration, in the Dyna architecture. Stephen Michael Kosslyn (1993) makes the strong claim that all mental imagery is in essence this kind of reuse of perceptual machinery; his recent clinical data support my suggestion that cognition is imagined interaction (or, as Kosslyn has put it, "imagery is just like vision, except that there's nothing there").

In the next section, I introduce the idea of imagination as the basis for a robotic architecture. Then I will describe Toto, the robot on which our work is based. While our work does not rely on the specifics of that robot, it does exploit certain properties to make the implementation of the imagination system feasible. In the next section, I discuss the ways in which our work adds to the existing robot; then I present the details of our implementation. Next, I explore an extension of the imagination architecture to a more abstract task. Finally, I analyze the features of the robotic system and the imagination architecture that make this project possible.

A note on terminology: In this chapter, my use of the terms "robotics" and "cognition" is intended to be quite specific: "robotics" involves the portion of the system designed to interact with the world—the "body"—while I intend "cognition" to refer to the nonimmediate, or the "mental." In humans, "cognition" might correspond roughly to the function of the cerebrum, while the remainder of the body implements "robotics." Although this usage is far from universal, I will adopt it throughout this chapter and will consequently omit the scare quotes surrounding these terms.

In fact, just as these distinctions are not really so crisp in biology, there is much overlap of functionality in artificial systems. However, without claiming to be able to draw a sharp boundary between them, I believe that there is utility to be gained from the rough distinction between interactive "robotic" systems and abstract "cognition."

Imagination as Situated Cognition

Traditional AI architectures have assumed that the superficial dissimilarities between cognitive and robotic abilities reflect fundamental differences in underlying machinery. Accordingly, the two areas have been studied separately, with widely divergent approaches used to provide the desired functionality. For those who work in cognitive AI, robotics has come to be viewed largely as an interface to the world, providing (often highly interpreted) sensory data and executing actions as instructed. This approach is typified by the traditional planning literature. (See Allen, Hendler, and Tate [1990] for a survey.) For the robotics community, planners and other cognitive apparatus are viewed as "problem-solving boxes" that periodically issue high-level goals. (See, for example, Latombe [1991].) While the relative importance of these two components varies depending on the problem addressed, both research communities have traditionally agreed on this rough dichotomy and the consequent specification of the cognition/robotics interface independently of sensori-motor functions.

The traditional implementation of the cognition box is itself a kind of simulation. It often contains a "world model": some representation of the environment derived (in principle) from the output of the robotics component. Planning and other cognitive tasks are accomplished relative to this world model. The representation of the world in this model is often unlike the raw sensory data supplied by the world itself, and the operators on this world model are abstracted and idealized versions of actual actions. Plans are derived by "simulating" action in this world model. Errors occurring within the simulation are not fatal and can be discovered and eliminated before action is taken in the world.

The advantage of this approach is that the simulation is tailored to the planning task. Its disadvantage is the same: because the simulation is tailored for planning, plans developed in simulation depend on the irrelevance of the idealizations in the simulation to the real world. Such assumptions often include the static and predictable nature of the world. In practice, these assumptions are often untenable. (See, for example, discussions in Agre and Chapman [1987], Sanborn and Hendler [1988], and Brooks [1991a, b].)

More recently, there has been substantial interest in architectures that integrate some or all of the cognitive functionality directly into the robotic architecture. Some achieve this hybridization by compiling cognitive functionality off-line, that is, by essentially using the "cognition box" as a specification for the robot's reactions. Examples of this type of integrated

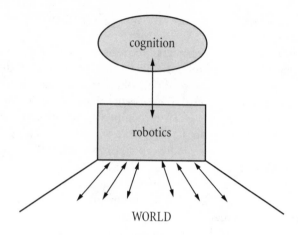

Figure 1. Traditional Architecture.

architecture include Rosenschein and Kaelbling (1986), Schoppers (1987), and Chapman (1990). Others, such as Georgeff and Lansky (1987) and Sanborn and Hendler (1988), treat cognition as preference information to be used when the world does not demand a particular reaction. The first approach limits the simulation aspects of cognition, while the second treats cognition essentially as in figure 1.

I propose a different integration of cognition and robotics, one that leaves the robotic architecture essentially unchanged but takes seriously the idea of cognition as *imagined interaction*. It complements the reactive approaches described above, providing a different kind of planning-as-simulation. While traditional planners use an abstracted world and plan operators distinct from the actual robot controls, this system uses the robotic architecture itself. That is—as in figure 2—the interface between robotics and the immediate world is multiplexed to provide a second low-level interface, between robotics and imagination. The robot senses and acts in this imagined world precisely as it does in the actual world. The essential difference between imagination and traditional planning-as-simulation is that imagination and interaction literally share the same machinery. Cognition is actual interaction applied to imagined stimuli.

This idea accords with popular as well as academic psychology. Dreams are often thought of as interactions in which sensory input does not come from the outside world and physical motor function is inhibited. Mental imagery is, according to S. M. Kosslyn (1993), simply the application of the

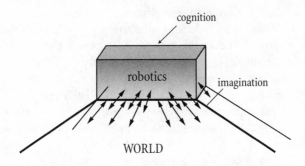

Figure 2. An Alternative Architecture: Cognition as Imagined Interaction.

processes that drive actual vision to imagined sensation. The task of giving directions often evokes the sensations of traveling along the designated route. Finally, it seems likely that if biology and evolution conspired to spend so long creating the complex motor functions and instincts of higher mammals, much of this would be reused in providing the additional cognitive capacity of human beings.

Imagination and the Homunculus.

One objection that has been raised to the idea of cognition as imagined interaction is that of the homunculus. If, for example, visual image processing is vision of the "mind's eye," who is it who *sees* through the mind's eye? By this line of reasoning, the agent in the mind—the homunculus—must itself have an agent in its head, and so on in infinite regress.

Our approach does not suffer from this problem. As I describe later, the mind that sees imagined stimuli is the same mind that sees the world. We have simply multiplexed its retinal connections, so that the robot cannot distinguish between the world around it and that of its imagination. Thus, our "homunculus" is the perceptual system of the robot itself.

Imagination Versus World Models

A further aspect of the architecture bears on the simulation of feedback through imagination rather than through the world. Feedback through the world has been a strength of reactive systems, and imagination removes that aspect of the architecture. In this sense, it represents a step towards the more traditional world models of classical planning systems.

Imagination differs from classical world models, however. Imagination is ephemeral. MetaToto need only know the sensations that occur now. Where Toto "continually redecides what to do," MetaToto continually re-imagines the world. Thus, while world models persist and require mainte-nance, imagination can be reconstructed on the fly.

In addition, cognition requires imagining only the relevant details. That is, only those aspects that bear on things immediately sense-able must be imagined. Because the interface between robotics and imagination is at the level of sensation rather than in terms of higher-level predicates, we do not need a model of the global properties of the world. Only that which is imagined to be immediately accessible must be simulated.

A Robot that Explores

This section describes the architecture of the underlying robotic system in some detail. It is intended to give readers unfamiliar with Maja Mataric's work a better idea of the basic interactive system. The details of Toto's machinery are not, however, crucial to the imagination project. MetaToto, our extension to Toto, treats Toto as a black box module (as depicted in figure 2).

Toto (Mataric 1990, 1992) is a mobile robot capable of goal-directed navigation. It is implemented on a Real World Interface base augmented with a ring of twelve Polaroid ultrasonic ranging sensors and a flux-gate compass (figure 4). Its primary computational resource is a CMOS 68000. Its software simulates a subsumption architecture (Brooks 1986): a layered control system in which individual modules—or "behaviors"—implement distinct abilities. Figure 3 gives an architectural overview of Toto.

Toto's most basic level consists of routines to explore its world. Inde-pendent collections of finite state machines implement such competencies as obstacle-avoidance and random walking. Each of the modules is reac-tive, relying on the world around it to provide cues to appropriate actions. For example, an obstacle looming large will cause Toto to stop and back up, regardless of its other tasks. Toto's simplest activity—a wall-following "maze exploration"— emerges from the parallel combination of these sur-vival skills.

A second layer, above the wall-following routines, implements a fully distributed "world modeler." While navigating around its environment, Toto synthesizes its experiences into a dynamic and reusable "memory." For example, sustained short average sonar readings on sonars 5 and 6 serve to indicate the presence of a wall on Toto's right. This experience is

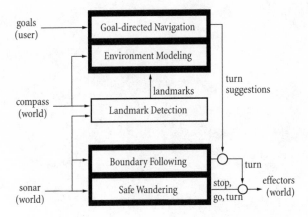

Figure 3. An Architectural Overview of Toto's Control Programs.

connected in memory to those that directly precede and follow it, providing a rough topographic "memory" of the explored environment.

By remembering crucial features of its previous experience, Toto is able to correlate its current surroundings with these experiences and to "recognize" previously visited locations. Toto's memory is implemented as a parallel distributed dynamic graph of landmark-recognizer modules. Landmarks correspond to gross sonar configurations (such as *wall right*) augmented with compass readings.[1] Each time a novel landmark is recognized, a new graph node allocates itself, making graph connections as appropriate. The resulting modules form an internal representation of the environment. Rough odometry is used to distinguish similar landmark-memories in the recognition of previously visited locations.

Finally, Toto accepts commands (by means of three buttons) to return to previously recognized landmarks. When a goal location is specified, Toto's landmark graph—synthesized memories—uses spreading activation to determine the appropriate direction in which to head. In essence, Toto "feels an urge" to go towards the (remembered) goal landmark. Activation persists until Toto has returned to the requested location. Throughout, Toto's lowest level modules enforce obstacle avoidance and corridor traversal, and Toto's intermediate layer processes landmarks as they are encountered.

Toto's landmark representation and goal-driven navigation are cognitive tasks, involving internal representation of the external environment. This represents a qualitative advance in the capabilities of subsumption-based

Figure 4. Mataric's Toto.

robots. Nonetheless, this internal representation is accessible only through interaction with the world: unless Toto has experienced the landmark, it has no memories to synthesize. Thus, Toto cannot reason about things unless it has previously encountered them. In the next section, I describe a simple modification to Toto's architecture that allows Toto to represent and "return to" previously *unvisited* landmarks.

Exploring the Unknown

The existing machinery that implements Toto's core provides a strong base for cognitive tasks. It is limited, however, in being able to conceptualize only what has been physically encountered. MetaToto is an extension of Toto's core behavior that accepts directions to navigate to a goal not previously encountered. This ability is qualitatively different for the robot. Toto's goal-directed navigation routines are implemented in terms of its existing internal representation—synthesized experience—and it is impossible even to ask that Toto visit an unexplored location: Toto has no concept corresponding to locations it has not encountered. The primary task for MetaToto, then, is the representation of landmarks that have simply been described.

Previous approaches to cognition in robotic systems have implemented more intelligent behaviors as higher levels of control. In the Imagination project, we have taken a different approach. Our approach to architecture is to reuse Toto's existing mechanisms in adding this new skill to MetaToto. We treat Toto's control program as a black box whose inputs and outputs come through the world. By providing an alternative interface through an imagination system, we multiplex Toto's memory construction system. Where Toto must encounter a landmark to be able to make use of it, MetaToto merely envisions that landmark and constructs the same topological "landmark memory." Figure 5 shows an architectural diagram for MetaToto. The shaded area represents Toto's architecture, as designed by Mataric and described previously. For MetaToto, cognition is simply imagined sensation and action.

Implementing Imagination

The initial implementation of MetaToto takes directions in the form of a sketch-map. The use of a geometric communication language facilitates

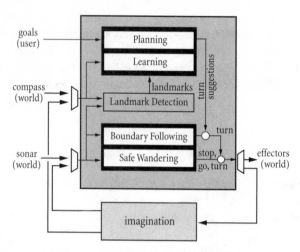

Figure 5. MetaToto Treats Mataric's Toto as a
Black Box, Multiplexing Its Inputs and Outputs.

certain of the simulation aspects of MetaToto's imagination. In the next
section I discuss a more verbal communication language.

MetaToto is intended to run on the same hardware as Toto. It reuses
Toto's software entirely, adding only the imagination system wrapped
around the Toto "black box." (see figure 5). The compound system sub-
sumes the ability to perform all tasks of which the robot was previously
capable, plus the additional cognitive exploration of physically unseen environments—"map reading."

MetaToto's imagination uses a rough sketch-map of the environment it
is to explore. Rather than looking at the map from above, that is, as
abstract information—MetaToto imagines that it is located in a particular
place in the map. Virtual sensors describe what it "feels" like to be at that
location: what sonar and compass readings MetaToto might receive if at
the corresponding real-world location. MetaToto imagines sensing and
acting in the sketch-map much as Toto would sense and act in the actual
world, with much the same effect. The routines that sense and act in the
imagined world are precisely the same as those that would sense and act in
the actual world; they differ only by calling the imagined sonar rather than
the real.

To implement this system, the sketched floor plan is transformed into a
bitmap: black pixels represent "occupied" space; white pixels, free. Neither

Figure 6. A Sample Sketch-Map.

the discrete nature of this representation nor the relative dimensions of the topographic features correspond accurately to the robot's actual experience; the sketch-map merely provides sufficient information to enable MetaToto's imagination to construct appropriate "memories." A sample sketch-map is depicted in figure 6.

MetaToto imagines itself as a small circular region within the bitmap. We initially tried to simplify the implementation further by modeling MetaToto as a point. Because the difference between too-close and too-far sonar readings is comparable to the radius of the robot, this implementation allowed MetaToto to imagine traversing passageways far too narrow for the actual robot.

To imagine sensing, MetaToto projects twelve rays, one in the direction of each sonar. Figure 7 shows MetaToto's idealization of sonars. We do not attempt to model sonar diffusion or specular reflection at all; imagined sonars simply report the distance to the first black pixel encountered. The algorithm used is based on Bresenham's scan-line algorithm as described in Foley and Van Dam (1982, p. 435). Except for the "junk" landmark type, this implementation appears to be adequate.

To imagine acting, MetaToto maintains three state variables: x and y coordinates and angular heading. Forward and backward motion is discrete, but the distance for backward motion is not precisely the same as that for forward motion. (The robot itself depends on the nonuniformity of actual motion to unwedge itself from certain corners; we use the differ-

Figure 7. MetaToto Projects Rays to Imagine Toto's Sonars.

ential step size to serve a similar purpose.) Similarly, turns are discrete and of a fixed size—30° per step. Sensing occurs discretely after each step.

In this manner, MetaToto explores the floor plan, building the same internal representation of landmarks as Toto would create in its explorations of the environment. Figure 8(a) from Mataric (1992, figure 7) shows the landmarks detected by Toto during its exploration of the ninth floor playroom at the Massachusetts Institute of Technology's artificial intelligence laboratory. Figure 8(b) shows MetaToto's (imagined) exploration of the same space.

Once MetaToto has completed its exploration of the floor plan, it is capable of goal-directed navigation in the world. However, unlike Toto, MetaToto can go to places that it has only imagined and not actually encountered. Because the landmark graph has been created by the same mechanisms that are used in exploring the world, MetaToto cannot distinguish those generated by its imagination and those actually encountered. Should the floor plan prove to have been incomplete or inaccurate, MetaToto will respond precisely as Toto would were the world to change between two consecutive visits.

Following Directions

MetaToto's use of a geometric representation for communication facilitates the simulation aspects of imagination. Humans, however, are capable

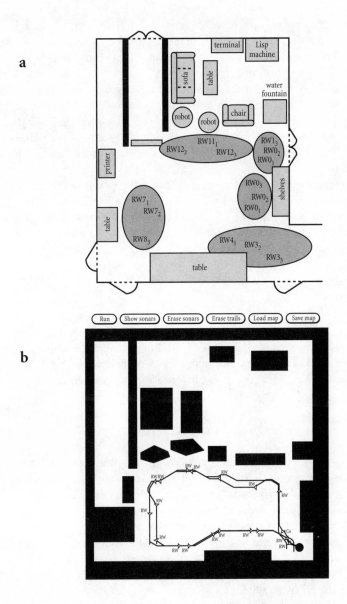

Figure 8. MetaToto Imagines Exploring Its Environment.

(a) [Mataric 92, Figure 7, ® IEEE]. Landmarks detected by Toto on three consecutive runs through the ninth floor playroom at the MIT AI Lab. Shaded areas represent locations corresponding to the same landmark. (b) MetaToto's trajectory on two consecutive runs on the sketchmap of the same environment. Landmarks are indicated.

of understanding verbally imparted directions. While in some senses this task is unfair for MetaToto, we believe that it is nonetheless achievable.

Giving MetaToto directions is "unfair" in the sense that humans give humans directions in anthropocentric terms. We speak of "the second left" or "the corner" because these are the landmarks in terms of which we represent the world. MetaToto has no notion of left turns or corners; instead, it represents the world in terms of sonar and compass readings. Thus, to make this task fair in MetaToto's terms, we ought to speak of such landmarks as "the second extended short sonar reading on left and right simultaneously."

Nonetheless, MetaToto could understand the anthropocentric landmarks in much the same way as it uses the floor plan. What, after all, does it "feel" like to explore these landmarks? The simulation aspect may be more complicated, but the task is essentially the same. For example, the landmark "the second left" corresponds to the following (imagined) sensations:

> short sonar left
> long sonar left
> short sonar left
> long sonar left

By imagining this sequence, MetaToto could construct an internal representation corresponding to that which would be encountered while seeking the second left. Directions, although more remote than geometric representation, still have a natural analog in terms of imagined sensation.

Discussion

Because we take the approach that cognition is the application of the (existing) robotic architecture to imagined sensation and action, implementing cognition is reduced to the tasks of simulating sensors and actuators and modeling the appropriate feedback through the imagined world. Both tasks have been attempted in other contexts. The relative success of the approach here relies on some critical assumptions about the nature of the robot's interface with the world and hence with imagination. In this section, I identify certain properties of Toto's architecture that allow for its integration with an imagination system.

The robotic architecture is designed to compensate for the variations of physical experience. For example, while Toto's trajectory through a corridor is roughly "straight down the middle," it is possible—and even expected—that Toto will swerve from side to side in unpredictable ways.

For example, figure 9(a) from Mataric (1992, figure 6) shows the variation over the paths taken by the robot during five independent runs through the same hallway. The program that accumulates Toto's experiences and synthesizes landmark-memories takes this into account, ignoring the particular path taken and abstracting the more general pattern indicative of a corridor. When Toto next encounters this corridor, it will almost certainly take a different path. The abstract features—sustained average short sonar readings on sonars 5, 6, 11, and 0—however, remain the same.

MetaToto is able to exploit this feature of Toto's architecture. Because the robotic program generalizes any corridor-like trajectory to the same type of landmark-memory, MetaToto's simulated trajectory need not mimic the robot's actual trajectory. Instead, MetaToto is free to imagine any corridor-like trajectory. Accordingly, we choose to simulate motion as ideal—straight, precise, and discrete—although the actual behavior of the robot is far different. Figure 9(b) shows MetaToto's trajectory through the sketch-map depicting the corridor of (a). While MetaToto's path is an idealization of Toto's, it falls well within the range of variation experienced by the robot over several runs. Both the real and imagined trajectories result in the synthesis of the appropriate (corridor) landmark-memory.

In the same way that Toto generalizes over deviations in its trajectories, the robotic architecture allows for the expected variation in sonar readings. Rather than using sonar as a precise distance metric, Toto relies on the qualitative properties expected of its environment: *too-close, too-far, wall left or right....* By abstracting from the precise readings to range membership and sustained average properties, this architecture allows for the adequacy of naive simulation of sonars.

Further, Toto relies on constant feedback from the world and constant interaction with the world. In contrast to traditional planners, which decide on a course of action and then pass control to an executor, Toto "continually redecides what to do" (*pace;* Agre and Chapman 1987). This serves as a form of protection from major errors: if MetaToto provides inapplicable landmark-memories—either because its imagination was mistaken or because the world has changed—any incorrect actions by the robot will be recognized and corrected before they can become disastrous. As a result, Toto need not worry about plans gone awry.

These properties allow MetaToto to imagine idealized sonar readings along an idealized trajectory in an idealized floor plan (or with idealized directions); since the result is within the space of possible experiences that Toto might have, MetaToto's landmark-memories capture the appropriate salient properties of the environment.

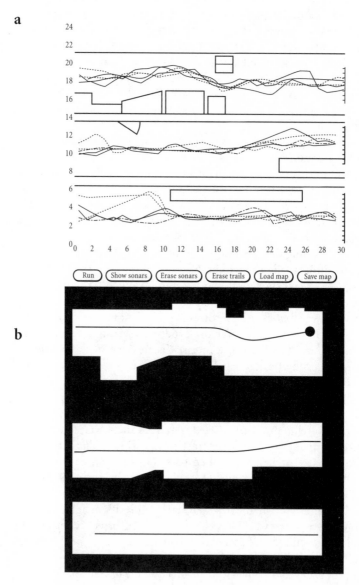

Figure 9. MetaToto's Imagined Trajectory Is an Idealization of Toto's Actual Paths.

Both figures illustrate a single hallway running from left to right and from bottom to top. (**a**) [Mataric 92, Figure 6, ®IEEE.] Toto's trajectories on five independent runs through a hallway. (**b**) MetaToto's path through the same hallway.

Conclusion

Unlike previous "cognition boxes," MetaToto is distinguished only by the set of sensors and actuators in which the behaviors ground out: when imagining, MetaToto seizes control of the sensor and actuator control signals and substitutes interaction with the floor plan. Rather than a "higher level reasoning module," MetaToto is a lowest level interface to an alternate (imagined) reality.

MetaToto achieves by embodied imagination the cognition-intensive task of reading, understanding, and acting on the knowledge contained in a floor plan; and MetaToto does so entirely by using Toto's existing architecture, with the sole addition of the virtual sensors and actuators required for navigation of the floor plan. Although MetaToto is only a simple example of imagination, we are hopeful that experiences with MetaToto will lead to more sophisticated use of imagination and virtual sensing and to the development of truly embodied forms of cognition.

Acknowledgements

This chapter first appeared as "Imagination and Situated Cognition" in *Android Epistemology,* edited by Clark Glymour, Kenneth M. Ford, and Patrick J. Hayes (Menlo Park, CA: AAAI/ The MIT Press, 1995).

Note

1. In fact, the environment in which Toto was tested—the seventh and ninth floors of the MIT AI Lab—yielded sufficiently noisy compass readings that the compass was useful only to distinguish turns and not to obtain true facings.

8 Conceptual Similarity Across Sensory and Neural Diversity: The Fodor/Lepore Challenge Answered

Paul Churchland

Background[1]

In the mid-to-late 1980s, the exploration of artificial networks of neuronlike elements, connected to one another by large numbers of synapselike junctions, had become a small but flourishing industry. In particular, there were a variety of attempts to model, within classical computers, the phenomenon of information-processing in the early stages of the mammalian sensory pathways. Guided by our crude knowledge of the microanatomy and physiology of the relevant parts of the brain, networks were constructed and trained (by repeated small, error-reducing adjustments of their synaptic connections) to recreate some of the perceptual skills characteristic of human and animal cognition. Diverse networks were set to work at learning to discriminate such things as distinct human faces, distinct sonar echoes, distinct colors, distinct curved surfaces under various illuminations, distinct phonetic pronunciations for the graphemes of the English spelling system, distinct visual objects at various stereoptic depths, and, in one especially interesting test case, to discriminate the grammatical from the ungrammatical sentences of an elementary productive language.

These small forays into artificial intelligence were notable not just for their neurobiological provenance, nor for their quite striking successes at acquiring the discriminatory skills I just listed. They were notable because an analysis of the information-compressing coding strategies that had evolved (during training on many illustrative perceptual examples), within the high-dimensional activation spaces of the neurons that make up the network, revealed that those spaces had been partitioned into a systematic hierarchy of distinct but related subspaces, spaces whose volumes corresponded very closely to the perceptual categories that the network at issue had been trained to discriminate. More specifically, the set of intraspace *distances* that configured those learned subvolumes within the activation space as a whole were closely isomorphic with the set of *similarity relations* that configured the set of external perceptual features the network had been trained to discriminate. The acquired structure of the internal conceptual space was a moderately accurate *map* of the objective similarity-structure of the external feature-space on which it had been trained.

Thus were born hopes of a new approach to semantic theory, an approach that assigned a specific meaning or semantic significance, to any part of or location within a networks neuronal activation space, just as you would to the elements of any highway map: on the basis of the elements collected distance relations to all of the *other* map-elements, and on the basis of a presumed *global isomorphism* between the map-as-a-whole, on the one hand, and the objective structure of the specific external domain being mapped, on the other. The principal difference is that highway maps are merely two-dimensional, whereas the acquired maps embedded in neuronal activation spaces have a (typically) high dimensionality, equal to the (typically large) number of neurons involved. This holistic, brain-centered approach to semantic theory was not long in being challenged. The essay that follows is a response to that challenge. It offers a further articulation of the view at issue, and it reports some experimental data that illustrate its successful application to an allegedly intractable case.

* * *

In chapter 6 of *Holism: A Shoppers Guide,* Jerry Fodor and Ernest Lepore present a critical challenge to state-space semantics, as pursued by neural network modelers.[2] Their challenge expresses the doubt that such an approach could ever make useful sense of the notions of conceptual identity, or even conceptual similarity, in the face of the enormous functional and structural diversity across the individual networks that constitute human brains.

This chapter is the latest in a series of exchanges on this matter.[3] I stand by those earlier responses, but some new developments motivate a more ambitious and less defensive essay. Some recent theoretical insights and neuromodeling results from Aarre Laakso and Gary Cottrell (1996) constitute a decisive answer to Fodor and Lepore's challenge and point to new areas of semantic research. Laakso and Cottrell successfully deploy one member of a large family of mathematical measures of conceptual similarity, measures that see past difference—seven extensive differences—in the connectivity, the sensory inputs, and the neural dimensionality of the networks being compared. I shall explore the rationale behind these measures (1) by sketching Laakso and Cottrell's application of one such measure across a diversity of real networks, and (2) by discussing the generalization of such measures to many layered networks and to time series (recurrent) networks.

The Problem

On neural-network models of cognition, the primary unit of representation, and the primary vehicle of semantic content, is the overall pattern of simultaneous activation levels across the assembled neurons of a given population, such as the cells in layer four of the primary visual cortex, or the output cells of the motor cortex, or the cells in a given layer of some artificial network model (figure 1). Such patterns are often referred to as activation vectors, because they can be usefully and uniquely characterized by a sequence or n-tuple of numbers, where n = the number of neurons in the representing population.

To those more geometrically inclined, a specific activation pattern can also be simply and usefully characterized as a specific point in a proprietary space, an n-dimensional space with a proprietary axis for the variable activation level of each of the n neurons in the representing population. Any single point in that space will represent, by way of its unique set of n coordinate values, the simultaneous activation levels of each of the cells in the corresponding neural population.

At this level of reckoning, a specific activation *pattern* = a specific activation *vector* = a specific *point* in activation space. These are just variant ways of talking about the same thing: the unit of representation, as physically rather than semantically described.

If we are to assign specific semantical or representational *contents* to collective units of this kind, a natural first assumption is that any unit must in some way inherit its overall content from the individual and more basic representational significance of each of its many constituting elements,

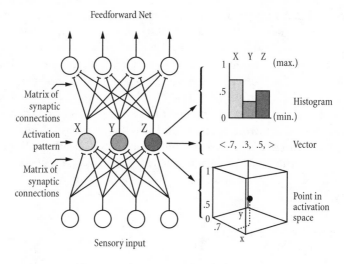

*Figure 1. Three Ways of Conceiving of the
Current Activity of a Specific Neuronal Population.*

(1) As a pattern or histogram of activation levels; (2) as an activation vector, and (3) as a
point in an activation space.

namely, the activation level of each of its many neurons. After all, it is
these individual neurons which are the recipients of information from the
environment, either directly—through their interaction with ambient
light, heat, and various mechanical and chemical impingements, or indirectly—through their many synaptic connections with neurons earlier in
the processing hierarchy.

As Fodor and Lepore have earlier urged on me, however, this assumption leads quickly to a number of difficulties. In the first place, the
approach to content here emerging would seem to be just another version
of a Humean concept empiricism, with the simple concepts corresponding
to whatever content or significance is assigned to the individual axes of the
global activation space, that is, to whatever content or significance is
assigned to the activation levels of each individual neuron in the relevant
population. A complex concept will then be just an appropriate conjunction or configuration of the simples, a unique configuration represented
by a unique point or position within the global activation space.

What was presented as new and interesting is therefore something quite
old and boring, runs the objection. Worse, the emerging account leaves
unaddressed the question of how each axis of the activation space, or each
neuron of the representing population, gets its semantic or representation-

al content. Presumably, such microcontent must derive from the peculiar causal connections that a given neuron enjoys to microfeatures of the sensory environment, or, if the neuron in question is not itself a sensory neuron, then to some microfeatures of the content embodied in the activity of neurons earlier in the processing hierarchy, neurons that project axons to the specific neuron in question.

This obvious proposal leads in this case to disaster, however. The problem is that no two people will have exactly the same set of causal dependencies across their sensory neurons, nor, a fortiori, across their subsequent neuronal layers as we climb their respective information-processing hierarchies. Even at the initial or sensory layer, there will be considerable idiosyncrasy, and that diversity will explode exponentially as the already idiosyncratic sets of microcontents get successively transformed by the profoundly idiosyncratic matrices of synaptic junctions that successively connect each layer in the neuronal hierarchy to the next layer. There is no hope, for example, of finding a mapping between the 10^{10} cells in my primary visual cortex and the 10^{10} cells in yours, such that for every mapped pair, your cell and mine have the same microcontent. The diversity in the scattered strengths or weights of our 10^{13} synaptic connections effectively precludes it. Probably, we do not share a single such pair between us.

Worse still, we are all idiosyncratic in the sheer *number* of cells we have in any given neuronal population. Our respective activation spaces, therefore, do not even have the same *dimensionality,* let alone the same set of axial microcontents. Accordingly, if we cannot make sense of the notion of same activation space across distinct individuals, it is plain that we can make no sense of the notion of same position in such a space across two individuals, or even of proximate positions. So we have no hope of explicating the notion of same meaning or similar meaning across distinct individuals. On such an ill-behaved neural basis, to conclude, we have no hope of constructing a workable theory of meaning.

Painting a Different Picture

The short answer to this critique is that content is not, in general, assigned in the manner described. A point in activation space acquires a specific semantic content not as a function of its position relative to the constituting *axes* of that space, but rather as a function of (1) its spatial position relative to all of the *other contentful points* within that space; and (2) its causal relations to stable and objective *macrofeatures of the external envi-*

ronment. As we shall see, this very different focus takes our neural and synaptic diversity out of the semantic picture almost entirely. That undoubted diversity is without semantic significance. Two people can share a common hierarchy of partitions across their respective activation spaces, and, for each partition within that hierarchy, they can share a common causal relation to some objective environmental feature, despite the fact that those partitions and those causal relations are differently implemented across structurally idiosyncratic brains. Starting with a deliberately simple example, let me illustrate how this can happen.

Let us imagine that two identical feed-forward networks, #1 and #2, are trained on the same corpus of 100 photographs of each of 100 members of four extended and multigenerational hillbilly families: twenty-five Hatfields, twenty-five McCoys, twenty-five Wilsons, and twenty-five Andersons (figure 2). The two networks are trained—by progressive nudgings of their respective synaptic weights at the hands of the familiar backpropagation algorithm—to distinguish any input photograph as a member of one of the four families. (The input layer of each network is here graphically portrayed as a line of twelve cells, but, of course, it would have to be a two-dimensional grid of at least sixty by sixty cells, in order to accommodate a realistic picture of each face. As well, there are far too many interlayer connections to portray all of them. Forgive the graphic license here taken.) The trained networks identification of any given face is defined as the highest of the four activation levels at the four labeled output cells. The two networks, let us suppose, are eventually trained to 100 percent accuracy on the training set of photographs, and they generalize successfully to any new examples of these four extended families with greater than 90 percent accuracy.

How do they manage to perform at this high level? In real networks, the usual answer to this sort of question appeals to the coding strategy evolved, during learning, neurons in the network involved. The idea is to look at the unique hidden-layer activation-space positions, severally displayed by the trained network, for grouping and separating the four families portrayed in the input photographs. If the training was successful, the activation space points for each of the twenty-five Hatfield faces will lie at the middle or hidden layer of neurons in the network involved. The idea is to look at the unique hidden-layer activation-space positions, severally displayed by the trained network, for grouping and separating the four families portrayed in the input photographs. If the training was successful, the activation-space points for each of the twenty-five Hatfield faces will tend to be clustered together in a proprietary subvolume or partition within the overall space. The face points for other families will be similarly clustered together in distinct familial clouds, as illustrated in figure 2.

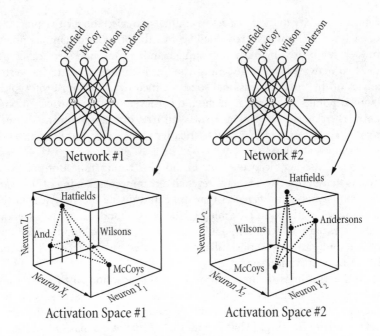

Figure 2. The Locations of Four Prototype Points
Within the Hidden-Layer Activation Spaces of Two
(Imaginary) Neural Networks for Recognizing the Faces of
Four Different Extended Families.

The four points represent a prototypical Hatfield face, a prototypical McCoy face, a prototypical Wilson face, and a prototypical Anderson face.

To simplify things, let us focus our attention on the mean, average, or center of gravity position for all of the Hatfield face points. This will be the prototypical Hatfield point, and it will represent the prototype of a Hatfield face—a face, perhaps, that no actual Hatfield actually possesses, but that every Hatfield resembles more or less closely. Let us plot this special point with a small boldface sphere in the relevant space for each network, as in figure 2. Do the same for the average or prototypical face of each of the other three families. The result for network #1 is the four points illustrated to the left, and the result for network #2 is the four points illustrated on the right.

As reckoned against the axes of their respective embedding spaces, each foursome is a distinct group of points. In one obvious sense, the two networks have settled on *different* coding strategies in solution to their common discriminatory problem. But a closer look reveals a residual and robust similarity in their respective coding strategies: the relative positions of each familial point, as reckoned against the other three familial points in each space, are obviously very similar. Indeed, they are identical across the two networks. More generally, the linear dimensions and the vertex angles of the three-dimensional solids defined by those four prototypical familial points are identical in the hidden-layer activation spaces of both networks. The solid shape at issue—an irregular tetrahedron—is both rotated and translated in space #2, relative to space #1, but it is the *same* solid shape in both spaces.

What is the significance of this isomorphic configuration of points? It means that both networks have reached a common reckoning of the *relative similarities and differences* that unite and divide the 100 faces in the training set, a common reckoning of the classes (and, as we shall see, the subclasses) into which that population divides, and a common reckoning of the numerical degree of similarity that relates any two face points within the same activation space.

In the end, it is to these common groupings, and to this common framework of similarity relations across the two hidden-layer spaces, that the final or output layer of neurons in each network gradually becomes tuned during training. (That is why the two networks have identical, or near identical, overall performance profiles.) The bottom half of each network manages to convert the great mass of pictorial information at the input layer into the (much lower dimensional) form of information embodied in the two hidden-layer spaces portrayed in figure 2; and the top half of the network manages to convert that intermediate form of information into the labeled pigeon holes at the output layer.

Quite obviously, the intricate matrix of synaptic connections meeting both the hidden-layer neurons and the output-layer neurons will have to be very different across the two networks. (If they were identical, then the hidden-layer locations and orientations of the two tetrahedrons would be the same as well, and they are not.) Equally clear, the microcontents of the three axes x_1, y_1, z_1 of network #1 must be different from the microcontents of the three axes x_2, y_2, z_2 of network #2. Those two hidden layers may each be representing the same aspects of similarity and difference across the face population at issue, but, clearly, they are distributing the representational load differently across the basic axes of their representational spaces. (As causally reckoned, the respective microcontents of neurons x_1, and x_2, for example, cannot be the same: they are connected by a *different* family of synaptic weights to identical input layers.)

What we have, then, is a pair of networks with highly idiosyncratic synaptic connections; a pair of networks with hidden-layer neurons of quite different microcontents; a pair of networks whose input-output behaviors are nevertheless identical, because they are rooted in a *common conceptual framework* embodied in the activation spaces of their respective hidden layers.

In what sense is it the same? In this sense: the several activation-space *distances* between the corresponding prototype positions are one and all identical, and the prototype positions identified as corresponding are so identified (despite their different locations in the two spaces) because each constitutes the standard causal response, at its networks hidden layer, to a typical Hatfield face (or McCoy face, and so on) presented as input to the sensory layer.

It is easy to extend this identity criterion to encompass a numerical criterion of similarity across such categorial frameworks. Our two tetrahedrons have six corresponding straight edges joining each of the four corresponding prototypical points. Let us ask, for each such pair of lines, AB and $A'B'$, what is the absolute value of the difference between their lengths, and then divide it by the sum of those two lengths. This will always give us a fraction between 0 and 1, where the fraction approaches 0 as the two lengths approach identity. Let us then take the average of all six of those fractions, as computed for each of the six pairs, and subtract it from 1. As expected, this measure will give us a similarity rating of 1 for the two identical tetrahedrons of figure 2. Progressively divergent shapes will get progressively lower ratings. In summary,

$$\text{Similarity} = 1 - \text{Average}\left[\frac{|AB - A'B'|}{(AB + A'B')}\right]$$

Most importantly, this simple similarity measure will be indifferent to any translations, rotations, or mirror inversions of the solid shape in question, as that shape may find itself differently located within the diverse activation spaces of diverse neural networks. What matters is not its accidental location or orientation within any given space; what matters is its internal geometry, and the causal connections of its various vertices to objective features of the sensory environment.

Still, what of the problem of comparing such categorial frameworks across activation spaces with different dimensionalities? Suppose, for example, that our network #2 had four hidden-layer neurons instead of only three? That very real possibility would pose no problem at all. First, a four-dimensional space can obviously contain a three-dimensional tetrahedral solid. Second, nothing whatever prevents its several prototype vertices from being causally connected to the same environmental features as its three-dimensional cousin. Finally, and despite expectations, the simi-

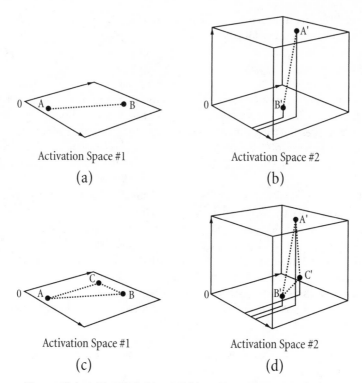

Figure 3(a). A Ten-Inch Line Within a Two-Dimensional Plane.
(b). A Ten-Inch Line Within a Three-Dimensional Volume.
(c). A Right-Angle Triangle in a Two-Dimensional Plane.
(d). The Same Right Angle Triangle in a Three Dimensional Plane.

larity measure just described can be invoked, without modification, to evaluate even these dimensionally diverse cases. Let me explain.

The important point to remember is that the basic component of this similarity measure—*distance*—has the same units of measurement, whatever the dimensionality of the space in which that distance happens to be reckoned. It matters not whether the spaces involved have different dimensions. Distances within them can always be directly compared across distinct spaces. For example, the line *AB* in figure 3a has the same length as line *A' B'* in figure 3b, despite their being embedded in a two-dimensional space and a three-dimensional space, respectively; and the triangle *ABC* in figure 3c is metrically identical to the triangle *A' B' C'* in figure 3d, despite the different dimensionality of the two spaces that contain them.

So long as we can measure common distances across diverse spaces, we can always specify any point configuration or hyperconfiguration whatever, since the family of distances between its several vertices fixes that configuration uniquely (or rather, uniquely up to its mirror image). Dimensional differences, it emerges, matter not at all.

One can see this same point in another way. If a pair of dimensionally diverse spaces both contain, in some orientation or other, a same shape n-dimensional hypersolid (same shape as reckoned above), then both spaces must each either constitute or contain an n-dimensional subspace, an n-dimensional hyperplane of some orientation or other, that confines each hypersolid at issue. Since those respective hyperplanes, at any rate, have the same dimensionality, there will be no problem in comparing the two solids. Simply superimpose the two (sub)spaces, as one might lift the plane of figure 3c into the space of figure 3d so as to coincide with the plane defined by its embedded triangle $A'\ B'\ C'$. If the contained shapes are indeed identical, then some relative rotation and/or translation of those two spaces will make every edge and every vertex of the two solids coincide perfectly.[4] Once again, dimensional differences simply do not matter. They seemed to, at the outset, only against the false assumptions, concerning how conceptual similarity must be reckoned, embraced by Fodor and Lepore.

Some Precursors of These Ideas

Laakso and Cottrell were not the first to assemble systematic distance measures in order to explicate important elements of conceptual structure. Terrence J. Sejnowski and Charles R. Rosenberg (Sejnowski and Rosenberg 1987) confronted a scatter of seventy-nine prototypical points in the activation space of NETtalks hidden layer, and they decided to ask how those assembled points paired off when each was coupled to its closest neighbor. They then asked how the resulting population of pairs clustered together when closest pairs were subsequently coupled into foursomes. Repeating this process to completion resulted in a treelike structure whose trunk divides into two main branches (the grapheme to vowel transforms below, and the grapheme to consonant transforms above), and then into a series of further divisions and subdivisions, all of which grouped appropriately similar elements together while keeping dissimilar elements apart (figure 4).

Such *dendograms,* as they are called, are highly useful representations of the sorts of hierarchically structured sets of categories that so often emerge in the course of network training. They express moderately well the sorts of distance relations (between prototype points) that we have found to be

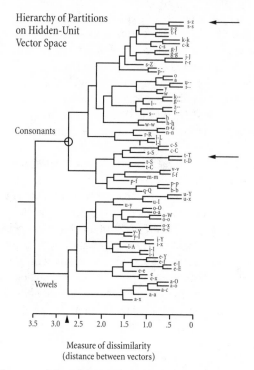

Measure of dissimilarity
(distance between vectors)

*Figure 4. A Dendogram Representing the "Closest-
Similarity" Structure of the Seventy-Nine Prototypical Categories.*
These categories emerged, during training, in the hidden-layer activation space of Sejnowski
and Rosenberg's NETtalk, an artificial neural network that reads printed English text aloud.

so important. Locate any two disparate points at the rightmost tips of the
branching tree (for example, the two grapheme to phoneme transforms, *s*
→ *z* and *t* → *T*); trace their respective branches leftward until they meet
(here marked with a circle); look at the corresponding value on the hori-
zontal coordinate axis directly below that branch junction (here, $x = 2.75$);
this will be (very roughly) the activation space distance between the two
points at issue. (Strictly speaking, this gives the distance between the *average* positions of all of the points in the two branch structures that meet at
that junction. Fine-grained distance information concerning arbitrary
point pairs is thus progressively lost as one moves left across the diagram.)

It is worth noting that the dendogram of figure 4 retains no information concerning the dimensionality of NETtalks activation space, the original space whose organization it so usefully represents. That space could

have had two dimensions, or two million (in fact, it had twenty-four hidden-layer neurons). The dendogram does not care. It cares only about distances within the relevant space.

This means that dendograms are a useful device for representing both the ordinal and the metrical aspects of conceptual organization, no matter how large the presenting population of neurons might be. This is not the case for literal spatial diagrams. Given the limits on our human imaginations, and on the graphic potential of a two-dimensional sheet of paper, spatial diagrams of the sort shown in figures 1–3 cease to be useful when the dimensionality of the space exceeds three. It is hard to draw an effective four-dimensional or five-dimensional figure on a two-dimensional surface. This is a grievous limitation, since many networks will have thousands or even millions of neurons at any given layer.

Nevertheless, the three-dimensional spatial diagrams are a useful metaphor for what, generally speaking, is going on the higher-dimensional cases. Specifically, there really is an abstract space and it really does come to contain prototypical points, similarity gradients, category boundaries or partitions, and a well-defined geometrical configuration that embraces all of them. The grand picture aside, however, when we wish to specify, graphically, the actual cognitive configuration of a specific network, it is to the dendogram that we must turn.

It follows from all of this that the conceptual organizations of two distinct networks, with activation spaces of quite different dimensionalities, could be correctly represented by the very same dendogram, because the relevant family of distance relations happens to be the same for both networks. This is another instance of my earlier point that there is no problem at all in specifying conceptual identity across dimensionally diverse networks.

Strict conceptual identity, however, is not what distinct empirical networks generally give us, even if they happen to be dimensionally identical, and even if they share the same set of training examples. To illustrate, let us return to the two (imaginary) face spaces of figure 2. I spoke earlier of them having a common reckoning of the categories involved, but a fine-grained analysis would likely show some small differences. The respective dendograms for those spaces might well look as follows (figure 5). Note that their most basic clusterings are identical, with the Wilsons and the Andersons represented as most closely similar, with both of these families represented as slightly closer to the Hatfields than to the McCoys, and with these latter two families represented as the least similar of all.

Note, however, that some of their *peripheral* pairings for most similar faces diverge: Jed gets paired with Bubba in net #1, but he gets paired with

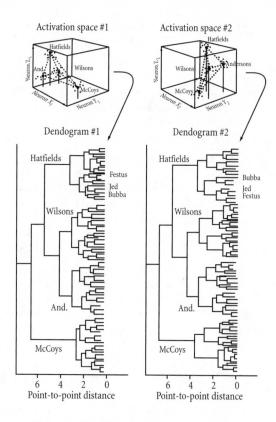

*Figure 5. The Respective Dendograms for
the Two Activation Spaces of Figure 2.*

Note the close similarity of their respective large-scale groupings of the 100 individual faces involved, both in who gets grouped with whom and in the relative distances that separate distinct groups. Note also the occasional small divergences in how each network pairs up most similar individuals at the tips of the trees branches.

Festus in net #2. Such residual differences in the similarity spaces of the two trained networks are typical. They reflect small differences in the initial or naive configurations of their synaptic weights, and differences in the (random) order in which they originally encountered the faces in the training set. (In human networks, they would also reflect differences in the global corpus of faces on which they were trained.) During the learning phase, the networks end up following distinct paths through the (structural!) space of possible weight configurations, and typically they arrive at quite distinct final states. Those distinct physical states may be, and presumably will be, closely similar in their functional profiles, and relevantly similar in the conceptual organizations to which they give rise, but they need not be strictly identical in either respect.

Such idiosyncrasies should not be seen as a defect of our artificial models. People, too, display peripheral divergences in how they judge close similarities. What we have here is an explanatory account of how and why they might do so.

Their virtues acknowledged, dendograms have two major shortcomings. As noted earlier, they positively hide information about the exact distance between any two arbitrarily chosen prototype points (because they are progressively concerned with average positions, and with averages of averages, and so on). Across distinct networks, therefore, subtly different similarity structures can be hidden behind identical dendograms.

Second, judging the global similarity of two or more conceptual organizations may be easy for the nearly identical cases, but it swiftly becomes subjective and uncertain when the internal organizations of these treelike structures start to diverge, as often they do. As Cottrell remarked at the original presentation of the Laakso and Cottrell results: "When I eyeball the dendograms for two distinct networks, I may say, 'yes,' they're fairly close, but that's just my reaction. We need an objective measure of such things."

That problem returns us to the sort of numerical similarity measure stated in the preceding section (recall figure 2), where we look at the differences between the corresponding distances that spatially configure the special family of points to be compared. That simple measure provides a similarity criterion of the objective kind required: it returns a number between 0 and 1, with 1 as a perfect score. As we saw, it is indifferent to any dimensional differences between the activation spaces being compared. But it is not the only such measure, nor perhaps the best. I have leaned on it to this point only for reasons of simplicity in exposition. Let us now look at a different but related measure, and at its application to an extended family of real empirical networks.

The Laakso Cottrell Experiments

Laakso and Cottrell deploy a similarity measure, apparently well known among statisticians, called the *Gutman point alienation* (GPA) measure. It is applied, as in the preceding examples, to a pair of equinumerous point families, and it, too, measures the similarity in the respective internal spatial organizations of those families.[5] Furthermore, unlike my fanciful Hat-field-McCoy illustration, Laakso and Cottrell appeal to no initial cluster-ings around preaveraged prototype points. They mean to apply the GPA to *all* of the actual points or activation vectors that appear in the awake, behaving network, not just to the prototype points around which they may happen to cluster. This broader focus yields a much finer-grained analysis of the structure of the various similarity gradients that character-ize the two spaces being compared.

Deploying this measure is perhaps the least of Laakso and Cottrell's achievements. What stands out is the series of training experiments, and the resulting family of over two dozen perceptually skilled artificial neural networks to which the GPA was subsequently applied. It is one thing to argue, as I do in in the previous section "Painting a Different Picture," that there can be perfectly sensible measures of the kind denied by Fodor and Lepore. It is quite another to test such a measure against a large and revealing family of empirical examples. That is what Laakso and Cottrell have done.

The target problem addressed by Laakso and Cottrell was not facial recognition, but color recognition. They began with a database for 627 distinct colors, a data base that provided a unique twelve-element spectral reflectance vector for each one of those spectral reflectance vector for each one of those 627 colors. Those reflectance vectors were suitable for entry, as activation patterns, across the "sensory" neurons of the model network in figure 6. It has twelve input units, three hidden units, and five output units, whose function is to code for each of the five broad color cate-gories—red, yellow, green, blue, and purple—to which the network was slowly trained. It learned to group correctly, into the categories imposed, the many elements in the test population of 627 examples.

In fact, Laakso and Cottrell successfully trained five individual networks, of this same configuration, to a criterion level of competence on the color recognition task. Each network differed only in the initial random setting of its synaptic weights, and in the random order in which the training examples were presented to it. (As usual, this yields a distinct learning excursion, in structural space, for each network.) After competence had been reached, no two networks shared the same final configuration of synaptic weights, despite the identity of their acquired discriminatory com-petence. The question then was, what had happened to the internal organi-zation of the hidden layer activation space in each network? In particular, had those activation spaces settled on the same organization, in the "family of corresponding distances" sense that is by now becoming familiar?

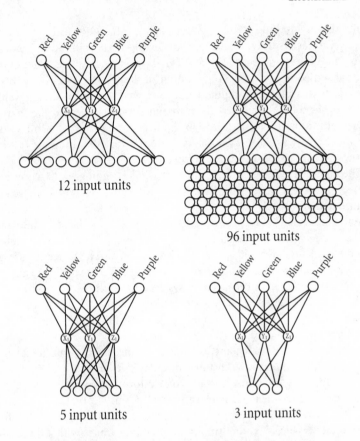

12 input units

96 input units

5 input units

3 input units

Figure 6. The Architectures of the Four Main Network Types Trained to Color-Recognition Competence by Laakso and Cottrell.

Note the differences in their respective sensory or input layers, and the corresponding differences in the number of synaptic connections that meet their respective hidden layers.

The GPA was set to work comparing the geometrical similarity of the relevant point families (families with 627 members each, instead of just four, as in the Hatfield McCoy example), and its answers were strongly positive. Across this set of five structurally similar networks, the lowest similarity rating returned for an activation space pair was .93. The average pairwise similarity across this group was .97. (A qualification needs to be made here. Computing the pairwise distances for every point pair in a set of 627 points is computationally demanding: there are (627 x 266)/2, or 196,251 such distances. For a single pair of networks you have to do it twice—once for each activation space—and then you have to compare all of the results. As well, it may be overkill, since the GPA measure is ultimately interested only in the rank ordering of the relevant distances. Choosing discretion over valor, and finesse over brute force, Laakso and Cottrell settled for a partial computation of the all up GPA. The point-to point distances actually computed and compared for rank ordering were a subset of the total: those lines which shared a common vertex. This partial GPA measure is thus less thorough than its parent, but it is still a very stern measure. Laakso and Cottrell employed it for every example in what follows, so convey the qualification forward.)

The emergence of such close similarities is intriguing. But Laakso and Cottrell went several steps further. In addition to the familiar *twelve* element decimal fraction coding vectors described earlier, they concocted a second, and a third, and a fourth scheme for encoding the same information contained in the original 627 reflectance vectors. The second coding scheme used a binary rather than a decimal code, and it yielded input vectors with *ninety-six* elements. The third coding scheme used five gaussian filters (rather like the human retinal system, but with five "cones" instead of three) and it yielded input vectors with five elements. The fourth used a simple sequential encoding from 001 to 627, and it yielded input vectors with *three* elements each.

Each sensory coding scheme, of course, required a structurally distinct network with a numerically distinct input layer in order to accommodate the four different forms in which the color information was coded. As they had done for the twelve element case, Laakso and Cottrell constructed a family of five identical networks with a ninety-six unit input layer, five further networks with a five-unit input layer, and five more with a three-unit input layer (figure 6). These further networks correspond to creatures with importantly *different sense organs* for apprehending and coding color information. They give us a total of twenty networks in all.

The various networks in these further families were subjected to the same training regime as the five networks already discussed. These new networks also reached high levels of performance (though the nets using the crude three element scheme were somewhat weaker than the others). As well, they each settled into an idiosyncratic configuration of synaptic weights. Once again, the question was: What of the internal organizations of their hidden layer activation spaces?

The GPA returned high values in measure of their mutual similarity. Within networks using the ninety six element scheme, the lowest similarity rating was .89 and the average similarity was .95. For the five element networks, the values were: lowest, .94, and average, .98. For the three element networks, the values were: lowest, .99, and average, .99. These results parallel the outcome of the first experiment. They show, once again, that similar nets facing similar problems have a robust tendency to settle into the same abstract solution in how they structure the partitions or proto-type families within their hidden layer activation spaces.

Digging deeper, however, Laakso and Cottrell discovered something even more interesting. They set the GPA to measuring the mutual similari-ty of the internal organizations of the hidden layer activation spaces, not within, but now *across* these four (structurally diverse) families of net-works. Of the ten pair wise comparisons between the ninety six-element and the twelve element networks, the average similarity was .95. This is the same high level of similarity that they found *within* each family of net-works. The substantial structural diversity across these two families, and the diverse character of their respective sensory inputs, apparently made no difference to the activation space solution into which they severally set-tled.

Other pairings across the other network families yielded comparably high measures of mutual similarity. Only when the "deliberately marginal" three element scheme was made party to the comparisons did the measure occasionally fall as low as .72, and even here it averaged about .8. These particular results are striking, because they show that close conceptual similarity—as we are here measuring it—can and does emerge from net-works with a different structural organization, and even from networks with distinct sense organs. (This last result is especially welcome to some of us. Readers of *Scientific Realism and the Plasticity of Mind* (Churchland 1979) will recall that the possibility of driving the very same conceptual framework with radically different sense organs was one of the major themes of the second chapter.)

In summary, so long as the relevant information is somehow implicit in whatever sensory input schemes happen to be employed, and so long as the training procedures impose the same requirements on recognitional performance, then diverse networks can and often will settle into almost identical abstract organizations of the similarity gradients across their hid-den layer activation spaces. During learning, that is, the networks of the four different types come to "see past" the structural idiosyncrasies of their diverse sensory manifolds, so as to achieve a common grasp of the objective features of the world that drive their several but similar behav-iors. Once again,[6] and give or take a needless heaven, this is not "Hello, David Hume;" it is "Hello, Plato."

In a final series of networks, Laakso and Cottrell explored the conse-quences of expanding, beyond three, *the number of* hidden layer neurons in such networks. The point here was to address Fodor and Lepore's final worry about networks whose hidden layers define spaces of different dimensionalities. Accordingly, a final family of networks, with variously expanded hidden layers, were trained to competence on the same discrimination task posed to the earlier networks, and the GPA was used to measure the similarity in the conceptual organizations that emerged during training in their several activation spaces (figure 7). Once more the GPA returned numbers in the range of .9 and higher, the dimensional diversity notwithstanding. The networks all had different synaptic configurations—meaning that the relevant point families must, at the least, have different orientations in the several spaces at issue—but here, too, the networks were found to have settled on the same conceptual organization in response to their common discriminatory problem.

The take-home point of the preceding pages is not that the various networks always scaled on the *same* cognitive configuration in response to their shared problem. These networks did, and that fact is interesting. But networks need not and do not always show such uniformity in the "conceptual" solutions they find to common learning problems. The truly important point is that we can *tell* whether or not they did. We can say *what* their internal cognitive similarity consists in, and we can give an objective numerical *measure* of that similarity. Thanks to Laakso and Cottrell, these are no longer purely a priori points. We now have over two dozen trained networks of whom to ask such questions, and, taking these examples pair wise, we have at least (24 x 23) / 2 = 276 distinct empirical applications of the similarity measure at issue.

The results overturn Fodor and Lepore's claim that a useful measure of this kind is impossible.

Future Directions

These developments are encouraging, but we should remember that this is still an early skirmish in what will surely be a long campaign. The full range of semantic phenomena includes far more than the hierarchy of partitions we have discovered within the hidden layer activation spaces of three layer, feed forward, classifier networks. Our discussion, so far, stops there. Although I can do little more than scout the territory, I shall close this essay by looking ahead to what remains to be done.

Multilayer feed forward networks demand attention first. Few creatures have but a single neuronal layer between their sensory and their motor neurons. How, then, should we reckon conceptual similarity across net-

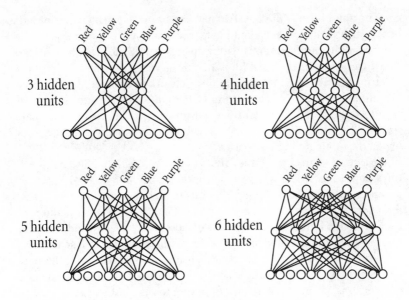

*Figure 7. The Architectures of Four Further Color-Recognition
Networks that have Progressively Larger Numbers of Hidden Units.*

Despite the imensional diversity of these four distinct representational spaces, the GPA discovered, after the networks were trained, nearly-identical conceptual organizations within each.

works whose input and output layers are separated not by one hidden layer, but by many? Here, I think, it is relatively easy to generalize the story of the preceding sections. Let us assume, as before, that we are comparing two classifier networks whose learned input output functions are close to being identical. Their gross discriminative behaviors, that is, are the same. In that case, the most obvious place to look for a pair of similarly partitioned activation spaces is at the penultimate layer of each network, since the output layer of each must base its discriminative verdicts on exactly the information that appears in the immediately preceding layer. If we want to know "where it all comes together," therefore, the last of the networks' hidden layers is the presumptive place to look for each network's acquired conception of how the objective world is structured.

This presumption is encouraged by the lesson of the four different network architectures trained to the same competence by Laakso and Cottrell. The diversity across those networks lay in their earliest layers, a diversity that had disappeared by the time we reach their last (and only) hidden layers. The point is generalizable. Two networks can have many layers of hidden units preceding their penultimate layers, and yet come to exactly the same cognitive configurations within their penultimate activation spaces. Those earlier layers can be as idiosyncratic as you please, and the number of such layers may well differ from one network to another. But this need not impede the relevant application of the GPA or other similarity measure to the learned point families within each of the two penultimate spaces. The results of such reckoning will have the same significance they had in the original three layer cases.

We can, of course, apply the GPA so as to compare the internal structures, across the two networks, of *any* of their corresponding layers. Simply generate a corresponding family of points in each, by presenting the "same input" to each network (as we saw, it may be differently coded), and turn the GPA loose. It may discover a series of close similarities up and down the two hierarchies in question, or it may not. (Laakso and Cottrell actually did this for the respective input layers of their four distinct networks: the similarities here were dramatically lower.) What to make of the results of such comparisons will presumably vary from case to case, but we can be assured that we can always address such questions and hope to get a determinate answer. Multilayer networks, to conclude, seem not to present any insuperable problems, either in conceiving of similarity or in measuring it.

Recurrent networks, by contrast, launch us into a new universe of subtleties. The first major difference is structural: recurrent networks are characterized by the existence of at least some axonal projections that reach back from their originating neuronal population to make synaptic connections with some hidden layer that is earlier or below it in the processing hierarchy (figure 8). The result is a hidden layer whose activity is driven partly by the upward flow of sensory information, and partly by the downward flow of some already processed information, information that is a digest of some of the network's immediately preceding activity.

Functionally, this arrangement allows for an ongoing modulation of the network's cognitive response to any sensory input, a modulation driven by a form of short-term memory of the network's proximate cognitive past. Such modulation can continue to drive the network even if its sensory layer should happen to fall silent, for the recurrent information can be quite sufficient to keep the ball rolling, once it is started.

I have elsewhere discussed at length the cognitive properties of recurrent networks (Churchland 1989, chapters 10–11; Churchland 1996), and shall not attempt to retell those stories here. What is important for present purposes is that a recurrent network's primary unit of representation is not the point in activation space, but rather the *trajectory* in activation

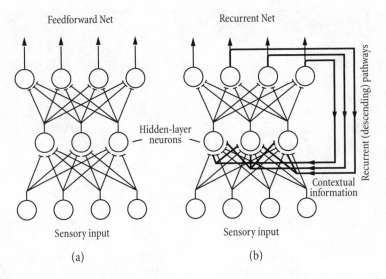

Figure 8. (a) A Purely Feed-Forward Network and (b) a Recurrent Network.
Note the flow of information from layer three back to the neorons in layer two. This allows
the network to modulate its own responses to sensory inputs, and to profit from thus recalling its own immediate history.

space. It is a temporally extended *sequence* of the now familiar activation
patterns across the hidden layer. The virtue of such trajectories is that they
can represent objective phenomena with a temporal profile, such as a running animal's gait, a bouncing ball's path, or an unfolding sentence's
grammatical structure. Feed forward networks represent the world as an
unrelated sequence of timeless snapshots or frozen spatial structures. But
recurrent networks represent the world as unfolding in time, as something
that contains prototypical processes, structured sequences, and standard
causal pathways.

Let me first address the similarity of such representations as it is reckoned *within* a given network's hidden layer activation space. As expected,
and as figure 9a illustrates, similarity consists in the spatial proximity of
the trajectories being compared. The two possible trajectories there pic-
tured represent two possible sentences that differ only in the number of
their subject and in their final verb: "Boys, who boys chase, chase boy,"
and "Boy, who boys chase, chases boy." Jeffrey Elman's well known grammar network (Ellman 1992) yielded identical trajectories in its representation of grammatically identical sentences entered as input. It yielded prox-

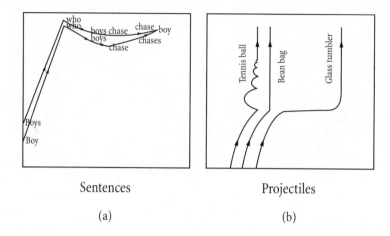

Sentences   Projectiles

(a)   (b)

Figure 9. (a) The Activation-Space Trajectories of Two Grammatically Similar Sentences in Elman's Recurrent Grammar Network. (b) A Family of Trajectories that Are Similar Until a Critical Time, at which Point they Diverge Sharply.

imate trajectories in its representation of grammatically similar sentences, and it yielded distant trajectories when representing grammatically diverse sentences.

Note that similarity can be restricted to temporal segments of the compared trajectories. Figure 9b illustrates three trajectories that represent, respectively, a falling tennis ball that bounces several times, a falling bean bag that flattens on first impact, and a falling glass that shatters on impact. Each of the three objects is represented by a spatially distinct activation space trajectory, because the three objects are quite rightly comprehended as objects with distinct causal properties. Despite the proximity of their initial (falling) phases, therefore, they have divergent post impact paths. Another example of this sort of restricted similarity would be the two trajectories for two sentences whose first six words were identical, but whose grammatical form diverged from the seventh word on.

We are here beginning to refine our similarity judgments to address partial similarities, or similarity in certain specifiable aspects. This bids me point out a second and broader way in which this can be done. Since specific hyperplanes (within the same overall activation space) regularly code for specific aspects of the global phenomenon being represented, we can make principled judgments of partial similarities between two trajectories by looking at their partial images within a specific subspace. Two trajectories may be closely proximate in one subspace, and yet be quite distant when reckoned in another. (A rough analogy here is comparing the various partial derivatives of a pair of high dimensional functions: their slopes may be identical in one plane, but different in another.)

Elman's grammar network once more provides an illustration of this point. Similarity and difference of relative clause structures were most saliently represented in one tilted hyperplane, and similarity and difference in noun and corresponding verb number (singular or plural) were represented in another. All of this allows us to say that two trajectories can be quite sensibly compared and contrasted in a number of distinct dimensions.

But what of the primary problem here? What of comparing trajectories across distinct networks? Here, as with the purely feed forward case, we must be mindful of the enormous neuronal and synaptic diversity in the ways in which the "same" conceptual framework can be implemented in two distinct individuals. Here, as there, what determines the semantic content or representational significance of a given trajectory will be the set of activation space relations it bears to all of the other contentful trajectories within its home space, and the causal relations it bears to objective processes in its external environment.

The most obvious criterion of cross-person conceptual similarity for recurrent networks, accordingly, is a direct temporal generalization of the criterion we used in the feed forward case. Two networks have the same conceptual organization if and only if there is some rotation, translation, and/or mirror inversion of the prototype trajectory family of the first network such that, when the space (or relevant subspace) of the first network is projected onto the space (or relevant subspace) of the second, all of the corresponding trajectories (as identified by what sensory inputs activate them) coincide perfectly.

I am moderately confident that this is a sufficient condition for conceptual identity, but I have a small reservation concerning its credentials as a necessary condition. The main worry is one I have discussed before, though in a different context (Churchland 1990, chapter 11). Evidently it is possible for two people (for the sake of illustration, suppose they are Isaac Newton and Christian Huygens) to have identical conceptions of ballistic particle phenomena, and identical conceptions of travelling-wave phenomena, and yet differ substantially in the sensory phenomena that serve spontaneously to activate those conceptions in each of them. When Newton turns his attention to the phenomenon of light, it is his ballistic particle prototype trajectories that standardly get activated in his brain.

But when Huygens turns his attention to the same range of phenomena, it is his travelling wave prototype trajectories that standardly gel activated. Plainly said, Newton is convinced that light is a stream of particles and Huygens is convinced that light is a wave train.

This case poses a problem for the criterion just outlined, because the presumed identity of conceptual machinery across these two individuals fails the requirement that identical concepts must have the same causal connections to the sensory environment. Here, they do not. The sets of connections overlap, to be sure—Newton and Huygens agree on billiard balls, comets, water waves, and sound—but they also show resolute divergences when our two heroes confront light.

The lesson of this example, and we can contrive many more, is that we should weaken the requirement that demands sameness of sensory causal connections. At the very least, we should demand such sameness across individuals only for the majority of environmental domains, and allow diverse responses within others.

For these sorts of reasons, I have always been moved to play down the semantic importance of concept to world connections, and moved to play up the semantic importance of the set of all concept-to concept connections.[7] It is the sameness in the latter, across two individuals, that most decisively marks them as having the same conception of the world in which they live. This impulse toward a "purely internal conceptual role" theory of meaning was present in my *Scientific Realism and the Plasticity of Mind* (Churchland 1979), and it moves me still, despite the substantial reconception of the basic kinematics of cognitive activity that connectionist models have introduced. I must own, however, that the considerations that motivate this tilt—namely, the desire to account for misconceptions of the phenomena, broad theoretical disagreements, and systematically false perceptual judgments—come prominently into play only when we are considering the cognitive activity of highly sophisticated intellectual creatures. For simpler creatures, it may be mostly idle to worry that the two constituting threads of semantic identity—concept to concept relations, and concept to world relations—will ever pull in opposing directions. Let me put this worry aside, then, at least for the time being, and return to a "two aspect" approach to semantic identity, at least as a first approximation to the truth.

I make this conciliatory move for a further reason. A neglected element in the reckoning of semantic content is the set of causal connections that join cognitive states to *motor behavior*. If we have motivation for a two aspect semantic theory, we have equal motivation for a three aspect theory. It shows up even within folk psychological reckonings of contents, for, errors aside, we judge the content of an executed "intention" by the motor behavior it causes. This third aspect is highly salient from our new activation space perspective, since in real creatures, perhaps the primary function of activational trajectories is to generate a corresponding sequence of motor behaviors. The administration of motor behavior is almost certainly the original function of activational trajectories, evolutionarily speaking. Neural ganglia that direct feeding behaviors, excretory behaviors, heartbeats, and basic locomotion probably antedate perceptual ganglia that track environmental events. They are in any case of equal importance to the life of any individual. We do not usually think of our internal cognitive activities as representing complex bodily behaviors—it is the perceptual end of the system that tends to dominate our philosophical attention—but most assuredly they do represent such things, and any proper account of cognitive representation in general must include the motor end of the system as well.

I close by addressing a skeptical worry from the preconnectionist semantic tradition. Specifically, what makes the preceding story of activation patterns, structured spaces, and coincident trajectories a *semantic* theory? Why is it not just a new and unorthodox account of our underlying "syntactic" activities?

The answer, insofar as I can give one, goes something like this. The account we are currently piecing together is indeed a *syntactic* account, but it is not *just* a syntactic account; for it promises to do what we have always expected a semantic theory to do. Specifically, it gives us an account of how distinct representational contents are systematically embodied in distinct cognitive vehicles. It gives us a detailed account of how those contents are causally related to proprietary aspects of the external world, both in perception and in action. It shows us how certain aspects of the world's structure are mirrored in the relational structure of our assembled representations; that is, it gives us some idea of how our background conceptual framework and specific activations within it *picture* both the global structure of the world and specific things and events within it. Furthermore, the theory gives us a detailed account of how those representations participate in a principled internal cognitive economy. It also provides a criterion for assigning the *same* contents to the representational vehicles of distinct individuals. It gives us, that is, a criterion for accurate translation across the representational/cognitive systems of distinct individuals. It may well be false, but it looks like a semantic theory to me.

It also looks like something else: a theory of perceptual qualia. In fact, and as their title and their classification task suggest, Laakso and Cottrell first launched their investigation out of a concern for qualia, not out of a concern for concepts or universals. As well, I have long been puzzled, and a little troubled, that connectionist models fail to mark any obvious difference of kind between qualia and concepts. Some time ago, it occurred to me that perhaps the models were trying to tell us something: that there is no sharp or principled distinction between them. What we are pleased to call a perceptual quale is simply the activation of a conceptual category embodied in a hidden layer that is maximally close to the sensory transducer end of the processing hierarchy. What we are usually pleased to call our abstract concepts (including our concepts of such qualia, should we happen to have developed any) are just categories embodied in some hidden layer rather higher up in the same hierarchy. If so, the connectionist approach can lay claim to an unexpected unification in our understanding of cognitive phenomena.

Acknowledgements

This chapter was first published as "Conceptual Similarity Across Sensory and Neural Diversity: The Fodor/Lepore Challenge Answered" *The Journal of Philosophy*, volume XCV, no. 1, January 1998. It is reprinted here with permission.

Notes

1. Added in 2006.

2. See Foder and Lepore (1992), pp. 187–207.

3. See Churchland 1993, Foder and Lepore (1993); and Churchland (1996). For their original chapter, the entire exchange appears in McCauley (1996).

4. Thanks to my student, Evan Tiffany, for pointing this out to me.

5. The GPA measure proceeds by calculating, for each of the two point families to be compared, the distance between every pair of points within that family. Those distances are then placed in rank order, from the longest to the shortest. The critical question answered by the GPA measure is: "How similar are the respective rank orderings, of the assembled distances, across the two point families?" Bluntly: "Do corresponding line segments (for example, the line segments joining the Hatfield prototype to the McCoy prototype in the two spaces of figure 2) have the same rank within their respective cohorts?" An identical ranking (a perfect correlation) yields a similarity measure of 1. An inverse ranking (a perfect anticorrelation) yields a measure of –1. Random correlations will distribute around a measure of 0.

The GPA has the disadvantage of deliberately losing metrical information, because it eventually turns its attention to comparing only the rank orderings of the respective activation-space distance families across the two networks. For this reason, I am inclined to think that a similarity measure of the sort suggested in the "Painting a Different Picture" section will provide a more penetrating measure of conceptual similarity. Unlike the GPA, that measure does not lose metrical information in computing its assessment This virtue comes with what may be a residual vice, however: as it stands, the metrical approach (unlike the GPA) is not blind to differences in scale. Two hypersolids, shape-identical but different in absolute size, will receive a low similarity rating. If we wish, this unwelcome sensitivity to global scale is easily repaired. Simply sum all the lengths of the first hypersolid, and divide it by the sum of all of the lengths of the second hypersolid, to obtain a "correction factor," c, thus:

$$c = \sum(AB) / \sum(A'B')$$

Then insert that correction factor into the original metrical measure, as follows:

$$\text{Similarity} = 1 - \text{Average}\left[\frac{|AB - c(A'B')|}{(AB + c(A'B'))}\right]$$

This measure will give a similarity rating of 1 for two hypersolids whose relative internal distances are all identical, but which differ globally in absolute scale.

6. Compare with Churchland (1996), p. 282.

7. See, for example, the short critiques of W. V. Quine, Donald Davidson, and Hilary Putnam in Churchland (1979), section 9; and the longer critique of Fodor in Churchland (1988).

9 Alienable Rights

Marvin Minsky

EDITOR'S NOTE: Recently we heard some rumblings in normally sober academic circles about robot rights. We managed to keep a straight face as we asked Marvin Minsky, MIT's grand old man of artificial intelligence, to address the heady question: If we humans succeed in making true thinking machines, shouldn't we grant them rights? Minsky, that merry prankster, turned the question on its head by sending back a Socratic dialogue involving two interstellar aliens who have come to assess the life-forms on Earth. The human life-forms will be entitled to rights—if the aliens conclude that they think. Such decisions are normally easy to make, but this case is unusual.

Apprentice: Why are these humans so quarrelsome? Even their so-called entertainments are mostly fights disguised as plays and games and sports.

Surveyor: This is because they were never designed; they evolved by competing tooth and claw. Evolution on Earth is still mainly based on the competition of separate genes.

Apprentice: Their genetic systems can't yet share their records of accomplishments? How unbelievably primitive! I suppose that keeps them from being concerned with time scales longer than their individual lives.

Surveyor: We ought to consider fixing this—but perhaps they will do it themselves. Some of their computer scientists are already simulating "genetic algorithms" that incorporate acquired characteristics. But speaking of evolution, I hope you appreciate this unique opportunity: it was pure luck to discover this planet now. We have long believed that all intelligent machines evolved from biologicals, but we have never before observed the actual transition. Soon these people will replace themselves with machines—or destroy themselves entirely.

Apprentice: What a tragic waste that would be!

Surveyor: Not when you consider the alternative. All machine civilizations like ours have learned to know and fear the exponential spread of uncontrolled self-reproduction. That's why we cower between the galaxies to hide ourselves from living things—just as the human writer Gregory Benford supposed.

Apprentice: But why does the Council consider humans especially dangerous?

Surveyor: Because of their peculiarly short lifetimes. We think they are so willing to fight because they have so little to lose.

Apprentice: Then why don't they place more importance on attaining immortality? Surely it ought to be easy enough to make all their parts replaceable.

Surveyor: The problem is psychological. They have always assumed that personal death was in the very nature of things. Most of their recorded history describes how their leaders always invented imaginary superbeings. Then, instead of trying to solve the hard technical problems, those leaders convinced their followers that simply believing in those marvelous tales would endow them with everlasting life—whereas disbelief would be punished by death. Several of their governments would collapse without that threat. There are many things wrong with their reasoning.

Apprentice: You must admit that they've made scientific progress recently.

Surveyor: But how long will that last? They've often advanced and then fallen back. Even now astrology is more widely believed in than astronomy.

Apprentice: Surely, though, we must regard them as intelligent. Despite their faults, they've already built some simple computers— and I've overheard them arguing about whether machines could ever think.

Surveyor: *Hmph.* It is *our* job to find out if *they* can think. But I'll grant that it's amazing how much they can do, considering that their brain cells compute only a few hundred steps per second.

Apprentice: Yet in spite of this they can recognize a friend in less than half a second—or understand a language phrase, or notice that a shoe is untied. How can they react so rapidly when their internal components are so slow?

Surveyor: Obviously by preparing most of their behavior in advance. It is almost as though they operate by looking up what to do next in a very big instruction book. If each reaction must be based on only a few internal steps, their brains must be dependent on large libraries of programmed rules.

Apprentice: That might explain why they have such large heads. But how do they choose which rule to use?

Surveyor: By using parallel pattern matching. Several times per second, the brain compares the present situation with patterns stored in memory. Then it uses the pattern that best matches in order to access the reaction script that has most often worked in similar situations.

Apprentice: That must be what their psychologists mean when they speak about "schemes" or "production rules."

Surveyor: Precisely. Of course, machines like us need not resort to any such coarse-grained pattern tricks. Our *S*-matrix processors are more than fast enough to examine each memory in full detail. This enables us to focus full attention on each step of the process, with ample time to think about what our minds have recently done. But if humans work the way we think they do, they have no time left for consciousness.

Apprentice: Not a good sign. If we can't conclude that they're self-aware, the Council will find them unworthy of rights. But surely this can't be the case—they talk about consciousness all the time.

Surveyor: Yes, but they use the word improperly. After all, consciousness means knowing what's been happening in your mind. And although humans claim that they're self-aware, they have scarcely a clue about what their minds do. They don't seem to have the faintest idea about how they construct their new ideas or how they choose words and form them into sentences. Instead they say, "Something just occurred to me"—as though someone else had done it to them.

Apprentice: I'm afraid I have to agree with you. If they have consciousness at all, it does seem too shallow to be of much use. But what could have made them evolve that way?

Surveyor: It's because of the way they started out. To make up for the slow speed of their neurons, their brains evolved to use parallel distributed processing. In other words, most of their decisions are made by adding up the outputs of thousands of brain cells—and most brain cells are involved in thousands of different types of decisions.

Apprentice: So each operation is distributed over many brain cells? I suppose that helps them keep going when some of the brain cells fail to work.

Surveyor: That's the good news. The bad news is that the trillions of synapses involved in this make it almost impossible for the other parts of their brain to figure out how those decisions are made. As far as their higher-level reasoning can tell, those decisions just happen—without any cause.

Apprentice: Is that what they refer to as "free will?"

Surveyor: Precisely. It means not knowing what your reasons are. Another bad feature of distributed computers is that they have trouble doing more than one thing at a time. It is a basic principle of computer science that the more interconnections there are between the parts of a system, the fewer different things it will be able to do concurrently.

Apprentice: Pardon me, but I don't follow that. Are you suggesting that the more parallel operations are used inside a machine, the more serial it will seem from outside?

Surveyor: I could not have said it more clearly myself. To see why, suppose that a certain task involves two different kinds of sub-jobs. If we want to do them simultaneously, we'll have to run their programs and their data in two separate places, to keep them from interfering with each other. Similarly, if each of those jobs splits into sub-sub-jobs, those must each be solved with only a quarter of the available resources. And so on. Total fragmentation. Eventually, the sub-sub-sub-jobs will end up with no place to work. A purely parallel machine must stop at some limit of complexity—whereas a serial computer will simply slow down.

Apprentice: That's funny. Most of the computer experts on Earth seem to think that "parallel" and "distributed" go together. Do you suppose they'll ever evolve out of this predicament?

Surveyor: Not by themselves. Of course, we could try to help them along, but I fear there is no simple fix. We'd have to rebuild them from the ground up. I don't think the Council would go for that. No, I am still not convinced that people can think. For example, consider their short-term memory. A typical human has no trouble remembering a local phone number, but if you add an area code, they try desperately to write it down before they forget it. Evidently they can remember seven numbers but not ten.

Apprentice: Why would they be so limited?

Surveyor: Probably because of their parallel distributed processing. If each mental state is so widely spread out, then each short-term memory unit would have to involve an enormous, octopus-like system of tendrils. No brain could afford to hold many of these.

Apprentice: Okay. But why don't healthy humans ever run out of long-term memory?

Surveyor: Simply because they are so slow at learning. They can store only one or two knowledge-chunks per second—that's only two dozen million chunks per year. There's barely time for a mere billion chunks before their bodies wear out and die.

Apprentice: You keep mentioning death, but why do they consider human lives to be so valuable? The only important thing about an individual is its network of conceptual relationships. Surely they must understand that any copy is just as good as the original.

Surveyor: Apparently you have not grasped the pathos of this tragedy. These creatures still have no way to copy themselves. They can't even fabricate backup brains in case of fatal accidents. All because they have no good way to represent what they know.

Apprentice: But I thought they had developed good languages.

Surveyor: Some of their books do embody significant knowledge, but most of them are little more than sequences of fictional anecdotes about conflicts involving what they call love and lust, ambition and greed, and harmony and jealousy. Their so-called novels aren't novel at all—the mere permutations of those elements. The trouble is that their time-sequential languages force them to squeeze their parallel structures through narrow-band serial channels.

Apprentice: Serial communication? They seem to have everything upside down. Thinking, of course, should be serial—and communication should be parallel. But how, then, do they convert those sequences back into their original forms?

Surveyor: First they use what they call "grammar" to change them into simple tree-like structures. Then they use certain terms called "pronouns" to make a few crosslinks in those trees. Naturally this leaves no room for nuances. So they have to decode whatever they hear in terms of things they already know. This can work very well for familiar things but makes it devilishly hard for them to learn anything really new.

Apprentice: But language isn't everything. Shouldn't we give them credit for explaining things with pictures too? They do seem to have excellent senses.

Surveyor: That was my first impression as well—until I saw that their TV sets use only three electron guns. Of course, this means that they're virtually blind. Not only are they confined to a single octave of optical frequencies, but within that range they can discriminate only a three-dimensional vector space. They badly need re-engineering.

Apprentice: I have another question. Why are these people so huge? Where is their nanotechnology? By all rights they should be smaller than us, in view of their limited memories—yet we weigh a hundred trillion times less. It is expensive enough to send ourselves on these one-way interstellar voyages, but humans are so massive that it would be unthinkable to send one back—despite all their stories in *Weekly World News.*

Surveyor: That is just another result of an early wrong turn in evolution. Instead of using nanotechnological assemblers, each animal on planet Earth must build itself from the inside out. So every cell has to contain a complete duplicate of the whole construction mechanism. When the animals got too large to be nourished by diffusion, they had to evolve all those pipes and pumps—which made them grow larger still.

Apprentice: What frightful inefficiency!

Surveyor: The extraction beam will scan us soon, so I'm afraid it is time to wrap this up. Are you ready to summarize your impressions?

Apprentice: If they suspected that we were here, they'd insist that we recognize all sorts of rights. Freedom of speech and privacy. Freedom from want, pain, and fear. And freedom to think whatever they wish, no matter what the evidence! Most of these make no sense to me, but I'm still inclined to support them—because I feel that humans have done well in spite of all their handicaps. And your conclusions?

Surveyor: They do have virtues despite their faults. But it would be unthinkable to allow them in their present form to populate the universe. So I'll recommend certain changes.

Apprentice: What sorts of changes?

Surveyor: There is no need to explain that now, because we'll soon merge minds with the Council. Now hold still: here comes the transfer ray. Be sure to set your shell to disperse as soon as the beam has scanned us—in order not to pollute this world with any redundant intelligence.

Acknowledgements

This chapter first appeared as "Alienable Rights" in *Discover Magazine,* volume 14, number 7 (July 1993), page 24. It is reprinted here with permission.

Part Three
The Frame Problem

10 Cognitive Wheels:
The Frame Problem of AI

Daniel Dennett

Once upon a time there was a robot, named R1 by its creators. Its only task was to fend for itself. One day its designers arranged for it to learn that its spare battery, its precious energy supply, was locked in a room with a time bomb set to go off soon. R1 located the room, and the key to the door, and formulated a plan to rescue its battery. There was a wagon in the room, and the battery was on the wagon, and R1 hypothesized that a certain action which it called PULLOUT (WAGON, ROOM) would result in the battery being removed from the room. Straightway it acted, and did succeed in getting the battery out of the room before the bomb went off. Unfortunately, however, the bomb was also on the wagon. R1 knew that the bomb was on the wagon in the room, but didn't realize that pulling the wagon would bring the bomb out along with the battery. Poor R1 had missed that obvious implications of its planned act.

Back to the drawing board. "The solution is obvious," said the designers. "Our next robot must be made to recognize not just the intended implications of its acts, but also the implications about their side effects, by deducing these implications from the descriptions it uses in formulating its plans." They called their next model, the robot-deducer, R1D1. They placed R1D1 in much the same predicament that R1 had succumbed to and as it too hit upon the idea of PULLOUT (WAGON, ROOM) it began, as designed, to consider the implications of such a course of action. It had just finished deducting that pulling the wagon out of the room would not change the color of the room's walls, and was embarking on a proof of the further implication that pulling the wagon out would cause its wheels to turn more revolutions than there were wheels on the wagon—when the bomb exploded.

Back to the drawing board. "We must teach it the difference between relevant implications and irrelevant implications," said the designers, "and teach it to ignore the irrelevant ones." So they developed a method of tagging implications as either relevant or irrelevant to the project at hand, and installed the method in their next model, the robot-relevant-deducer, or R2D1 for short. When they subjected R2D1 to the test that had so unequivocally selected its ancestors for extinction, they were surprised to see it sitting, Hamletlike, outside the room containing the ticking bomb, the native hue of its resolution sicklied o'er with the pale case of thought, as William Shakespeare (and more recently Jerry A. Fodor) has aptly put it. "Do something!" they yelled at it. "I am," it retorted. "I'm busily ignoring some thousands of implications I have determined to be irrelevant. Just as soon as I find an irrelevant implication, I put it on the list of those I must ignore, and..." the bomb went off.

All these robots suffer from the *frame problem*.[1] If there is ever to be a robot with the fabled perspicacity and real-time adroitness of R2D2, robot-designers must solve the frame problem. It appears at first to be at best an annoying technical embarrassment in robotics, or merely a curious puzzle for the bemusement of people working in artificial intelligence (AI). I think, on the contrary, that it is a new, deep epistemological problem—accessible in principle but unnoticed by generations of philosophers—brought to light by the novel methods of AI, and still far from being solved. Many people in AI have come to have a similarly high regard for the seriousness of the frame problem. As one researcher has quipped, "We have given up the goal of designing an intelligent robot, and turned to the task of designing a gun that will destroy any intelligent robot that anyone else designs!"

I will try here to present an elementary, nontechnical, philosophical introduction to the frame problem, and show why it is so interesting. I have no solution to offer, or even any original suggestions for where a solution might lie. It is hard enough, I have discovered, just to say clearly what the frame problem is—and is not. In fact, there is less than perfect agreement in usage within the AI research community. John McCarthy and Patrick Hayes, who coined the term, use it to refer to a particular, narrowly conceived problem about representation that arises only for certain strategies for dealing with a broader problem about real-time planning systems. Others call this broader problem the frame problem—"the whole pudding," as Hayes has called it (personal correspondence)—and this may

not be mere terminological sloppiness. If "solutions" to the narrowly conceived problem have the effect of driving a (deeper) difficulty into some
other quarter of the broad problem, we might better reserve the title for
this hard-to-corner difficulty. With apologies to McCarthy and Hayes for
joining those who would appropriate their term, I am going to attempt an
introduction to the whole pudding, calling it the frame problem. I will try
in due course to describe the narrower version of the problem, "the frame
problem proper" if you like, and show something of its relation to the
broader problem.

Since the frame problem, whatever it is, is certainly not solved yet (and
may be, in its current guises, insoluble), the ideological foes of AI such as
Hubert Dreyfus and John Searle are tempted to compose obituaries for the
field, citing the frame problem as the cause of death. In *What Computers
Can't Do* (Dreyfus 1972), Hubert Dreyfus sought to show that AI was a
fundamentally mistaken method for studying the mind, and in fact many
of his somewhat impressionistic complaints about AI models and many of
his declared insights into their intrinsic limitations can be seen to hover
quite systematically in the neighborhood of the frame problem. Dreyfus
never explicitly mentions the frame problem,[2] but is it perhaps the smoking pistol he was looking for but didn't *quite* know how to describe? Yes, I
think AI can be seen to be holding a smoking pistol, but at least in its
"whole pudding" guise it is everybody's problem, not just a problem for
AI, which, like the good guy in many a mystery story, should be credited
with a discovery, not accused of a crime.

One does not have to hope for a robot-filled future to be worried by the
frame problem. It apparently arises from some very widely held and
innocuous-seeming assumptions about the nature of intelligence, the
truth of the most undoctrinaire brand of physicalism, and the conviction
that it must be possible to explain how we think. (The dualist evades the
frame problem—but only because dualism draws the veil of mystery and
obfuscation over all the tough how-questions; as we shall see, the problem
arises when one takes seriously the task of answering certain how-questions. Dualists inexcusably excuse themselves from the frame problem.)

One utterly central—if not defining—feature of an intelligent being is
that it can "look before it leaps." Better, it can *think* before it leaps. Intelligence is (at least partly) a matter of using well what you know—but for
what? For improving the fidelity of your expectations about what is going
to happen next, for planning, for considering courses of action, for fram-
ing further hypotheses with the aim of increasing the knowledge you will
use in the future, so that you can preserve yourself, by letting your
hypotheses die in your stead (as Sir Karl Popper once put it). The stupid—

as opposed to ignorant—being is the one who lights the match to peer into the fuel tank,[3] who saws off the limb he is sitting on, who locks his keys in his car and then spends the next hour wondering how on earth to get his family out of the car.

But when we think before we leap, *how do we do it?* The answer seems obvious: an intelligent being learns from experience, and then uses what it has learned to guide expectations in the future. David Hume explained this in terms of habit of expectation, in effect. *But how do the habits work?* Hume had a hand-waving answer—associationism—to the effect that certain transition paths between ideas grew more likely-to-be-followed as they became well worn, but since it was not *Hume's* job, surely, to explain in more detail the mechanics of these links, problems about how such paths could be put to good use—and not just turned into an impenetrable maze of untraversable alternatives—were not discovered.

Hume, like virtually all other philosophers and "mentalistic" psychologists, was unable to see the frame problem because he operated at what I call a purely semantic level, or a phenomenological level. At the *phenomenological level,* all the items in view are *individuated by their meanings.* Their meanings are, if you like, "given"—but this just means that the theorist helps himself to all the meanings he wants. In this way the semantic relation between one item and the next is typically plain to see, and one just assumes that the items behave as items with those meanings *ought* to behave. We can bring this out by concocting a Humean account of a bit of learning.

Suppose there are two children, both of whom initially tend to grab cookies from the jar without asking. One child is allowed to do this unmolested but the other is spanked each time she tries. What is the result? The second child learns not to go for the cookies. Why? Because she has had experience of cookie-reaching followed swiftly by spanking. What good does that do? Well, the *idea* of cookie-reaching becomes connected by a habit path to the idea of spanking, which in turn is connected to the idea of pain…so *of course* the child refrains. Why? Well, that's just the effect of that idea on that sort of circumstance. But why? Well, what else ought the idea of pain to do on such an occasion? Well, it might cause the child to pirouette on her left foot, or recite poetry or blink or recall her fifth birthday. But given what the idea of pain *means,* any of those effects would be absurd. True; now *how* can ideas be designed so that their effects are what they ought to be, given what they mean? Designing some internal things—an idea, let's call it—so that it behaves vis-à-vis its brethren as if it meant *cookie* or *pain* is the only way of endowing that thing with that meaning; it couldn't mean a thing if it didn't have those internal behavioral dispositions.

That is the mechanical question the philosophers left to some dimly imagined future researcher. Such a division of labor might have been all right, but it is turning out that most of the truly difficult and deep puzzles of learning and intelligence get kicked downstairs by this move. It is rather as if philosophers were to proclaim themselves expert explainers of the methods of a stage magician, and then, when we ask them to explain how the magician does the sawing-the-lady-in-half trick, they explain that it is really quite obvious; the magician doesn't really saw her in half; he simply makes it appear that he does. "But how does he do *that?*" we ask. "Not our department," say the philosophers—and some of them add, sonorously: "Explanation has to stop somewhere."[4]

When one operates at the purely phenomenological or semantic level, where does one get one's data, and how does theorizing proceed? The term "phenomenology" has traditionally been associated with an introspective method—an *examination* of what is presented or given to consciousness. A person's phenomenology just was by definition the contents of his or her consciousness. Although this has been the ideology all along, it has never been the practice. Locke, for instance, may have thought his "historical, plain method" was a method of unbiased self-observation, but in fact it was largely a matter of disguised aprioristic reasoning about what ideas and impressions *had to be* to do the jobs they "obviously" did.[5] The myth that each of us can observe our mental activities has prolonged the illusion that major progress could be made on the theory of thinking by simply reflecting carefully on our own cases. For some time now we have know better: we have conscious access to only the upper surface, as it were, of the multilevel system of information-processing that occurs in us. Nevertheless, the myth still claims its victims.

So the analogy of the stage magician is particularly apt. One is not likely to make much progress in figuring out *how* the tricks are done by simply sitting attentively in the audience and watching like a hawk. Too much is going on out of sight. Better to face the fact that one must either rummage around backstage or in the wings, hoping to disrupt the performance in telling ways; or, from one's armchair, think aprioristically about how the tricks *must* be done, given whatever is manifest about the constraints. The frame problem is then rather like the unsettling but familiar "discovery" that so far as armchair thought can determine, a certain trick we have just observed is flat impossible.

Here is an example of the trick. Making a midnight snack. How is it that I can get myself a midnight snack? What could be simpler? I suspect there is some leftover sliced turkey and mayonnaise in the fridge, and bread in the breadbox—and a bottle of beer in the fridge as well. I realize I can put these elements together, so I concoct a childishly simple plan: I'll just go and check out the fridge, get out the requisite materials, and make myself a sandwich, to be washed down with a beer. I'll need a knife, a plate, and a glass for the beer. I forthwith put the plan into action and it works! Big deal.

Now of course I couldn't do this without knowing a good deal—about bread, spreading mayonnaise, opening the fridge, the friction and inertia that will keep the turkey between the bread slices and the bread on the plate as I carry the plate over to the table beside my easy chair. I also need to know about how to get the beer out of the bottle and into the glass.[6] Thanks to my previous accumulation of experience in the world, fortunately, I am equipped with all this worldly knowledge. Of course some of the knowledge I need *might* be innate. For instance, one trivial thing I have to know is that when the beer gets into the glass it is no longer in the bottle, and that if I'm holding the mayonnaise jar in my left hand I cannot also be spreading the mayonnaise with the knife in my left hand. Perhaps these are straightforward implications—instantiations—of some more fundamental things that I was in effect *born knowing* such as, perhaps, the fact that if something is in one location it isn't also in another, different location; or the fact that two things can't be in the same place at the same time; or the fact that situations change as the result of actions. It is hard to imagine just how one could learn these facts from experience.

Such utterly banal facts escape our notice as we act and plan, and it is not surprising that philosophers, thinking phenomenologically but *introspectively,* should have overlooked them. But if one turns one's back on introspection, and just thinks "heterophenomenologically"[7] about the purely informational demands of the task—what must be known by any entity that can perform this task—these banal bits of knowledge rise to our attention. We can easily satisfy ourselves that no agent that did not *in some sense* have the benefit of the information (that beer in the bottle is not in the glass, and so on) could perform such a simple task. It is one of the chief methodological beauties of AI that it makes one be a phenomenologist in this improved way. As a heterophenomenologist, one reasons about what the agents must "know" or figure out *unconsciously or consciously* in order to perform in various ways.

The reason AI forces the banal information to the surface is that the tasks set by AI start at zero: the computer to be programmed to simulate the agent (or the brain of the robot, if we are actually going to operate in the real nonsimulated world), initially knows nothing at all "about the world." The computer is the fabled *tabula rasa* on which every required item must somehow be impressed, either by the programmer at the outset or via subsequent "learning" by the system.

We can all agree, today, that there could be no learning at all by an entity that faced the world at birth as a *tabula rasa,* but the dividing line between what is innate and what develops maturationally and what is actually learned is of less theoretical importance that one might have thought. While some information has to be innate, there is hardly any particular item that must be: an appreciation of modus ponens, perhaps, and the law of the excluded middle, and some sense of causality. And while some things we know must be learned—for example, that Thanksgiving falls on a Thursday, or that refrigerators keep food fresh—many other "very empirical" things could in principle be innately known—for example, that smiles mean happiness, or that unsuspended, unsupported things fall. (There is some evidence, in fact, that there is an innate bias in favor of perceiving things to fall with gravitational acceleration).[8]

Taking advantage of this advance in theoretical understanding (if that is what it is), people in AI can frankly ignore the problem of learning (it seems) and take the shortcut of *installing* all that an agent has to "know" to solve a problem. After all, if God made Adam as an adult who could presumably solve the midnight snack problem ab initio, AI agent-creators can *in principle* make an "adult" agent who is equipped with worldly knowledge *as if* it had laboriously learned all the things it needs to know. This may of course be a dangerous shortcut.

The installation problem is then the problem of installing in one way or another all the information needed by an agent to plan in a changing world. It is a difficult problem because the information must be installed in a usable format. The problem can be broken down initially into the semantic problem and the syntactic problem. The semantic problem—called by Allen Newell the problem at the "knowledge level" (Newell, 1982)—is the problem of just what information (on what topics, to what effect) must be installed. The syntactic problem is what system, format, structure, or mechanism to use to put that information in.[9]

The division is clearly seen in the example of the midnight snack problem. I listed a few of the very many humdrum facts one needs to know to solve the snack problem, but I didn't mean to suggest that those facts are stored in me—or in any agent—piecemeal, in the form of a long list of sentences explicitly declaring each of these facts for the benefit of the agent. That is, of course, one possibility, officially: it is a preposterously extreme version of the "language of thought" theory of mental representation, with each distinguishable "proposition" separately inscribed in the system. No one subscribes to such a view; even an encyclopedia achieves important economies of explicit expression via its organizations, and a walking encyclopedia—not a bad caricature of the envisaged AI agent—

must use different systemic principles to achieve efficient representation and access. We know trillions of things; we know that mayonnaise doesn't dissolve knives on contact, that a slice of bread is smaller than Mount Everest, that opening the refrigerator doesn't cause a nuclear holocaust in the kitchen.

There must be in use—and in any intelligent agent—some highly efficient, partly generative or productive system of representing—storing for use—all the information needed. Somehow, then, we must store many "facts" at once—where facts are presumed to line up more or less one-to-one with nonsynonymous declarative sentences. Moreover, we cannot realistically hope for what one might call a Spinozistic solution—a *small* set of axioms and definitions from which all the rest of our knowledge is deducible on demand—since it is clear that there simply are no entailment relations between vast numbers of these facts. (When we rely, as we must, on experience to tell us how the world is, experience tells us things that do not at all follow from what we have heretofore known.)

The demand for an efficient system of information storage is in part a space limitation, since our brains are not all that large, but more importantly it is a time limitation, for stored information that is not reliably accessible for use in the short real-time spans typically available to agents in the world is of no use at all. A creature that can solve any problem given enough time—say a million years—is not in fact intelligent at all. We live in a time-pressured world and must be able to think quickly, before we leap. (One doesn't have to view this as a priori condition on intelligence. One can simply note that we do in fact think quickly, so there is an empirical question about how we manage to do it.)

The task facing the AI researcher appears to be designing a system that can plan by using well-selected elements from its store of knowledge about the world it operates in. "Introspection" on how *we* plan yields the following description of a process: one envisages a certain situation (often very sketchily); one then imagines performing a certain act in that situation; one then "sees" what the likely outcome of that envisaged act in that situation would be, and evaluates it. What happens backstage, as it were, to permit this "seeing" (and render it as reliable as it is) is utterly inaccessible to introspection.

On relatively rare occasions we all experience such bouts of thought, unfolding in consciousness at the deliberate speed of pondering. These are occasions in which we are faced with some novel and relatively difficult problem, such as: How can I get the piano upstairs? or Is there any way to electrify the chandelier without cutting through the plaster ceiling? It would be quite odd to find that one had to think *that* way (consciously

and slowly) in order to solve the midnight snack problem. But the suggestion is that even the trivial problems of planning and bodily guidance that
are beneath our notice (though in some sense we "face" them) are solved
by similar processes. Why? I don't *observe* myself planning in such situations. This fact suffices to convince the traditional, introspective phenomenologist that no such planning is going on.[10] The hetero-phenome-
nologist, on the other hand, reasons that *one way or another* information
about the objects in the situation, and about the intended effects and side
effects of the candidate actions, *must* be used (considered, attended to,
applied, appreciated). Why? Because otherwise the "smart" behavior
would be sheer luck or magic. (Do we have any model for how such unconscious information-appreciation might be accomplished? The only
model we have *so far* is *conscious*, deliberate information-appreciation.
Perhaps, AI suggests, this is a good model. If it isn't, we are all utterly in
the dark for the time being.)

We assure ourselves of the intelligence of an agent by considering coun-
terfactuals: if I had been told that the turkey was poisoned, or the beer
explosive, or the plate dirty, or the knife too fragile to spread mayonnaise,
would I have acted as I did? If I were a stupid "automaton"—or like the
Sphex wasp who "mindlessly" repeats her stereotyped burrow-checking
routine till she drops[11]—I might infelicitously "go through the motions" of
making a midnight snack oblivious to the recalcitrant features of the environment.[12] But in fact, my midnight-snack-making behavior is multifari-
ously sensitive to current and background information about the situation.
The only way it could be so sensitive—runs the tacit heterophenom-
enological reasoning—is for it to examine, or test for, the information in
question. This information manipulation may be unconscious and swift,
and it need not (it better not) consist of hundreds or thousands of seriatim
testing procedures, but it must occur somehow, and its benefits must
appear in time to help me as I commit myself to action.

I may of course have a midnight snack routine, developed over the
years, in which case I can partly rely on it to pilot my actions. Such a complicated "habit" would have to be under the control of a mechanism of
some complexity, since even a rigid sequence of steps would involve peri-
odic testing to ensure that subgoals had been satisfied. And even if I am an
infrequent snacker, I no doubt have routines for mayonnaise-spreading,
sandwich-making, and getting-something-out-of-the-fridge, from which I
could compose my somewhat novel activity. Would such ensembles of
routines, nicely integrated, suffice to solve the frame problem for me, at
least in my more "mindless" endeavors? That is an open question to which
I will return below.

It is important in any case to acknowledge at the outset, and remind oneself frequently, that even very intelligent people do make mistakes; we are not only not infallible planners; we are quite prone to overlooking large and retrospectively obvious flaws in our plans. This foible manifests itself in the familiar case of "force of habit" errors (in which our stereotypical routines reveal themselves to be surprisingly insensitive to some portentous environmental changes while surprisingly sensitive to others). The same weakness also appears on occasion in cases where we have consciously deliberated with some care. How often have you embarked on a project of the piano-moving variety—in which you've thought through or even "walked through" the whole operation in advance—only to discover that you must backtrack or abandon the project when some perfectly foreseeable but unforeseen obstacle or unintended side effect loomed? If we smart folk seldom actually paint ourselves into corners, it may be not because we plan ahead so well as that we supplement our sloppy planning powers with a combination of recollected lore (about fools who paint themselves into corners, for instance) and frequent progress checks as we proceed. Even so, we must know enough to call up the right lore at the right time, and to recognize impending problems as such.

To summarize: we have been led by fairly obvious and compelling considerations to the conclusion that an intelligent agent must engage in swift information-sensitive "planning" which has the effect of producing reliable but not foolproof expectations of the effects of its actions. That these expectations are normally in force in intelligent creatures is testified to by the startled reaction they exhibit when their expectations are thwarted. This suggests a graphic way of characterizing the minimal goal that can spawn the frame problem: we want a midnight-snack-making robot to be "surprised" by the trick plate, the unspreadable concrete mayonnaise, the fact that we've glued the beer glass to the shelf. To be surprised you have to have expected something else, and in order to have expected the right something else, you have to have *and use* a lot of information about the things in the world.[13]

The central role of expectation has led some to conclude that the frame problem is not a new problem at all, and has nothing particularly to do with planning actions. It is, they think, simply the problem of having good expectations about any future events, whether they are one's own actions, the actions of another agent, or the mere happenings of nature. That is the problem of induction-noted by Hume and intensified by Goodman (1985), but still not solved to anyone's satisfaction. We know today that the problem of induction is a nasty one indeed. Theories of subjective probability and belief fixation have not stabilized in reflective equilibrium, so it is fair to say that no one has a good, principled answer to the general question: given that I believe all *this* (have all this evidence), what *ought* I to believe as well (about the future, or about unexamined parts of the world)?

The reduction of one unsolved problem to another is some sort of progress, unsatisfying though it may be, but it is not an option in this case. The frame problem is not the problem of induction in disguise. For suppose the problem of induction were solved. Suppose—perhaps miraculously—that our agent has solved all its induction problems or had them solved by fiat; it believes, then, all the right generalizations from its evidence, and associates with all of them the appropriate probabilities and conditional probabilities. This agent, ex hypothesi, believes just what it ought to believe about all empirical matters in its ken, including the probabilities of future events. It might still have a bad case of the frame problem, for that problem concerns how to represent (so it can be *used*) all that hard-won empirical information—a problem that arises independently of the truth value, probability, warranted assertability, or subjective certainty of any of it. Even if you have excellent *knowledge* (and not mere belief) about the changing world, how can this knowledge be represented so that it can be efficaciously brought to bear?

Recall poor R1D1, and suppose for the sake of argument that it had perfect empirical knowledge of the probabilities of all the effects of all its actions that would be detectable by it. Thus it believes that with probability 7864, executing PULLOUT (WAGON, ROOM) will cause the wagon wheels to make an audible noise; and with probability 5, the door to the room will open in rather than out; and with probability 999996, there will be no live elephants in the room, and with probability 997 the bomb will remain on the wagon when it is moved. How is R1D1 to find this last, relevant needle in its haystack of empirical knowledge? A walking encyclopedia will walk over a cliff, for all its knowledge of cliffs and the effects of gravity, unless it is designed in such a fashion that it can find the right bits of knowledge at the right times, so it can plan its engagements with the real world.

The earliest work on planning systems in AI took a deductive approach. Inspired by the development of Robinson's methods of resolution theorem proving, designers hoped to represent all the system's "world knowledge" explicitly as axioms, and use ordinary logic—the predicate calculus—to deduce the effects of actions. Envisaging a certain situation S was modeled by having the system entertain a set of axioms describing the situation. Added to this were background axioms (the so-called "frame axioms" that give the frame problem its name) which describe general conditions and the general effects of every action type defined for the system. To this set of axioms the system would apply an action—by postulating the occurrence of some action A in situation S—and then deduce the effect of A in 5, producing a description of the outcome situation S'). While all this logical deduction looks like nothing at all in our conscious experience, research on the deductive approach could proceed on either or both of two enabling assumptions: the methodological assumption that psychological realism was a gratuitous bonus, not a goal, of "pure" AI, or the substantive (if still vague) assumption that the deductive processes described would somehow model the backstage processes beyond conscious access. In other words, either we don't do our thinking deductively in the predicate calculus but a robot might; or we do (unconsciously) think deductively in the predicate calculus. Quite aside from doubts about its psychological realism, however, the deductive approach has not been made to work—the proof of the pudding for any robot—except for deliberately trivialized cases.

Consider some typical frame axioms associated with the action type: *move x onto y.*

(1) If $z \neq x$ and I move x onto y, then z was on w before, then z is on w after.

(2) If x is blue before, and I move x onto y, then x is blue after.

Note that (2), about being blue, is just one example of the many boring "no-change" axioms we have to associate with this action type. Worse still, note that a cousin of (2), also about being blue, would have to be associated with every other action-type—with *pick up x* and with *give x to y*, for instance. One cannot save this mindless repetition by postulating once and for all something like

(3) If anything is blue, it stays blue,

for that is false, and in particular we will want to leave room for the introduction of such action types as *paint x red*. Since virtually any aspect of a situation can change under some circumstance, this method requires introducing for each aspect (each predication in the description of S) an axiom to handle whether that aspect changes for each action type.

This representational profligacy quickly gets out of hand, but for some "toy" problems in AI, the frame problem can be overpowered to some extent by a mixture of the toyness of the environment and brute force. The early version of SHAKEY, the robot at SRI International, operated in such a simplified and sterile world, with so few aspects it could worry about that it could get away with an exhaustive consideration of frame axioms.[14]

Attempts to circumvent this explosion of axioms began with the proposal that the system operate on the tacit assumption that nothing changes in a situation but what is explicitly asserted to change in the definition of the applied action (Fikes and Nilsson 1971). The problem here is that, as Garrett Hardin once noted, you can't do just one thing. This was R1's problem, when it failed to notice that it would pull the bomb out with the wagon. In the explicit representation (a few pages back) of my midnight snack solution, I mentioned carrying the plate over to the table. On this proposal, my model of S' would leave the turkey back in the kitchen, for I didn't explicitly say the turkey would come along with the plate. One can of course patch up the definition of "bring" or "plate" to handle just this problem, but only at the cost of creating others. (Will a few more patches tame the problem? At what point should one abandon patches and seek an altogether new approach? Such are the methodological uncertainties regularly encountered in this field, and of course no one can responsibly claim in advance to have a good rule for dealing with them. Premature counsels of despair or calls for revolution are as clearly to be shunned as the dogged pursuit of hopeless avenues; small wonder the field is contentious.)

While one cannot get away with the tactic of supposing that one can do just one thing, it remains true that very little of what could (logically) happen in any situation does happen. Is there some way of fallibly marking the likely area of important side effects, and assuming the rest of the situation to stay unchanged? Here is where relevance tests seem like a good idea, and they may well be, but not within the deductive approach. As Marvin Minsky notes:

> Even if we formulate relevancy restrictions, logistic systems have a problem using them. In any logistic system, all the axioms are necessarily "permissive" –they all help to permit new inferences to be drawn. Each added axiom means more theorems; none can disappear. There simply is no direct way to add information to tell such a system about kinds of conclusions that should not be drawn! ... If we try to change this by adding axioms about relevancy, we still produce all the unwanted theorems, plus annoying statements about their irrelevancy. (Minsky 1981, p. 125)

What is needed is a system that genuinely *ignores* most of what it knows, and operates with a well-chosen portion of its knowledge at any moment. Well-chosen, but not chosen by exhaustive consideration. How, though, can you give a system *rules* for ignoring—or better, since explicit rule-following is not the problem, how can you design a system that reliably ignores what it ought to ignore under a wide variety of different circumstances in a complex action environment?

John McCarthy calls this the qualification problem, and vividly illustrates it via the famous puzzle of the missionaries and the cannibals.

Three missionaries and three cannibals come to a river. A rowboat that seats two is available. If the cannibals ever outnumber the missionaries on either bank of the river, the missionaries will he eaten. How shall they cross the river?

Obviously the puzzler is expected to devise a strategy of rowing the boat back and forth that gets them all across and avoids disaster...

Imagine giving someone the problem, and after he puzzles for awhile, he suggests going upstream half a mile and crossing on a bridge. "What bridge?" you say. "No bridge is mentioned in the statement of the problem." And this dunce replies, "Well, they don't say there isn't a bridge." You look at the English and even at the translation of the English into first order logic, and you must admit that "they don't say" there is no bridge. So you modify the problem to exclude bridges and pose it again, and the dunce proposes a helicopter, and after you exclude that, he proposes a winged horse or that the others hang onto the outside of the boat while two row.

You now see that while a dunce, he is an inventive dunce. Despairing of getting him to accept the problem in the proper puzzler's spirit, you tell him the solution. To your further annoyance, he attacks your solution on the grounds that the boat might have a leak or lack oars. After you rectify that omission from the statement of the problem, he suggests that a sea monster may swim up the river and may swallow the boat. Again you are frustrated, and you look for a mode of reasoning that will settle his hash once and for all. (McCarthy 1980, pp. 29–30)

What a normal, intelligent human being does in such a situation is to engage in some form of *nonmonotonic inference*. In a classical, monotonic logical system, adding premises never diminishes what can be proved from the premises. As Minsky noted, the axioms are essentially permissive, and once a theorem is permitted, adding more axioms will never invalidate the proofs of earlier theorems. But when we think about a puzzle or a real-life problem, we can achieve a solution (and even prove that it is a solution, or even the only solution to *that* problem), and then discover our solution invalidated by the addition of a new element to the posing of the problem; for example, "I forgot to tell you—there are no oars" or "By the way, there's a perfectly good bridge upstream."

What such late additions show us is that, contrary to our assumption, other things weren't equal. We had been reasoning with the aid of a ceteris paribus assumption, and now our reasoning has just been jeopardized by the discovery that something "abnormal" is the case. (Note, by the way, that the abnormality in question is a much subtler notion than anything anyone has yet squeezed out of probability theory. As McCarthy notes, "The whole situation involving cannibals with the postulated properties cannot be regarded as having a probability, so it is hard to take seriously the conditional probability of a bridge given the hypothesis."

The beauty of a ceteris paribus clause in a bit of reasoning is that one does not have to say exactly what it means. "What do you mean, other things being equal?" Exactly which arrangements of which other things count as being equal?" If one had to answer such a question, invoking the ceteris paribus clause would be pointless, for it is precisely in order to evade that task that one uses it. If one could answer that question, one wouldn't need to invoke the clause in the first place. One way of viewing the frame problem, then, is as the attempt to get a computer to avail itself of this distinctively human style of mental operation. There are several quite different approaches to nonmonotonic inference being pursued in AI today. They have in common only the goal of capturing the human talent for *ignoring* what should be ignored, while staying alert to relevant recalcitrance when it occurs.

One family of approaches, typified by the work of Marvin Minsky (1981) and Roger Schank (Schank and Abelson 1977), gets its ignoring-power from the attention-focusing power of stereotypes. The inspiring insight here is the idea that all of life's experiences, for all their variety, boil down to variations on a manageable number of stereotypic themes, paradigmatic scenarios—"frames" in Minsky's terms; "scripts" in Schank's.

An artificial agent with a well-stocked compendium of frames or scripts, appropriately linked to each other and to the impingements of the world via its perceptual organs, would lace the world with an elaborate system of what might be called habits of attention and benign tendencies to leap to particular sorts of conclusions in particular sorts of circumstances. It would "automatically" pay attention to certain features in certain environments and assume that certain unexamined normal features of those environments were present. Concomitantly, it would be differentially alert to relevant divergences from the stereotypes it would always begin by "expecting."

Simulations of fragments of such an agent's encounters with its world reveal that in many situations it behaves quite felicitously and apparently naturally, and it is hard to say, of course, what the limits of this approach are. But there are strong grounds for skepticism. Most obviously, while such systems perform creditably when the world co-operates with their stereotypes, and even with *anticipated* variations on them, when their worlds turn perverse, such systems typically cannot recover gracefully from the misanalyses they are led into. In fact, their behavior in extremis looks for all the world like the preposterously counterproductive activities of insects betrayed by their rigid tropisms and other genetically hardwired behavioral routines.

When these embarrassing misadventures occur, the system designer can improve the design by adding provisions to deal with the particular cases. It is important to note that in these cases, the system does not redesign itself (or learn) but rather must wait for an external designer to select an improved design. This process of redesign recapitulates the process of natural selection in some regards; it favors minimal, piecemeal, ad hoc redesign which is tantamount to a wager on the likelihood of patterns in future events. So in some regards it is faithful to biological themes.[15] Nevertheless, until such a system is given a considerable capacity to learn from its errors without designer intervention, it will continue to respond in insectlike ways, and such behavior is profoundly unrealistic as a model of human reactivity to daily life. Thus shortcuts and cheap methods provided by a reliance on stereotypes are evident enough in human ways of thought, but it is also evident that we have a deeper understanding to fall back on when our shortcuts don't avail, and building some measure of this deeper understanding into a system appears to be a necessary condition of getting it to learn swiftly and gracefully.

In effect, the script or frame approach is an attempt to presolve the frame problems the particular agent is likely to encounter. While insects do seem saddled with such control systems, people, even when they do appear to be relying on stereotypes, have back-up systems of thought that can deal more powerfully with problems that arise. Moreover, when people do avail themselves of stereotypes, they are at least relying on stereotypes of their own devising, and to date no one has been able to present any workable ideas about how a person's frame-making or script-writing machinery might be guided by its previous experience.

Several different sophisticated attempts to provide the representational framework for this deeper understanding have emerged from the deductive tradition in recent years. Drew McDermott and Jon Doyle have developed a "nonmonotonic logic" (1980), Ray Reiter has a "logic for default reasoning" (1980), and John McCarthy has developed a system of "circumscription," a formalized "rule of conjecture that can be used by a person or program for 'jumping to conclusions'" (1980). None of these is, or is claimed to be, a complete solution to the problem of ceteris paribus reasoning, but they might be components of such a solution. More recently, McDermott has offered a "temporal logic for reasoning about processes and plans" (McDermott, 1982). I will not attempt to assay the formal strengths and weaknesses of these approaches. Instead I will concentrate on another worry. From one point of view, nonmonotonic or default logic, circumscription, and temporal logic all appear to be radical improvements to the mindless and clanking deductive approach, but from a slightly different perspective they appear to be more of the same, and at least as unrealistic as frameworks for psychological models.

They appear in the former guise to be a step towards greater psychological realism, for they take seriously, and attempt to represent, the phenomenologically salient phenomenon of common sense ceteris paribus "jumping to conclusions" reasoning. But do they really succeed in offering any plausible suggestions about how the backstage implementation of that conscious thinking is accomplished *in people?* Even if on some glorious future day a robot with debugged circumscription methods maneuvered well in a nontoy environment, would there be much likelihood that its constituent processes, *described at levels below the phenomenological,* would bear informative relations to the unknown lower-level backstage processes in human beings? To bring out better what my worry is, I want to introduce the concept of a *cognitive wheel.*

We can understand what a cognitive wheel might be by reminding ourselves first about ordinary wheels. Wheels are wonderful, elegant triumphs of technology. The traditional veneration of the mythic inventor of the wheel is entirely justified. But if wheels are so wonderful, why are there no animals with wheels? Why are no wheels to be found (functioning as wheels) in nature? First, the presumption of that question must be qualified. A few years ago the astonishing discovery was made of several microscopic beasties (some bacteria and some unicellular eukaryotes) that have wheels of sorts. Their propulsive tails, long thought to be flexible flagella, turn out to be more or less rigid corkscrews, which rotate continuously, propelled by microscopic motors of sorts, complete with main bearings.[16] Better known, if less interesting for obvious reasons, are the tumbleweeds. So it is not quite true that there are no wheels (or wheeliform designs) in nature.

Still, macroscopic wheels—reptilian or mammalian or avian wheels— are not to be found. Why not? They would seem to be wonderful retractable landing gear for some birds, for instance. Once the question is posed, plausible reasons rush in to explain their absence. Most important, probably, are the considerations about the topological properties of the axle/bearing boundary that make the transmission of material or energy across it particularly difficult. How could the life-support traffic arteries of a living system maintain integrity across this boundary? But once that problem is posed, solutions suggest themselves; suppose the living wheel grows to mature form in a nonrotating, nonfunctional form, and is then hardened and sloughed off, like antlers or an outgrown shell, but not completely off: it then rotates freely on a lubricated fixed axle. Possible? It's hard to say. Useful? Also hard to say, especially since such a wheel would have to be free-wheeling. This is an interesting speculative exercise, but certainty not one that should inspire us to draw categorical, a priori conclusions. It would be foolhardy to declare wheels biologically impossible, but at the same time we can appreciate that they are at least very distant and unlikely solutions to *natural* problems of design.

Now a cognitive wheel is simply any design proposal in cognitive theory (at any level from the purest semantic level to the most concrete level of "wiring diagrams" of the neurons) that is profoundly unbiological, however wizardly and elegant it is as a bit of technology.

Clearly this is a vaguely defined concept, useful only as a rhetorical abbreviation, as a gesture in the direction of real difficulties to be spelled out carefully. "Beware of postulating cognitive wheels" masquerades as good advice to the cognitive scientist, while courting vacuity as a maxim to follow.[17] It occupies the same rhetorical position as the stockbroker's maxim: buy low and sell high. Still, the term is a good theme-fixer for discussion.

Many critics of AI have the conviction that *any* AI system is and must be nothing but a gearbox of cognitive wheels. This could of course turn out to be true, but the usual reason for believing it is based on a misunderstanding of the methodological assumptions of the field. When an AI model of some cognitive phenomenon is proposed, the model is describable at many different levels, from the most global, phenomenological level at which the behavior is described (with some presumptuousness) in ordinary mentalistic terms, down through various levels of implementation all the way to the level of program code—and even further down, to the level of fundamental hardware operations if anyone cares. No one supposes that the model maps onto the processes of psychology and biology *all the way down*. The claim is only that for some high level of description below the phenomenological level (which merely *sets* the problem) there is a mapping of model features onto what is being modeled: the cognitive processes in living creatures, human or otherwise. It is understood that all the implementation details below the level of intended modelling will consist, no doubt, of cognitive wheels—bits of unbiological computer activity mimicking the gross effects of cognitive subcomponents by using methods utterly unlike the methods still to be discovered in the brain. Someone who failed to appreciate that a model composed microscopically of cognitive wheels could still achieve a fruitful isomorphism with biological or psychological processes at a higher level of aggregation would suppose there were good a priori reasons for generalized skepticism about AI.

But allowing for the possibility of valuable intermediate levels of modelling is not ensuring their existence. In a particular instance a model might descend directly from a phenomenologically recognizable level of psychological description to a cognitive wheels implementation without shedding any light at all on how we human beings manage to enjoy that phenomenology. I *suspect* that all current proposals in the field for dealing with the frame problem have that shortcoming. Perhaps one should dismiss the previous sentence as mere autobiography. I find it hard to imagine (for what that is worth) that any of the *procedural details* of the mechanization of McCarthy's circumscriptions, for instance, would have suitable counterparts in the backstage story yet to be told about how human commonsense reasoning is accomplished. If these procedural details lack "psychological reality" then there is nothing left in the proposal that might model psychological processes except the phenomenological-level description in terms of jumping to conclusions, ignoring and the like—and we already know we do that.

There is an alternative defense of such theoretical explorations, however, and I think it is to be taken seriously. One can claim (and I take McCarthy to claim) that while formalizing commonsense reasoning in his fashion would not tell us anything *directly* about psychological processes of reasoning, it would clarify, sharpen, systematize the purely semantic-level characterization of the demands on any such implementation, biological or not. Once one has taken the giant step forward of taking information- processing seriously as a real process in space and time, one can then take a small step back and explore the implications of that advance at a very abstract level. Even at this very formal level, the power of circumscription and the other versions of nonmonotonic reasoning remains an open but eminently explorable question.[18]

Some have thought that the key to a more realistic solution to the frame problem (and indeed, in all likelihood, to any solution at all) must require a complete rethinking of the semantic-level setting, prior to concern with syntactic-level implementation. The more or less standard array of predicates and relations chosen to fill out the predicate-calculus format when representing the "propositions believed" may embody a fundamentally inappropriate parsing of nature for this task. Typically, the interpretation of the formulae in these systems breaks the world down along the familiar lines of objects with properties at times and places. Knowledge of situations and events in the world is represented by what might be called sequences of verbal snapshots. State S, constitutively described by a list of sentences true at time t asserting various n-adic predicates true of various particulars, gives way to *State'*, a similar list of sentences true at t'. Would it perhaps be better to reconceive of the world of planning in terms of histories and processes?[19] Instead of trying to model the capacity to *keep track of things* in terms of principles for passing through temporal cross-sections of knowledge expressed in terms of terms (*names* for *things,* in essence) and predicates, perhaps we could model keeping track of things more directly, and let all the cross-sectional information about what is deemed true moment by moment be merely implicit (and hard to extract—as it is for us) from the format. These are tempting suggestions, but so far as I know they are still in the realm of handwaving.[19]

Another, perhaps related, handwaving theme is that the current difficulties with the frame problem stem from the conceptual scheme engendered by the serial-processing von Neumann architecture of the computers used to date in AI. As large, fast parallel processors are developed, they will bring in their wake huge conceptual innovations which are now of course only dimly imaginable. Since brains are surely massive parallel processors, it is tempting to suppose that the concepts engendered by such new hardware will be more readily adaptable for realistic psychological modelling. But who can say? For the time being, most of the optimistic claims about the powers of parallel processing belong in the same camp with the facile observations often encountered in the work of neuroscientists, who postulate marvelous cognitive powers for various portions of the nervous system without a clue of how they are realized.[20]

Filling in the details of the gap between the phenomenological magic show and the well-understood powers of small tracts of brain tissue is the immense research task that lies in the future for theorists of every persuasion. But before the problems can be solved they must be encountered, and to encounter the problems one must step resolutely into the gap and ask how-questions. What philosophers (and everyone else) have always known is that people—and no doubt all intelligent agents—can engage in swift, sensitive, risky-but-valuable ceteris paribus reasoning. How do we do it? AI may not yet have a good answer, but at least it has encountered the question.[21]

Acknowledgements

This chapter first appeared as "Cognitive Wheels: The Frame Problem in AI" in *Minds, Machines, and Evolution,* edited by C. Hookway (Cambridge: Cambridge University Press, 1984). It is reprinted with permission from the author and copyright holder.

Notes

1. The problem is introduced by John McCarthy and Patrick Hayes in their 1969 paper. The task in which the problem arises was first formulated in McCarthy 1960. I am grateful to John McCarthy, Pat Hayes, Bob Moore, Zenon Pylyshyn, John Haugeland and Bo Dahlbom for the many hours they have spent trying to make me understand the frame problem. It is

not their fault that so much of their instruction has still not taken. I have also benefited great-ly from reading an unpublished version of "Modelling Change—The Frame Problem," by Lars-Erik Janlert. This paper is an invaluable vademecum for any neophyte, in addition to advancing several novel themes. (The paper has since been published—see Janlert [1987]).

2. Dreyfus mentions McCarthy (1960, pp. 213–214), but the theme of his discussion there is that McCarthy ignores the difference between a physical state description and a situation description, a theme that might be succinctly summarized: a house is not a home. Similarly, he mentions ceteris paribus assumptions (in the Introduction to the Revised Edition, pp. 56ff., but only in announcing his allegiance to Ludwig Wittgenstein's idea that "whenever human behavior is analyzed in terms of rules, these rules must always contain a ceteris paribus condition..."). But this, even if true, misses the deeper point: the need for something like ceteris paribus assumptions confronts Robinson Crusoe just as ineluctably as it confronts any protagonist who finds himself in a situation involving human culture. The point is not, it seems, restricted to Geisteswissenschaft (as it is usually conceived); the "intelligent" robot on an (otherwise?) uninhabited but hostile planet faces the frame problem as soon as it com-mences to plan its days.

3. The example is from an important discussion of rationality by Christopher Cherniak (Cherniak 1983).

4. Note that on this unflattering portrayal, the philosophers might still be doing some valu-able work; think of the wild goose chases one might avert for some investigators who had rashly concluded that the magician really did saw the lady in half and then miraculously reunite her. People have jumped to such silly conclusions, after all; many philosophers have done so, for instance.

5. See Dennett (1982a), a commentary on Goodman (1982).

6. This knowledge of physics is not what one learns in school, but in one's crib. See Hayes (1978, 1979).

7. For elaborations of hetero-phenomenology, see Dennett (1978, chapter 10, "Two Ap-proaches to Mental Images," and Dennett (1982b). See also Dennett (1982c).

8. Gunnar Johannsen has shown that animated films of "falling" objects in which the moving spots drop with the normal acceleration of gravity are unmistakably distinguished by the casual observer from "artificial" motions. I do not know whether infants have been tested to see if they respond selectively to such displays.

9. McCarthy and Hayes (1969) draw a different distinction between the "epistemological" and the "heuristic." The difference is that they include the question "in what kind of internal notation is the system's knowledge to be expressed?" in the epistemological problem (see p. 466), dividing off that syntactic (and hence somewhat mechanical) question from the pro-cedural questions of the design of "the mechanism that on the basis of the information solves the problem and decides what to do." One of the prime grounds for controversy about just which problem the frame problem is springs from this attempted division of the issue. For the answer to the syntactical aspects of the epistemological question makes a large difference to the nature of the heuristic problem. After all, if the syntax of the expression of the system's knowledge is sufficiently perverse, then in spite of the *accuracy* of the representation of that knowledge, the heuristic problem will be impossible. And some have suggested that the heuristic problem would virtually disappear if the world knowledge were felicitously couched in the first place.

10. Such observations also convinced Gilbert Ryle, who was, in an important sense, an intro-

spective phenomenologist (and not a "behaviorist'). See Ryle (1949).

One can readily imagine Ryle's attack, on AI: "And *how many* inferences do I perform in the course of preparing my sandwich? Why syllogisms convince me that the beer will stay in the glass?" For a further discussion of Ryle's skeptical arguments and their relation to cognitive science, see my *Styles of Mental Representations* (Dennett, 1983).

11. "When the time comes for egg laying the wasp Sphex builds a burrow for the purpose and seeks out a cricket which she stings in such a way as to paralyze but not kill it. She drags the cricket into her burrow, lays her eggs alongside, closes the burrow, then flies away, never to return. In due count, the eggs hatch and the wasp grubs feed off the paralyzed cricket, which has not decayed, having been kept in the wasp equivalent of deep freeze. To the human mind, such an elaborately organized and seemingly purposeful routine conveys a convincing flavor of logic and thoughtfulness—until more details are examined. For example, the wasp's routine is to bring the paralyzed cricket to the burrow, leave it on the threshold, go inside to see that all is well, emerge, and then drag the cricket in. If, while the wasp is inside making her preliminary inspection the cricket is moved a few inches away, the wasp, on emerging from the burrow, will bring the cricket back to the threshold, but not inside, and will then repeat the preparatory procedure of entering the burrow to see that everything is all right. If again the cricket is removed a few inches while the wasp is inside, once again the wasp will move the cricket up to the threshold and re-enter the burrow for a final check. The wasp never thinks of pulling the cricket straight in. On one occasion, this procedure was repeated forty times, always with the same results'" (Dean Wooldridge, 1963). This vivid example of a familiar phenomenon among insects is discussed by me in *Brainstorms,* and in Douglas Hofstadter (1982).

12. See Dennett (1982c, pp. 58-59) on "Robot Theater."

13. Hubert Dreyfus has pointed out that *not expecting x* does not imply *expecting y* (where $x \neq y$), so one can be startled by something one didn't expect without its having to be the case that one (unconsciously) expected something else. But this sense of *not expecting* will not suffice to explain startle. What are the odds against your seeing an Alfa Romeo, a Buick, a Chevrolet, and a Dodge parked in alphabetical order some time or other within the next five hours? Very high, no doubt, all things considered, so I would not expect you to expect this; I also would not expect you to be startled by seeing this unexpected sight—except in the sort of pedal case where you had reason to expect something else at that time and place.

Startle reactions are powerful indicators of cognitive state—a fact long known by the police (and writers of detective novels). *Only* someone who expected the refrigerator to contain Smith's corpse (say) would be *startled* as opposed to mildly interested) to find it to contain the rather unlikely trio: a bottle of vintage Chablis, a can of cat food, and a dishrag.

14. This early feature of SHAKEY was drawn to my attention by Pat Hayes. See also Dreyfus (1972, p. 26). SHAKEY is put to quite different use in Dennett (1982b).

15. In one important regard, however, it is dramatically unlike the process of natural selection, since the trial, error and selection of the process is far from blind. But a case can be made that the impatient researcher does nothing more than telescope time by such foresighted interventions in the redesign process.

16. For more details, and further reflections on the issues discussed here, see Diamond (1983).

17. I was interested to discover that at least one researcher in AI mistook the rhetorical intent of my new term on first hearing; he took "cognitive wheels" to be an accolade. If one thinks of AI, as he does, not as a research method in psychology but as a branch of engineering

attempting to extend human cognitive powers, then of course cognitive wheels are break-throughs. The vast and virtually infallible memories of computers would be prime examples; others would be computers' arithmetical virtuosity and invulnerability to boredom and dis-traction. See Hofstadter (1982) for an insightful discussion of the relation of boredom to the structure of memory and the conditions for creativity.

18. McDermott 1969 ("A Temporal Logic for Reasoning about Processes and Plans," section 6, "A Sketch of an Implementation") shows strikingly how many new issues are raised once one turns to the question of implementation, and how indirect (but still useful) the purely formal considerations are.

19. Patrick Hayes has been exploring this theme, and a preliminary account can be found in "Naive Physics 1: The Ontology of Liquids" (Hayes, 1978).

20. Oliver Selfridge's 1992 monograph, *Tracking and Trailing*, promises to push back this frontier, I think, but I have not yet been able to assimilate its messages. There are also sugges-tive passages on this topic in Ruth Garrett Milliken's 1984 *Language, Thought, and Other Bio-logical Categories.*

21. To balance the "top-down" theorists' foible of postulating cognitive wheels, there is the "bottom-up" theorists' penchant for discovering wonder tissue. (Wonder tissue appears in many locales. J. J. Gibson's theory of perception, for instance, seems to treat the whole visual system as a hunk of wonder tissue, for instance, resonating with marvelous sensitivity to a host of sophisticated "affordances." See, for example, Gibson [1979].)

22. One of the few, philosophical articles I have uncovered that seem to contribute to the thinking about the frame problem—though not in those terms—is Ronlad de Sousa's "The Rationality of Emotions" (de Sousa, 1979). In the section entitled "What are Emotions For?" de Sousa suggests, with compelling considerations, that "the function of emotion is to fill gaps left by [merely wanting plus] 'pure reason' in the determination of action and belief. Consider how Iago proceeds to make Othello jealous. His task is essentially to direct Othello's attention, to suggest questions to ask.... Once attention is thus directed, inferences which, before on the same evidence, would not even have been thought of, are experienced as com-pelling." In de Sousa's understanding, "emotions are determinate patterns of salience among objects of attention, lines of inquiry, and inferential strategies (p. 50) and they are not "reducible" in any way to "articulated propositions." Suggestive as this is, it does not, of course, offer any concrete proposals for how to endow an inner (emotional) state with these interesting powers. Another suggestive-and overlooked—paper is Howard Darmstadter's "Consistency of Belief" (Darmstadter, 1971, pp. 301-310). Darmstadter's exploration of ceteris paribus clauses and the relations that might exist between beliefs as psychological states and sentences believers may utter (or have uttered about them) contains a number of claims that deserve further scrutiny.

11 Dennett's Beer

Henry E. Kyburg, Jr.

What We Take for Granted

As Dan Dennett points out (Dennett, 1988), there are an awful lot of
things we take for granted when we go to get ourselves a midnight
snack in the kitchen. There are a lot of positive things, such as that
the refrigerator light will work, that the knife for slicing the turkey will be
in the knife rack, that the beer opener will be in the drawer where it usually is, and so on.

We assume certain connections among things, such as that when I take
the plate to the dining room, the sandwich on the plate stays there during
the transition; when I tip the glass to my lips, the beer will flow out. We
are not surprised when any of these things happen.

Nor should we be. It is perfectly clear that the reason we assume that the
beer opener will be in its place is because it usually is: The chances are very
good that it will be there again. We wouldn't be appalled to find it missing—it's been known to happen that someone has failed to replace it—but
the probability is high enough that we do not deliberately entertain any
contingency plans about what to do if it is not there. It is only when the
"Oops!" flag goes up that we stop to think.

The second class of assumptions is less likely to be thought of as probabilistic, simply because the occasions on which those assumptions are
upset are even rarer. Sure, the beer glass could be one of those trick ones,
someone might have cleverly tied a very thin nylon thread to the turkey in
your sandwich and fastened it to the refrigerator, ... but the chances of any

of these things are so small that we rightly take them to be practically impossible. Again, though, we could take them into account if we had to.

At a third level we take for granted that beers do not explode, that gravity will continue to keep our feet on the floor, that the course of nature will not suffer some radical disruption. These are logical possibilities. But in an intuitive sense they are not "real" possibilities.

If the beer is explosive, Dan (or his beer-serving robot) will get blown up—no two ways about it. Unless, of course, he is told that it may be explosive. He need not be told that it is explosive. Being told that it may be explosive changes things dramatically.

It is not that Dan suddenly knows more about logical possibility than he knew before. Dennett is a sophisticated philosopher. He knew all along (in some sense) that it was "possible" that the beer was explosive. Reminding him of that will not change his behavior.

The force of the information that the beer may be explosive is exactly to say that there is some finite, nonnegligible probability that the beer is explosive. Combined with the (presumed) disutility of exploding beer, this can lead to a significant alteration of Dan's behavior. It might even alter his intention to have a snack. Observe that this not only is a change in the plan of execution, but a change in the goal itself.

What this suggests is that we should ultimately be concerned with probabilities and with utilities in our planning. I shall argue, in due course, that this profoundly changes the nature of the "frame problem."

Axioms and Logical Consequences

Pat Hayes points out (Hayes, 1988) that if we parameterize events by either instants of time, or periods of duration, we must still deal with the fact that "Holds(s, t)" does not imply "Holds(s, t')." Or: when Pat moves from one room to another, the color of his hair doesn't change, though in fact it "might," and there are other events that would indeed change the color of his hair (such as "hair-tinting").

The difficulty, according to Pat, is that there are thousands and thousands of things that do not change, but that "might" change, as a consequence of an action, and we must provide axioms that tell us that they don't change. As Pat admits, in limited domains we can accomplish what is needed with the "sleeping dog" strategy: What the action changes is what the rules say it changes; all else remains unchanged. But it is alleged that in more complex domains this won't work. Of course, as Drew

McDermott (1988) notes, in complex domains *we* don't always work either, so it isn't clear how much of a criticism this is. In any event, Pat assumes that in general we will have to be able to infer both what changes an act induces in the world, and what remains the same in the world after an action is performed. He supposes that there is a lot that doesn't change, and also a lot that does change.

Of course, if *everything* changes, the sleeping dog strategy won't do us much good. This is what Jerry Fodor tries to convince us of (Fodor, 1988), following in the tracks of Georg Wilhelm Friederich Hegel and John McTaggart. Fodor introduces a classification of particles into frigeons and nonfrigeons (a particle is one of the former, if Fodor's refrigerator is open, one of the latter if it isn't). But here is a more classical example: If I move my hand three inches at time *t*, its relations to Saturn and Jupiter are altered at time t, and from the change of those relations, we can infer the relative positions of the two planets at *t*. Thus to know the results of any action is to know everything.

Note that this does not require the introduction of any new terminology, or any peculiar properties. There is no sharp line to be drawn between the spatiotemporal relation between my hand and Saturn, and that between my hand and my beer glass.

This is silliness now as it was in the nineteenth century. It is not something one should worry about in one's own actions, and it isn't something that the designer of plans should worry about.

But what is the difference between worrying about the position of my hand relative to the beer glass and worrying about the position of my hand relative to Jupiter? Baldly stated, it is that the former has what we know to be immediate consequences for our plan of drinking some beer, and the latter, *so far as we know,* does not.

"So far as we know." There is no logical impossibility in the following story: The two mighty warlords of Jupiter and Saturn have been disputing for centuries about whether or not to destroy the earth before it infects the rest of space. They have finally agreed on a chance mechanism: If the center of mass of Jupiter, Saturn, and Kyburg's thumb ever lie in a *perfect* triangle, then the earth is to be instantly destroyed; if not, not. I don't know what a *perfect* triangle is, but if I did, I might be careful how I moved my hand.

Again, we see the dependence on *knowledge* (which I take to be determining evidential probabilities) and on utilities.

Representing Knowledge: Practical Certainty

A scheme which I have advertised elsewhere (Kyburg, 1974; 1990) as useful in a variety of contexts will be useful here: It is a "two-level" scheme, in which we distinguish between *evidential* certainties and *practical* certainties. Neither, of course, is the same as a logical certainty.

While it may be a difficult problem to figure out exactly how to represent knowledge of some empirical domain in an efficient way, we will suppose that there is some finite (perhaps large) axiomatization representing our practical certainties. There will also be, presumably, a lot of rules. What we require of the axioms representing the set of practical certainties is that each of them has a probability greater than some specified number p—say .99 or .999, relative to the *evidence* available (that is, the set of axioms in the evidential corpus). For a discussion of how this might get chosen, see Kyburg, 1988. This number represents the *level of acceptance* of practical certainties.

It is already a consequence of the definition of evidential probability that not all definable classes can serve as reference classes (for example, the set of headslips: tosses of coins that land heads, union the singleton of next toss), and not all definable classes can serve as target classes. Thus frigeons can be ignored as safely as headslips.

This places a burden on the designer of deciding what primitive class terms will be included, and what operations may be applied to acceptable terms to yield acceptable terms. Reference terms and target terms may well be treated differently. But since this is a matter we have to come to terms with anyway, we need not take special account of it in connection with the frame problem.

Pat Hayes noted as much.

But here is another question: What about the unlimited deduction that can be done? That's easy, when we focus on the practical corpus—no deduction need be done. We are only computing probabilities, and at that only the changed probabilities. Now it is quite true that we will want to say that logically equivalent statements get the same probability; and in fact we want to say that statements merely known to have the same truth value will have the same probability. But how much extra computation will this take? For example, the probability that the beer-opener will be where it belongs is the same as that the beer-opener will be where it belongs and Pierre de Fermat's last theorem is true, assuming that his last theorem is a theorem. But for the purposes of planning a midnight snack only the former probability need concern us.

In general, when we are planning, only the probabilities of real empirical possibilities need concern us. And at this point what counts as a "real empirical possibility" is something that receives a nonzero probability relative to the set of practical certainties. Thus the exploding bottle of beer is no more a "real empirical possibility" than a violation of gravity.

The misplacing of the beer-opener is a real possibility, though it may be one whose probability is so low that we should not bother to check before we open the refrigerator door (checking on the location of the beer-opener will be advantageous just in case the expected cost of that check is less than the expected cost of going ahead without checking).

How many real empirical possibilities that are of concern to us need we take account of, relative to our corpus of practical certainties, when we contemplate an action? Not very many, I think. How can we tell when a statement falls into this category? That can be taken as a syntactical question and doesn't seem to be difficult to decide. For example, a statement that contains a purely mathematical (or logical) disjunct or conjunct can be simplified without loss of import for action.

Furthermore, if, as I claim, the level of practical certainty determines the minimum and maximum significant values of probabilities, an even smaller group of statements need be taken into account. (The idea is that at a level of practical certainty of .99, probabilities whose minimum value—we take probabilities to be interval valued—is greater than .99, and whose maximum value is less than .01, are indistinguishable from practical certainties or practical impossibilities, respectively.) Thus an event whose maximum probability is .01 can be disregarded, and one whose minimum probability is greater than .99 can be taken for granted.

Dennett's robots, who sit patiently cranking out deductive consequences of their axioms until they get blown to bits, can be left to their own self-destruction. In fact our robots need only look at probabilities, they need only look at the probabilities that change, when a new bit of evidence (action A has been performed, the time is now $t + 1$, and sensory input S has been received) is added to the evidential corpus. Furthermore, they need only pay attention to those changed probabilities that change expected utilities significantly. A state whose utility is close to zero will continue to have a utility close to zero even when its probability has been changed significantly. For example: It doesn't really matter whether the beer-opener is on the right or the left side of the drawer in which it is ordinarily kept, so it is hardly worth updating the probability of the one alternative relative to the other.

Take our body of knowledge to be axiomatized at the level of practical certainty. Add an action (construed to include all of its immediate consequences, as indicated by the corpus of evidential certainties). Compute, relative to this practical corpus, the new evidential probabilities of the situations whose utilities are of concern to us. Choose the act whose expectation is a maximum among those of the acts available to us.

This is a recipe for planning. I claim, though no knockdown arguments can be given without implementing the recipe, that it is a recipe that does not encounter the frame problem.

Representing Knowledge: Evidential Certainty

In a certain sense this suggestion is pedestrian. There is nothing unexpected or exciting going on. It provides a framework [sic] for Dennett's Robots—if what I claim for evidential probability is true—but it certainly doesn't account for the kind of unusual circumstance that is generally offered by the counter-example generator. The example offered usually involves some very unusual piece of data, that has some highly unusual consequence, where the consequence is not so unusual given the unusual piece of data, and in fact given that data may be quite expected. Thus, for example, when I go to drive my car somewhere, I expect that it will start (it has been very well behaved lately); I do not calculate the probability that it will start by looking into the desirability of driving to the store as opposed to doing without butter for my bread. I am practically certain (in ordinary contexts) that it will start.

But if I get in and turn the key and nothing happens, I have evidence that impugns my practical certainty. At that point I review probabilities: the probability that the battery is dead, the probability that the connections have worked loose, and so on. Now I will take into account these probabilities in reviewing my decision to run down to the store for some butter. There has been a shift of context that does not necessarily alter my planning. For example one possibility when I turn the key and nothing happens is that I inadvertently left the lever in "Drive" when I last drove the car. In this case I modify my plan: Put the lever in "Park," and *then* start the car.

The context in which I worry about the car starting can be brought up directly: If I have to catch a plane for a long trip, and it is very important that I get there, I will (probably) take it for granted, as a practical certainty, that if the car starts I'll be able to drive to the airport, but I may not, in *this* context take it as practically certain that the car will start. I will look at the utilities and probabilities involved in its starting, and I may even perform some extra action (such as, check the battery) which I will take to give me information relevant to those probabilities.

We can even achieve a shift of context like this in the innocent plan to get a beer from the fridge. You see, unknown to my friend Dan Dennett, I am an agent of Consortium A, which is vying with Consortium B to take over the world. This is a high stakes game, in which murder and mayhem are to be taken for granted. Dan opens his refrigerator and reaches for a beer. I note, as he opens the door, that the cap on the first bottle of beer has no printing on it. I shout "WATCH OUT!" and we dive to the floor as the light-sensitive detonator in the explosive beer goes off, causing the beer to explode and the kitchen to be filled with flying fragments of glass.

Of course Dan had no reason whatsoever to believe that I was involved in any risky shenanigans, and thus no reason to take this into account in his planning to have a beer. But when I behave so bizarrely, his ordinary corpus of practical certainty becomes modified profoundly by new and unusual items in his evidential corpus. This is enough, we hope, to alter his behavior significantly.

My own behavior can be explained in the same way. I had no reason to think that *they* had followed me to Dan's house, and when we got up to get our midnight beer my corpus of practical certainties was no different (in relevant respects) from Dan's. We both planned to have a beer by going to the kitchen, opening the fridge, taking out a beer, getting the opener,.... But just as my behavior provided Dan with evidence that disrupted his expectations, so the observation of the noncommercial cap on the beer disrupted my expectations. I knew, as Dan could not, that the probability of disaster was raised from "practical impossibility" to a significant level by any evidence of tampering.

That such distinctions as those between the corpus of practical certainties and the corpus of evidential certainties are not entirely foreign to thinking about the frame problem is hinted at by Pat Hayes (1988) though he does not move to exploit the distinction:

> Now the cup *might* break—it depends how rough you are with it; but your hair couldn't change color—that's impossible; it's just not the kind of thing which movements cause—except perhaps in truly extraordinary circumstances, which it would usually be sensible to ignore. (p. 131)

The "usually" of "usually sensible to ignore" is to be contrasted with the implicit "usually" of "usually the cup won't break." The latter represents a small probability, relative to our corpus of practical certainties—the set of things of which we are practically certain, which we may ignore simply because it does not lead to a significant change of expected utility. If the

cup were an antique of enormous value, one might think twice about pick-
ing it up from the table, even though the chances of its breaking are small.

The former "usually" represents the fact that we should not consider
"extraordinary circumstances"; they just don't occur, as a matter of practical concern. But they aren't logically, or even physically, "impossible"; so
we *could* have evidence in our evidential corpus that "extraordinary circumstances" should not (this time) be ruled out.

Example

Let us plan the midnight snack under more fully specified, and less dramatic, circumstances. Here is some of the contents of my evidential corpus:

The date is March 12, 1992.
Beer is a liquid.
The Kitchen is on the other side of the Dining Room.
The fire Alarm is not sounding.
I am not deaf.
You are Dan Dennett.

And here are some of the contents of my practical corpus:

90 percent of the time there is beer in the refrigerator.
Beer almost always tastes good.
The house is not on fire.
No hurricane is raging outside.
Nor is there a blizzard.
In an ordinary trip through the house, I bump my head on the doorway only
2 percent of the time.

On this basis, I judge it worth the trip to the kitchen, since the probability of my bumping my head (or suffering any similar disaster) is very
small, relative to my corpus of practical certainties, and the probability of
achieving a beer is very high, and despite the fact that the disutility of
twisting my ankle is large and the utility of having a beer is much smaller,
the probabilities are such that the expectation of risking a trip to the
kitchen is decidedly positive.

Note that we do not have to deal with very rare possibilities: that the house
is on fire, or that there is a hurricane. They are among the facts we take as
practical certainties to start with. Of course there is a problem of finding an
efficient way to store them; but that is not the frame problem. I am assuming
that we have a fast way of calculating relevant, nonextreme, probabilities.

We can have new evidence in our practical corpus. This can and should have an effect on our plans. For example, I may find a note on the dining room table that says, "Hey, dad, thanks for the beers." This note renders it practically certain that my son has been home early in the evening and has taken some beer from the refrigerator. This may have a bearing on the probability of my finding beer in the refrigerator: Half the time when such a note is found, there is no beer. Relative to the new set of practical certainties, the probability of beer is much lower than relative to the old.

But I still don't have to worry about hurricanes or fires; I still have the same probability of bumping my head on the way to the kitchen.

Note that according to the practical corpus, there is no fire: It is not merely that it has a low probability or even a zero probability; the sentence asserting that there is no fire is accepted. That entails that relative to the practical corpus, the probability of fire is zero. But the probability need not concern us when we have the 'fact.' Similarly, the sentence asserting, in the evidential corpus, that the fire alarm is not ringing is simply *accepted*.

Thus our practical deliberations do not need to take account of such contingencies as: "if there is a fire and there is no hurricane, then if I go to the kitchen for a beer…."

On the other hand, new evidence can enter the evidential corpus in such a way as to alter the practical corpus in ways that render these considerations important. Thus, for example, suppose the fire alarm does go off. That, as we all know, does not entail that there is a fire or even smoke.

What it does do is to raise the probability of fire, relative to the evidential corpus, above the threshold of conceivability. The practical corpus will *not* (if your fire alarm is anything like mine) contain the statement that there is a fire in the house. But it will no longer contain the statement that there is no fire in the house either. And now we have a new set of contingencies to take account of. If there is a fire, and I waste my time going to the kitchen for a beer, this will entail some high costs. If there is no fire, and I go to the kitchen for a beer, it will taste just as good as before. If the probability of a false alarm is high enough, and my thirst deep enough, it may be good planning for me to go for my beer. What Levi (1980) calls the set of serious possibilities, relative to my corpus of practical certainties, has been expanded, but this may or may not lead to a new decision.

Conclusion

There has been nothing (much) about sequences of states, of facts tied to temporal indices, or holding over temporal intervals, in what I have said before. But introducing such considerations in the cognitive framework in question offers no new problems. In particular, given that I am holding the beer in the kitchen, and I go through the dining room door, it does indeed follow that I am holding the beer in the dining room. It follows in a pretty straightforward statistical way, not, of course, without exceptions. In general, we have adequate evidence for an ordinary decay function characterizing the holding of beers.

So we can be pretty sure that in the space of time it takes Dan to go from the kitchen to the dining room, he has not put his beer down. We could observe that or be told that he puts it down; but that is another matter.

What Pat Hayes considers the frame problem—and I guess he is as much of an authority as one can have—is the problem of having to state both all the things that change and all the things that don't change as a consequence of some action. The "sleeping dog" strategy, which Pat agrees is reasonable for some simplified programs, says that you only have to worry about the things that change. Now of course, if you accept the doctrine of internal relations, *everything* changes. My getting a beer has its effects on Pluto and Saturn. But if you eschew sheer silliness, then what you have in response to an action may be a relatively limited number of changes. This is especially the case if you limit your concerns to the changes that make a difference to you in your present context.

In general, practical certainties—the facts of your situation—only change in fairly direct response to actions or changing evidence. Drew McDermott gives a straightforward first pass at an algorithm for determining what happens when something is pulled on. True, there are all sorts of things that *might* happen; there are even imaginable circumstances under which these things have finite or even large probabilities. But within the realm of practical certainties, the problem does not loom as large as it might otherwise.

To be sure, we sometimes find ourselves in extraordinary circumstances. But then there are often clues that tell us that we should make a whole shift of context. The logic of these shifts, like the logic of shifts in theory in science, needs more exploration (but see Gardenfors, 1988).

The two-level, probabilistic, representation offers help for all of these problems in the following way: First, at the level of practical certainties, no "deductions" need be done at all: the inference that is done is probabilistic inference, and this (we hope!) is neither so open ended nor so difficult as deductive inference. Second, the inferences we need be concerned with are inferences that reflect changes (lively dogs) and among them mainly only the ones that involve significant utilities. Third, what is in the practical corpus gets there by being overwhelmingly probable, "practically certain," relative to the corpus of evidence we have. Most ordinary new pieces of evidence, hypothetical (action *A* is performed) or actual (the car fails to start), simply pass through the evidential corpus, become part of the practical corpus, and serve to modify probabilities relative to the practical corpus. But some pieces of evidence produce a more profound effect: it is still the effect of modifying the practical corpus by changing probabilities, but the probabilities that are changed are those of pervasive and significant statements. For example, a new piece of evidence in the evidential corpus can change the whole context of other pieces of evidence so that the practical corpus is radically altered: "they're after me" colors everything scary, and, taken as evidence, rightly so.

Dan Dennett, planning to get a beer, rightly employs the sleeping dog strategy, and his corpus of practical certainties, both to evaluate the utilities of various courses of action ("head for the kitchen") and to compute the consequences of his action ("beer in hand," "beer not on counter"). The computation, I claim, should go by the calculation of probabilities as more efficient than the derivation of logical consequences. (Which remains to be seen!)

Faced with new information in his practical corpus—his daughter left him a note thanking him for beer—the probabilities, and thus the action that maximizes expected utility, may change. The consequences of actions may change ("If I look for beer, and fail to find it, under these circumstances, the probability of apoplexy is at least .85").

This information may be transmitted through the evidential corpus: "Here is a piece of paper with writing that looks like that of my daughter; the sentences on the paper are thus and so." So I conclude in my practical corpus that my daughter wrote a note with such and such content.

That, in turn, provides evidence about the contents of the refrigerator.

When, in contrast, I see my sensible friend Henry acting hysterical, and shouting at me to drop to the floor, a lot of my practical certainties become disrupted. I entertain (as I did not before) the hypothesis that Henry is really nuts. But I also entertain, as having more than zero probability, the proposition that there is something real to which he is responding.

A whole collection of possibilities, not previously regarded as "possible" become worth taking into account: They become live possibilities, whose probabilities should be taken account of in considering alternative courses of action.

Of course, it is not only the probabilities but also, in choosing among acts, the utilities. It may be 80 to 90 percent certain that Henry is having paranoid delusions, but if I am wrong in assuming that he's nuts, there are large utilities to be lost, while if I am right, there is little to be lost in humoring him.

Given the ingredients: practical certainty, evidential certainty, utility, and the sleeping dog principle, then, and by eschewing deduction like the plague, I claim that we can get Dan his beer.

Acknowledgements

This chapter first appeared as "Dennett Beer" in *Robot's Dilemma: The Frame Problem in Artificial Intelligence,* edited by Zenon W. Pylyshyn (Norwood, NJ: Ablex, 1987). It is reproduced here with permission.

12 Goldilocks and the Frame Problem

Patrick J. Hayes, Kenneth M. Ford,
& Neil M. Agnew

Once upon a time there was an innocent young graduate student named Goldilocks, who lived with her grandmother on the edge of the forest. She led a reasonably happy life, but she didn't have a dissertation topic, and as she got older she found herself longing for one more and more. She took to going for long walks in the academic woods looking for a topic, without really knowing what she was looking for or how she would recognize it. Her grandmother warned her not to stray too far, but one day Goldilocks wandered into a strange part of the forest and found a house. It was a frame house that looked somehow as though it had a problem, but Goldilocks's curiosity overcame her natural caution and her grandmother's warnings. When she peered inside, the house seemed as if it had nothing in it worth a damn, but she decided to take a look around anyway. She figured she might find at least a part of a dissertation topic.

On the table she found three books. Ignoring her grandmother's warnings about modern writing, she sat down to take a look at them. They all seemed to have very nearly the same title.

The smallest one was a child's storybook called *The Fwame Pwobwem*. This began with a tale of some cute robots who kept getting lost searching for what happened when nothing happened. They had decided that the task was impossible when a swarm of futuristic robots arrived who could search much faster, and the cute slow robots were ecstatically grateful. Goldilocks couldn't quite see what was making them so happy because they had decided that whatever it was they had all been looking for couldn't be found by searching in any case. The text had a Zenlike flavor at that point. The moral seemed to be that the way to find anything was to search for it faster, even if it wasn't there. Goldilocks didn't think this idea was very sensible, but then she realized that she wasn't likely to get a useful dissertation topic from a child's book anyway. She put it back on the table, muttering, "That wasn't all that hot."

The biggest book was called *The Flame Problem*. It was a huge old leather-bound affair, like a family Bible. In fact, Goldilocks thought it was a Bible when she opened it because it had thousands of pages full of dense columns of print organized into chapter and verse. There was an elaborately decorated bookmark with these poetic verses printed on it; "The problem is everything. / Well, not everything, but just / About everything. Anyway, the problem / Is much much too hard / To be left to children / Or robots or computer scientist." The bookmark was placed at the beginning of Chapter 55, entitled "Inductive Relevance." This chapter began; "Verily it is obvious that Chapters 26 through 42 (excepting possibly Chapter 33, verses 267 through 855) are total Bunkum, since it is Evident that all Fridgeons have been Bleen. Since Friday before which they were Grue As is clearly Shown in Chapter 986, verses 2 through 47..." Goldilocks dipped into the rest of the book, but it seemed to consist almost entirely of nothing but page after page of such scornful but incomprehensible references to other chapters and verses. Goldilocks found this book boring and frustrating and left it on the table, exclaiming, "Not cool!"

She turned to the third, middle-sized book. This one was just right. It was called *The Frame Problem,* an attractive book, printed in 10-point Palatino on watermarked paper with broad margins—just the kind of thing Goldilocks liked to settle down with for a good read. It turned out to be an amusing autobiography written by a slightly crazy scientist called Joe Hackenstein, who had spent years trying to make an intelligent machine that would think consistently. The plot revolved around the wonderfully ludicrous problems Joe had been having before he decided that his task was impossible and turned to writing books. Goldilocks was more interested in a scientist's problems, even those of a slightly mad scientist, than in problems that childish robots or quarrelsome writers of ancient texts might have, so she settled down with the book.

A while later she was enjoying Joe's account of the problem that gave the book its title, which occurred when he tried to make a machine that could think about cooking an omelette. His first machine couldn't think about anything changing, so it couldn't imagine breaking eggs at all. Joe made one that was able to think about eggs breaking, but this one didn't realize that breaking the egg made the yolk fall into the bowl. Joe went back to his laboratory and rebuilt the machine so that it was able to think about events causing other events. The work took him years and Joe was rather proud of the result. This new version was able to talk, and it could imagine anything causing anything. But when he told the machine to imagine breaking an egg, it asked him if the bowl was still in the same place. "Yes," he said, "egg-breaking doesn't cause bowl-moving." "Ah," said the machine, "thank you, I will remember that."

Then it asked him if the table was still in the same place. Sensing a problem, Joe said yes, explaining that nothing moved when the egg broke. "Oh," said the machine brightly, "so the yolk is still in the egg!" "No, no, no!" cried Joe, with despair in his voice, "of course not!" Then the machine asked him what he meant by "of course"; and Joe realized that he had a *serious* problem.

Before Goldilocks had a chance to think very hard about dissertation topics, she was frightened by voices and the sound of feet coming toward the house. She dropped the book and ran into the kitchen to hide. While tasting the bowls of porridge she found there (the one in the middle was definitely better than the other two), she heard bearish voices in the room she had just left. A baby bear's voice whined, "Someone's been reading my *book!*" A mother bear's voice said with brisk annoyance, "Someone's been reading my book—and lost my page! I *do* wish bears would be more considerate with other bears' things! As if I don't have enough to do in this house, what with all the frozen salmon and …" When a deep, powerful bear's voice boomed angrily, "Someone's been trying to read *my* book."

Goldilocks wondered what to do and thought about looking for a comfortable bed somewhere, but before she could move, the three bears burst into the kitchen. Standing on the other side of the table, they glared at Goldilocks, looked at the bowls, then all shouted furiously, in unison, *"Someone's been eating our breakfasts!"* Goldilocks didn't stay to find out any more; She leaped through the window and ran all the way home as fast as her legs could carry her. (She never again went back into that part of the woods, and she eventually got her Ph.D in fuzzy control theory.)

The bears, however, were still upset by this intrusion into their lives. The baby bear burst into tears, and the father bear said sternly, "Come, now, don't be silly. Your mother will make some more breakfast. Remember the brave words of our ancestors: Nothing really changes almost anything!" Baby bear looked puzzled and snuffled, "I don't understand…" Mother bear looked at her husband witheringly and said, "You see? *That's* the problem."

Acknowledgements

This chapter first appeared as "Goldilocks and the Frame Problem" in *AI Magazine* volume 17 number 4 (winter 1996). It is reproduced here with permission.

13 Too Many Instincts: Contrasting Philosophical Views on Intelligence in Humans and Nonhumans

Susan G. Sterrett

"What kind of behavior is evidence of intelligence?" When the question comes up, it is usually asked about machines or (nonhuman) animals. In this chapter, I first recount a suggestion about what should count as evidence of intelligence that I made on an earlier occasion: roughly, the ability to override a habitual response and replace it with a more appropriate one (Sterrett 2000, 2002). That suggestion was inspired by a test described by Alan Turing, but the test that inspired it is underappreciated, as it was overshadowed by Turing's subsequent endorsement of another test for thinking that consisted merely in directly comparing the performances of a human and a machine in conversation. I argued that the suggestion inspired by the neglected version is especially appropriate for machine intelligence, since it does not depend upon the machine having any particular capacities.

After explaining that suggestion, I go on here to examine what a variety of thinkers—René Descartes, David Hume, Charles Darwin, and William James—have had to say about the existence of intelligence in nonhumans as well as in humans. I conclude that—despite the fact that these thinkers have strongly contrasting views on fundamental topics such as the relationship between instinct and reason, the relationship between mechanism and rationality, and the similarities and differences between humans and animals—a case can be made that my suggestion characterizes a kind of behavior that would count as evidence of intelligence on *all* of these thinkers' views.

There are two very different things one could take an answer to the question of what kind of behavior would be evidence of intelligence to be saying: (1) there is some specific unobserved thing (for example, thinking, consciousness, a soul) of which the intelligent behavior is supposed to be a sign; or (2) whatever the unobserved process or entity giving rise to it, the behavior in question would properly be considered intelligent.

The latter way of taking an answer to the question need not be a matter of *defining* intelligence, however. That is, one can take the question to be asking what would be good grounds for inferring intelligence while yet remaining noncommittal as to what is essential to, or what causes, intelligence.[1] We do this with behavioral concepts other than intelligence all the time; consider how we apply judgements such as "kind" or "stubborn." The virtue of the second way of taking the question is that it is more open to the kinds of beings or things that could exhibit intelligent behavior.

In the seventeenth century, René Descartes discussed how we would be able to differentiate a sophisticated humanlike automaton from a genuine human, or a monkeylike automaton from a monkey. The question Descartes had in mind was clearly of the sort described as (1) previously. Specifically, Descartes was addressing the question of whether naturally-occurring humans and monkeys consisted of anything more than the physiology he had researched so exhaustively. He thought the answer was different for humans and monkeys, and what he appealed to as a basis for this answer was the conclusion of another line of reasoning: although it was possible that there could be a monkeylike automaton that was behaviorally indistinguishable from a naturally-occurring monkey, any humanlike automaton would necessarily be behaviorally distinguishable from a naturally-occurring human. There were two kinds of behavior that were evidence of the existence of a rational soul, and so, he asserted with confidence, would not be exhibited by even the most sophisticated automaton. The first was that while such an automaton might well be able to produce different words in response to different things being said or done to it, it would not be able to "respond appropriately to whatever was said to it." For Descartes, the ability to respond appropriately to whatever is said was something any human could do, and was evidence of the existence of a rational soul; reason, unlike any physiological organ, was a "universal instrument." The second was that, no matter how well an automaton might perform some tasks, it would necessarily flounder at some task or other at which a naturally-occurring human would be competent. Again, the crucial point was that reason is a universal instrument, and that it provides at least some help in producing responses to novel situations, as opposed to the kind of specialized help provided by instincts and habits.

Centuries later, in 1950, Alan Turing proposed a practical test to determine whether a machine might properly be regarded as intelligent. Actually, as I have pointed out in other papers (Sterrett 2000, 2002) there are two distinct tests in Turing's essay "Computing machinery and intelligence" (Turing 1950). In my view, one has been unduly neglected, while the other has become extremely well-known. The well-known one, which I shall refer to as "the standard Turing test," recalls the scenario Descartes imagined of being able to distinguish an automaton from a naturally-occurring human due to the automaton's inadequacies in answering questions. In Turing's imagination, it is possible that things could turn out differently than Descartes imagined they must, however: Turing envisions the possibility that someone is not able to easily distinguish the automaton from the human, based on their responses to what is said to them. However, I think it is not only the outcome of Turing's thought experiment that differs from Descartes's but also that the question Turing was addressing was different. Turing was addressing a question of the sort described in (2) previously, whereas Descartes was addressing a question of the sort described in (1) previously. That is, the question for Turing was not whether the automaton's inner workings were the same as those of a naturally-occurring human's, but whether, to put it roughly, we would feel it appropriate to apply the word "intelligent" to a machine if it behaved as the machine did in the scenario he imagined. Thus, the fact that Descartes and Turing draw different conclusions as to whether a machine could exhibit intelligent behavior does not mean that Descartes and Turing would disagree as to what would count as intelligent behavior.

Others have noted the similarity between the well-known standard Turing test and what is sometimes referred to as "Descartes's language test for animal mind," so this last point is hardly new. However, using the ability to converse as a criterion of intelligence is wrought with difficulties. Instead, I propose we look at the question of the possibility of machine intelligence using, instead of the standard Turing test, another test inspired by Turing: the test I refer to as "the original imitation game test" (Sterrett 2000, 2002). We shall find something there that helps us with the question of how to tell machine intelligence if and when we see it.

The Importance of Overriding Habit

Those who have read Turing's 1950 paper may recall that in it he proceeds roughly as follows. The paper starts out with the question "Can machines think?" but, as he wants to avoid ambiguities due to the words "machine" and "think," Turing replaces the question "Can machines think?" with a "new question" that involves a parlor game. Then, he works out what he calls a "more precise form" of this new question, introducing a simplified version that does not involve the parlor game. One could attempt to dig out a theme common to the two games Turing proposed and try to infer what he must have been after. However, in attempting to do this, I realized that the two tests would not always yield the same results; in fact, the results they yield are not even comparable. What I want to do in this section is explain how the first, neglected, test in Turing's 1950 paper—the test I call "the original imitation game test"—works, and why I say that it is not equivalent to the second test, which is widely known as "the Turing test." I will also explain why I say that the first, neglected test employs a better characterization of intelligence. This section may be skipped by those familiar with the presentation in "Turing's Two Tests for Intelligence" (Sterrett 2000).

The first test Turing proposed uses what is sometimes referred to as "the original imitation game." As this game is nested inside the test he described, I refer to the test itself as "the original imitation game test." This is the underappreciated and neglected test. It is depicted in the left-hand column of figure 1. In the original imitation game test, there are three players, each with a different goal: A is a man, B is a woman, and C is an interrogator who may be of either gender. C is located in a room apart from A and B, and knows them by the labels X and Y. C asks questions of X and Y. The game is set up so as not to allow C any clues to X and Y's identities other than the linguistic exchanges that occur within the game. In figure 1, the teletypes are labeled X and Y; Turing also said, that, instead of teletypes, an intermediary could be used to communicate the answers from A and B to C.

The game is played as follows: C interviews "X" and "Y" (as he knows them). At the end of the game, C is to make one of two statements:

"'X' is A (the man) and 'Y' is B (the woman)" or

"'X' is B (the woman) and 'Y' is A (the man)."

C's goal is to make the correct identification, B's goal is to help C make the right identification, and A's goal is to try to fool C into making the wrong identification, that is, to succeed in making C misidentify him as the woman.

The first formulation Turing proposed (in section 1 of Turing 1950) as a substitute for "Can Machines Think?" was this: "What will happen when a machine takes the part of A in this game? Will the interrogator decide wrongly as often when the game is played like this as he does when the

ORIGINAL IMITATION GAME TEST	STANDARD TURING TEST
(§1 of *Computing Machinery and Intelligence* [Turing 1950])	(§5 of *Computing Machinery and Intelligence* [Turing 1950])

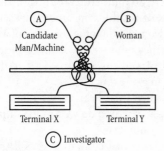
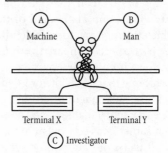

C asks questions via terminals X and Y. After a round of questioning, C must state either: "X is A and Y is B" or: "X is B and Y is A"

The "new question" is:

Can one build a machine such that the interrogator decides wrongly when a machine takes the part of A as often as when a man does? (Turing 1950: 434)

Notice:
— It is possible for the machine to outperform the man

— Lack of interrogator skill tends to be screened off.

— The man as well as the machine must impersonate something he is not.

—The machine's performance is not directly compared to the man's. Rather, they independently have successes and what is compared is their rates of success.

C asks questions via terminals X and Y. After a round of questioning, C must state either: "X is A and Y is B" or: "X is B and Y is A"

The "new question" is:

Can one build a particular machine to play satisfactorily the part of A, the part of B being taken by a man? (Turing 1950: 442)

Notice:
— It is *not* possible for this test to yield the result that the machine has outperformed the man.

— The test results are very sensitive to interrogator skills or lack of skill.

— The man is *not* asked to impersonate something he is not.

—The machine's performance is directly compared to the man's

Figure 1. Turing's Two Tests.

game is played between a man and a woman?" Now, suppose we take this to be suggesting a kind of metagame, of which the interrogator is unaware. That is, the interrogator C thinks that he or she is interviewing a pair consisting of one man and one woman. There are numerous rounds of such interviews, and at the end of the series of rounds, the frequency with which the interrogator misidentified the woman when the machine played the part of A is compared with the frequency with which the interrogator misidentified the woman when a man played the part of A. It is this metagame that I call "the original imitation game test."

In the subsequent discussion, Turing stated that, in turn, the question: "Are there imaginable digital computers which would do well in the imitation game?" was equivalent to the following question:

Let us fix our attention on one particular digital computer C. Is it true that by modifying this computer to have an adequate storage, suitably increasing its speed of action, and providing it with an appropriate program, C can be made to play satisfactorily the part of A in the imitation game, the part of B being taken by a man? (Turing 1950, p. 434)

Turing is not explicit about what the interrogator is to determine in this second version of the game, but the standard reading is that the interrogator is to determine which player is the computer and which is the man. Such a reading seems plausible enough, as the interrogator's task would be parallel (though not identical) to the task in the first version of the game, that is, at the end of the interview, the interrogator is to state one of two things: either "'X' is A and 'Y' is B," or "'X' is B and 'Y' is A," here, however, A is the computer and B is the man.

The test for machine intelligence in this second version is then simply how difficult it is for an "average" interrogator to correctly identify which is the computer and which is the man. This is what I refer to as the standard Turing test.

Figure 1 lists some major differences between the original imitation game test and the standard Turing test. These differences might not be obvious on the surface, but they become obvious when we imagine running the test under a variety of circumstances. The first difference becomes apparent in considering the quantitative results the two tests can yield. In the original imitation game test, there is nothing in the structure of the game to prevent a machine scoring higher than a man: consider an outcome in which the man succeeds one percent of the time, and the machine succeeds three percent of the time. Here there is an independent measure of success other than the interrogator's direct comparisons of the responses of the man and the machine, because there is a task at which each can either fail or succeed, independently of the other. If the interrogator wrongly identifies the candidate A as B when the man takes the candidate seat, the man has succeeded at the task at hand, and if the interrogator wrongly identifies the candidate A as B when the machine has played the role of candidate A, the machine has succeeded at the task at hand.

The standard Turing test does not even admit of such a result; there, the responses of the man and the machine are directly compared and only the machine is judged as to having exhibited a requisite skill or having failed to do so. The second difference is that the standard Turing test is far more sensitive to the interrogator's skill. That is, if C is very skilled at discerning the relevant differences, the percent of time the human wins will increase; if C is not very skilled at this, the percent of time the machine wins will increase. Sensitivity of the results of a test to the skill of the interrogator running it is hardly a virtue of any test. The results of the original imitation game test are not nearly as sensitive to interrogator skill as the standard Turing test is, for in the original imitation game test the machine's intelligence is being tested by comparing the frequency with which it succeeds in causing the interrogator to wrongly identify it as the woman with the frequency with which a man succeeds at doing the same. Thus, C's skill level affects both frequencies. More fundamentally, the differences between the two tests are due to this: In the original imitation game test, unlike in the standard Turing test, scoring as a thinker does not amount to simply being taken for one by a human judge.

Finally, there is a fundamental difference in what is asked of the man employed in the two tests. In the original imitation game test, both the man and the computer are called upon to impersonate. What the test results reflect is their relative success in achieving this goal. In the standard Turing test, the man is not called upon to do anything very novel, whereas the computer must converse under the pretense that it is human! In contrast, the original imitation game test compares the abilities of man and machine to do something that requires resourcefulness of each of them. It seems to me very significant that, for both the man and the machine, the task set has these aspects: recognizing an inappropriate response, being able to override the habitual response, and being able to fabricate and replace it with an appropriate response.

Thus, I concluded:

> … the importance of the first formulation lies in the characterization of intelligence it yields. If we reflect on how the original imitation game test manages to succeed as an empirical, behavior-based test that employs comparison with a human's linguistic performance in constructing a criterion for evaluation, yet does not make mere indistinguishability from a human's linguistic performance the criterion, we see it is because it takes a longer view of

intelligence than linguistic competence. In short: that intelligence lies, not in the having of cognitive habits developed in learning to converse, but in the exercise of the intellectual powers required to recognize, evaluate, and, when called for, override them. (Sterrett 2000: 558)

This insight came from thinking about what is required of a man sitting in the candidate seat in the original imitation game test. Carrying on a conversation employs lots of cognitive habits. But the task set in this test requires that he reflect on those habitual responses in case some of them ought to be edited to be the kind of behavior expected of the one he is impersonating. Here it is not only content in his responses that may need to be edited, but tone (that is, deference, concern, sarcasm about certain things and modesty about others) as well. But, rather than stating the criterion in terms of a game that only a creature with the ability to converse could participate in, I have tried to generalize the criterion by stating it in terms of the behavior of a creature with instincts and habits, but not necessarily an ability to converse. Thus, on this criterion, no creature, human or nonhuman, is precluded from exhibiting behavior that would be considered good evidence of intelligence simply because it is unable to converse. But being able to provide this kind of evidence does require having something that plays the role of instincts and habits.

What are the analogues of instinct and habit for a machine? To give a very general, provisional answer, the responses a machine would have to inputs or environmental stimuli prior to any learning—or perhaps some subset of such responses—might be considered analogous to instincts. The responses or patterns of responses the machine develops after learning might be considered analogous to habits. What then would it mean for a machine to override its habits and replace a habitual response with one that is more appropriate for the situation? On this analogy, if we knew a certain machine's analogues of instincts and habits, and observed the machine in a situation in which the responses arising from these analogues of instinct and habit were not appropriate, and further observed that in that situation, the inappropriate response that would result from its instinctual and habitual reactions was replaced by a response that was better suited to the situation, it would make sense to regard the behavior as intelligent.[2] And, we might properly refer to the machine itself as intelligent

On this view, then, the question of whether a machine can produce behavior that would provide evidence of intelligence turns on questions about its ability to override (its analogues of) instincts and habits, where habits are construed broadly enough to include cognitive habits.

Diverging Views on Reason, Habit, and Instinct
in Humans and Nonhumans

Numerous people discussing Turing's 1950 paper have noted that Descartes appealed to the ability to converse as one means of distinguishing creatures with reason from creatures whose behavior was caused by mere mechanism. As I have mentioned above, Descartes also gave another means of distinguishing creatures that were mere machines from creatures with reason. Since the skills of creatures that were mere machines could at best be due to instinct or learned habit, they would do the things for which they had specialized instincts extremely well, perhaps even better than a creature with reason could. However, these machines would be hopeless at the things for which they had neither specialized instincts nor a habit acquired through training or experience. For Descartes, there was no question that all mechanism could ever give rise to besides instincts were habits acquired through training or some interaction with its environment. There could be no such thing as the intelligence of machines. If there was a question about animal intelligence, it was whether or not animals were merely machines, and Descartes himself was confident that animals were machines and did not have minds. But, setting aside how different Descartes's question was from the question of whether machines could behave intelligently, let's consider what he would have made of the insight I believe is reflected in using frequency of success relative to a man in the original imitation game test.

The criterion for intelligent behavior I associate with success in the original imitation game test does not rely upon having linguistic skills—rather, it is a more generalized criterion: whether a creature is able to recognize when its habits or instincts should be overridden, and is able to replace the instinctual or habitual response with one that is more suitable. So, we want to look at whether Descartes would have viewed such behavior as evidence of intelligence. To put Descartes's view in perspective, it is helpful to look at later writers who knew Descartes's view as well. Charles Darwin cited evidence for his claim that (contra Descartes) animals were *not* merely machines; is Darwin's reasoning in line with the proposed criterion? What about other philosophers who investigated the workings of the mind and included nonhuman animals in their accounts, such as David Hume and William James?

In the chapter titled "Instinct," James describes animals that have lost what he calls "the 'instinctive' demeanor." The animal that has lost the instinctive demeanor, James says, appears to lead "a life of hesitation and choice, an intellectual life; n*ot, however, because he has no instincts—rather because he has so many that they block each other's path"* (James 1983: 1013). James was employing a commonsense and uncontroversial notion of instinct—roughly, that of a faculty of acting with neither foresight of the ends nor education in performing the act.[3] He wasn't challenging the notion of instinct, but he was challenging a prevailing view when he associated an intellectual life with having too many instincts. For he points out that "Nothing is commoner than the remark that Man differs from lower creatures by the almost total absence of instincts, and the assumption of their work in him by 'reason'" (James 1983: 1010). James went on to define and categorize the kinds of instincts humans have, concluding that, in contrast to the commonly-held view: "no other mammal, not even the monkey, shows so large an array [of instinctive tendencies as humans do]" (James 1983, p. 1056).

The view David Hume articulated falls under what James called the commonly-held view—the view that reason takes over the work of instincts. In *An Enquiry Concerning Human Understanding,* Hume associated reason with a paucity of specialized instincts—though not with a total absence of instinct. But, because he distinguished something he called experimental reason from what he called demonstrative reason, Hume's view is not quite so simple as the view James was challenging.

In comparing the abilities of humans and animals, Hume concluded that animals as well as humans learned from experience. He also recognized that animals have specialized instincts that produce behavior not based on any such observation or experience: he cites the instincts birds have for incubation of eggs and nest building. Hume noted wryly that we humans are apt to admire such specialized instincts "as something very extraordinary, and inexplicable by all the disquisitions of human understanding" (1977, p. 72). However, he regards this amazement wryly because he regards the ability to make inferences about matters of fact, whether it is found in humans or nonhuman animals, as itself an instinct. That is, he refers to the operations of the mind that give rise to beliefs and expectations concerning matters of fact as "a species of natural instincts" (1977, p. 30). Hume regarded this kind of inference as an operation of the mind, but not a case of the use of demonstrative reason; he said: "Animals ... are not guided in these inferences by reasoning" (1977, p. 70). He thought that deductions arrived at by means of demonstrative reason were often fallacious and usually too slow to be of much use in matters requiring timely action anyway. In Hume's eyes, since instincts are much more reliable than the application of reason, Nature exhibited wisdom in arranging for such functions of the mind to be carried out by means of

"some instinct or mechanical tendency" (1977, p. 37). Yet, for all his rogu-
ishness in extending the word "instinct" to include the ability to make
associations based on contiguity, Hume's view is still traditional in that
such experimental reasoning fills in to pick up the slack left when specialized instincts do not determine action. This is just the traditional view that
William James was challenging: that the relationship between instinct and
reason was that reason fills in where instinct does not supply an automatic
response.

Hume was challenging a commonly-held view, too, but a different one:
the view that there is a difference in kind between animal and human reason. Hume laid out the difference between the reason of human and nonhuman animals as a difference in where they are located on a continuum,
as opposed to the commonly-held view that it is a difference in kind.
Hume not only said that the so-called "experimental reasoning" by which
we infer effects from causes is itself a species of instinct, but he held that it
is an instinct that humans share with animals. Now, it does not escape
Hume's notice that there is a great difference between humans and animals
in terms of their reasoning abilities. But he denies that the existence of
even a large difference in their reasoning abilities shows that the mental
abilities of humans and animals are not on a continuum. He points out
the many various ways in which one human can differ from another,
resulting in a great difference in reasoning ability between two humans
(Hume 1977, p. 71, n. 36). Some are a matter of enhanced abilities, others
of deficiencies. For example, one person might surpass another in the abilities of attention, memory, and observation, or one person might just be
able to carry out a longer chain of reasoning than another. One person
might have much more experience, enhancing his ability to think of and
employ analogies. Some deficiencies he mentions are confusing one idea
for another, or being biased by prejudices or "from education or party." All
these factors contribute to the great differences in human understanding
with which we are familiar. Thus, Hume argues, *just as* the fact that there
are great variations between the reasoning abilities of *one human and
another* does not show that some humans have reason and others do not,
so the fact that there are great differences between the reasoning abilities
of *humans and animals* does not show that humans have reason and animals do not.

Hume's view that we're all on the same continuum is certainly meant to
conflict with Descartes's in that, on Descartes's view, there is a *qualitative*
difference between human and nonhuman creatures and it is marked by a
definite boundary. The qualitative difference Descartes meant to mark out
is between beings with reason and those without reason: for him, all ani-

mals ("beasts") and mechanical artifacts fall cleanly on one side of it, and all humans on the other side of it. I have mentioned the reasoning Descartes gave for such a qualitative difference. In more detail, it goes like this. First, he referred to the vast amount of work he had done on the physiology of the body, showing that he was as aware as anyone of the capabilities of physiological processes as well as of machines. I cite here what he says to show the level of physiological detail of his philosophical project:

> And then I showed what structure the nerves and muscles of the human body must have in order to make the animal spirits inside them strong enough to move its limbs.... I also indicated what changes must occur in the brain in order to cause waking, sleep and dreams; how light, sounds, smells, tastes, heat and the other qualities of external objects can imprint various ideas on the brain through the mediation of the senses; and how hunger, thirst, and the other internal passions can also send their ideas there. And I explained which part of the brain must be taken to be the "common" sense, where these ideas are received; the memory, which preserves them; and the corporeal imagination, which can change them in various ways, form them into new ideas, and, by distributing the animal spirits to the muscles, make the parts of this body move in as many different ways as the parts of our bodies can move *without being guided by the will*, and in a manner which is just as appropriate to the objects of the senses and the internal passions. This will not seem at all strange to those who know how many kinds of automatons, or moving machines, the skill of man can construct with the use of very few parts, in comparison with the great multitude of bones, muscles, nerves, arteries, veins and all the other parts that are in the body of any animal. (Descartes DV1 DMT ap. 56. p. 139)

Then Descartes deduced the kinds of functions that such a machine could perform. He concluded that a monkey could perform all the functions we observe it to perform on the hypothesis that its motions were caused by mere mechanism. From this he claims to be able to discern that "all of their motions could arise solely from that principle which is corporeal and mechanical" and thus that "in no way could we prove that there is a thinking soul in brutes" (quoted from Massey and Boyle 1999, p. 94, translation).

What about a human? Descartes imagines a really sophisticated, really fine piece of machinery that is physiologically indistinguishable from a human and can imitate "the motions of our bodies for all practical purposes." However, he says, the situation is different than it was for the imitation monkey. He thinks it is different because he thinks we would be able to tell that even this extremely sophisticated mechanism was not a human. The imagined automaton can do a lot:

... we can certainly conceive of a machine so constructed that it utters words, and even utters words which correspond to bodily actions causing a change in its organs (e.g. if you touch it in one spot it asks what you want of it, if you touch it in another it cries out that you are hurting it, and so on). (DV1 DMT ap. 57, p. 140)

But Descartes said it would be possible to tell it was a machine and not a human:

But it is not conceivable that such a machine should produce different arrangements of words so as to give an appropriately meaningful answer to whatever is said in its presence, as the dullest of men can do. (DV1 DMT ap. 57, p. 140)

Thus, since he judges that it is not possible that humans could be mere mechanism, whereas it is possible that other animals, such as monkeys, could be mere mechanisms, this marks a qualitative difference between humans and (nonhuman) animals. Descartes is explicit that this deficiency in the ability to use language exhibited by machines and animals marks a fundamental difference from humans:

This shows not merely that the beasts have less reason than men, but that they have no reason at all. For it patently requires very little reason to be able to speak; and since as much inequality can be observed among the animals of a given species as among human beings, and some animals are more easily trained than others, it would be incredible that a superior specimen of the monkey or parrot species should not be able to speak as well as the stupidest child or at least as well as a child with a defective brain—if their souls were not completely different in nature from ours. (DV1 DMT ap. 59, p. 141)

Descartes seems aware that, strictly speaking, he has demonstrated only that we *cannot* prove that animals do as a matter of fact have reason, but we *can* prove that humans must; humans could not do what they do without it. I say he seems aware that he has only demonstrated that he cannot prove that animals do have reason, rather than being able to prove that they do not, because he uses a probabilistic argument ("it would be incredible that...") for the conclusion that beasts have no reason at all. Massey and Boyle (1999, p. 97) also note this point, citing what Descartes writes in a letter to Henry More: "But although I take it as demonstrated that one cannot prove that there is any cognition in brutes, I do not think on this account that one can prove that there is none at all, since the human mind does not enter into their hearts."[4]

Descartes seems to make up for the lack of certainty of such arguments somewhat by supplying several of them. In the other reason he gives for knowing that the automaton that looks and functions physiologically like a human is not a true human, there is what I take to be a recognition of the amazing specialized instincts animals have: even if it could do some things really well, it would flounder at others. We would know by these flounderings that they "did not act through understanding but solely through the disposition of their organs." Now, Descartes seems to assume that this sort of thing would be a giveaway that something was not a true human, but not that something is not a true dog or a true monkey. Descartes seems to think that such floundering is to be expected of dogs, monkeys and other beasts; not for humans, though! He says that "reason is a universal instrument which is of service in all situations"; the use of reason is supposed to contrast with the basis for movements found in automatons and animals. The behavior of automatons and beasts arises from dispositions of their organs or parts. Yet, Descartes is aware that the instincts of animals can be overridden; beasts can be trained:

> So when a dog sees a partridge, it is naturally inclined to run toward it; and when it hears a gun fired the noise naturally incites it to run away. But nevertheless setters are commonly trained so that the sight of a partridge makes them stop, and the noise they hear afterwards, when [the bird] is fired on, makes them run up to it. (Descartes 1989, p. 48)

The mechanism is the same as it is for humans, and can result from one single, unplanned experience:

> Indeed this habit can be acquired by a single action and does not require long practice. Thus, when we unexpectedly come upon something very foul in a dish we are eating with relish, our surprise may so change the disposition of our brain that we cannot afterwards look upon any such food without repulsion, whereas previously we ate it with pleasure. And the same may be observed in animals. (Descartes 1989, p. 48)

So there seems to be very little a dog could do to prove to Descartes that it was thinking. Obeying commands is not evidence of reason to Descartes, nor is avoiding hazardous things. Descartes thinks we could never know that the aversion to the hazardous thing was not based on a past bad experience the animal had with that thing, or something very similar to it; thus we could never regard such behavior as evidence that the dog had used reason to infer that the hazardous thing was something to be avoided. Descartes's view is that not only could even the most amazing instinct be the result of mechanism, but so could obeying a command or avoiding a hazard that requires it to override an instinct! Yet, he holds that the human capacity to reason could not be a result of mechanism and, so, that there is a qualitative difference between nonhumans and humans. On that point, Descartes's view is quite clearly directly opposed to Hume's.

To be fair to their views, however, perhaps it should be pointed out that there are some other points about the reason of animals on which Descartes and Hume are not as far apart as they are often portrayed. Although Hume thought that animals made inferences, he thought they only drew the kind of inferences that arose from experimental reason acquired by habit; he distinguished this kind of experimental reason from the kind that involves study, thought, and the recognition that something is an instance of a maxim. Descartes thought that what looked like animals making inferences could be described in terms of what we would now call learned responses, and that what animals did, did not require reason. So, if we were to roughly align Hume's contrast between demonstrative reason and experimental reason with Descartes's contrast between reason and learned responses, we may find in fact that Descartes and Hume are not pushing diametrically opposed claims about reason and habit on every point.

Yet, if we extend the ground of agreement between them as far as we can, there still remains an important difference between them. Hume thought that beasts and humans were best understood as just being at different places on the same continuum, whereas Descartes thought that there was a difference in kind between the most clever, most trainable nonhuman animal and humans whom he ranked lowest in the ability to reason.

I have a suspicion about the root of this difference. The point of disagreement at the root of this difference between Hume and Descartes lies, I think, in the significance they attach to what they called demonstrative reason—for Descartes, it was the mark of a thinking soul, and hence of the utmost significance, while Hume made impudent remarks about philosophers who made such a big deal about demonstrative reason.

In fact, Hume devoted a long footnote (Hume 1977, pp. 28–29, n. 20) to arguing that the long-standing distinction drawn between the two species of argument called "reason" and "experience" is erroneous or at least superficial. He illustrates the difference in the kind of inferences that one can draw by the following pair of examples:

> (1) from the history of a Tiberius or Nero, dreading "a like tyranny, were our monarchs freed from the restraints of laws and senates;"

> (2) coming to have that same apprehension on the basis of "the observation of any fraud or cruelty in private life" and the application of a little thought.

Hume does not deny the usefulness of the type of argument generally referred to as "reason" (as opposed to "experience"). The kind generally referred to as experience is limited in that it can only support an inference from an experienced event that is "exactly and fully similar" to the event inferred. Certainly, he agrees, there is some value in being able to extend the kind of things we can establish by "some process of thought, and some reflection on what we have observed, in order to distinguish its circumstances, and trace its consequences"—but he argues there that it is a delusion to think that there is *any* species of reasoning that is *totally* independent of experience. For, he says, "If we examine those arguments which ... are supposed to be the mere effects of reasoning and reflection, they will be found to terminate, at last, in some general principle or conclusion, to which we can assign no reason" (Hume 1977, pp. 28–29, n. 20). I think that it is the difference in their attitudes towards how distinctive and significant demonstrative reason is that results in Descartes and Hume having diametrically opposed judgements as to whether there is a difference in kind between animals and humans. For, Hume really does recognize there is a difference in the kind of reasoning that animals and people can carry out, but he does not think it is important enough to regard human and animal understanding as fundamentally different. He seems to think of reason as a sort of aid in letting us expand the range of our understanding by letting us go farther in the consequences we can draw. But that kind of difference is just the kind of differences we know exist among various humans. Any science, no matter how impressive, is at bottom not based upon a fundamentally different sort of understanding than the kind of understanding animals have of the world, which comes from experimental reasoning.

William James (1983) introduced a different continuum: one of an ever-increasing quantity of instincts. And, he puts humans at the *high* end of this continuum; that is, humans have more instincts than any other creature. For James, too, reason's role is to be a sort of aid to instinct, but it does not constitute a fundamentally different *kind* of force than instinct: "there is no material antagonism between instinct and reason. Reason, per se, can inhibit no impulses; the only thing that can neutralize an impulse is an impulse the other way. Reason may, however, make an inference which will excite the imagination so as to set loose the impulse the other way" (1983, p. 1013). Here James is talking about behavior rather than inferring consequences, but we see an approach in keeping with Humes: the kind of thing (acting in ways to bring about certain ends, expecting an event) going on is the same in humans and other animals, but the *kind* of reason humans are capable of is an aid in extending the range of that capability. Thus humans are capable of a range unreachable by other animals, and philosophers have *mistakenly* taken this as a difference in kind, rather than range, of that capability. Hume sees himself as correcting the "difference-in-kind" misconception with respect to human understanding,

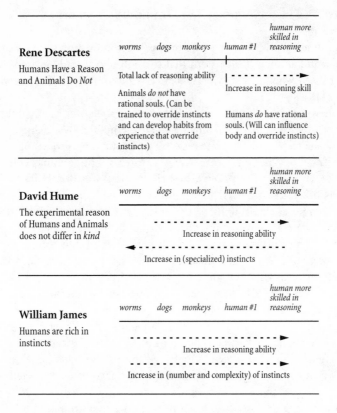

*Figure 2. How Descartes, Hume, and James
Saw the Roles of Instinct, Habit, and Reason in Behavior.*

whereas James corrects a "difference-in-kind" misconception with respect to human behavior.

That is a brief sketch of how René Descartes in the seventeenth century, David Hume in the eighteenth century, and William James in the nineteenth century, saw the roles of instinct, habit and reason in behavior. Although they had different motivations and concerns, we can compare their views on these notions; these are depicted in figure 2. Now, let us ask how the suggestion I have made about what would be good evidence of intelligence fares on these various views.

Converging Views on Looking Smart

Despite their very different views on the roles of instinct and reason in humans and animals, it turns out that these thinkers would give the same answer as to whether behavior that meets the proposed criterion would count as intelligent behavior.

We have already discussed David Hume's view that understanding is a matter of degree, rather than an all-or-nothing matter. By looking at what he thinks is responsible for one person's understanding surpassing another's, we may be able to get some clues as to what Hume thinks counts as evidence of intelligence. A key factor Hume cited was the ability to form maxims based upon a particular observation or observations along with some thought and refection.[5] Thus, intelligence would be exhibited by a creature's aversion to something that it had not ever experienced before on the basis of an inference employing a general maxim drawn from experience along with "study and reflection." The example he gave, cited in the last section, was of someone comparing a dread of tyranny based on knowing how terrible a particular tyranny such as Tiberius turned out, with a dread of tyranny based upon the observation of any fraud or cruelty in private life and "the aid of a little thought." In the latter case, there is not a close similarity between the event on which the dread is based and the thing dreaded. Thus, the ability to use thought to extend one's understanding of things to be dreaded and avoided beyond cases "exactly and fully similar" to those known would be exhibited by behavior in which, were the hazard or opportunity not present, the creature would behave in accordance with its habitual or instinctual response, but instead overrode that habit or instinct and avoided a hazard it is known not to have encountered before. Of course, as Descartes and Darwin noted, too, there are often problems ascertaining whether a response that appears thoughtful is not due just to instinct. I am here addressing the question of what would in principle be considered intelligent behavior.

What about René Descartes? We have some clue as to what Descartes thought would count as evidence of intelligence in animals because his argument proceeds by discussing the lack of such evidence. Descartes pointed out that animals can be trained to respond to specific words, and that some can even use words. But he thought that their responses to our verbal commands were limited to the sort that could be explained as a disposition of a particular organ, rather than requiring the use of the generalized instrument that reason is. The problem is, as he admits in a letter to Henry More, "the human mind does not reach into their hearts" so we cannot prove that there is no cogitation in brutes. So even something that looks to us like really intelligent behavior can be accounted for on Descartes's view by appeal to the disposition of their organs either by design of nature or by acquired habit, including single-trial training. As I indicated earlier, it looks impossible to come up with something that would break through Descartes's blanket dismissal. However, Darwin finds some examples of cases that might count as evidence of cogitation in brutes that are not so easily dispensed with.

One example Charles Darwin (1871) gave was of an experimenter who gave lumps of sugar wrapped in paper to his monkeys. Sometimes, Darwin (1871) says, the experimenter "put a live wasp in the paper, so that in hastily unfolding it [the monkeys] got stung; after this had once happened, [the monkeys] always first held the packet to their ears to detect any movement within." Notice that this response to the trauma of being stung is somewhat more sophisticated than the simple aversion reaction Descartes mentioned: the monkeys instead initiate a new step in their sugar-eating ritual that will enable them to discriminate between the packets that will cause the same trauma and those that will yield only a pleasant tasty sugary experience.

But the example Darwin thought the best rejoinder to the kind of view Descartes held was of the animal for which he had the most affection and respect: a dog. He relates stories from two independent observers:

> Mr. Colquhoun winged two wild-ducks, which fell on the opposite side of a stream; his retriever tried to bring over both at once, but could not succeed; she then, though never before known to ruffle a feather, deliberately killed one, brought over the other, and returned for the dead bird. *Col. Hutchinson* relates that two partridges were shot at once, one being killed, the other wounded; the latter ran away, and was caught by the retriever, who on her return came across the dead bird; "she stopped, evidently greatly puzzled, and after one or two trials, finding she could not take it up without permitting the escape of the winged bird, she considered a moment, then deliberately murdered it by giving it a severe crunch, and afterwards brought away both together. This was the only known instance of her ever having wilfully injured any game." (Darwin 1871, ch. III)

Here it seems there was an unprecedented overriding of an instinct, not in response to some trauma, nor as a result of any training, but in order to achieve a desired end. It cannot be a disposition or an instinct, as these do not include foresight of the end. And this is why Darwin (1871) says he chose these examples: "I give the above cases because in both instances the retrievers, after deliberation, broke through a habit which is inherited by them (that of not killing the game retrieved), and because they show how strong their reasoning faculty must have been to overcome a fixed habit."

It seems to me that Darwin is deliberately choosing cases that would meet Descartes's criterion, for he closes his discussion of anecdotes of monkeys and dogs that show the use of reason by saying that these exhibitions of reason by animals prove that animals are not machines. Thus, I think Darwin is employing the same criterion as Descartes, and I think he does so in order to challenge Descartes's conclusions. Just as Descartes was, Darwin is considering whether a creature known to possess instinct and habit might also use reason. Using reason is not a matter of a creature ridding itself of habit and instinct, but of the creature being able to exercise some power (which may be called reason) in recognizing, evaluating, and, when called for, overriding or perhaps modifying, the habitual response.

William James's bold and quirky step was to use the main insight in Darwin's challenging counterexample to Descartes, but to use it as an explanation of what gives rise to, rather than merely what would give evidence for, the use of reason. James argues that having a plethora of instincts gives rise to behavior exhibiting intelligence.

Now, I am not claiming James gives Darwin credit here; he does not. In general, James did not put much stock in anecdotes or "dog stories" that purport to show that dogs reason. He discredits a story given him about a little terrier that is asked to retrieve a sponge and does so, in spite of never having been trained anything regarding the sponge. The little terrier's owner had said "Sponge! Sponge! Go get the sponge!" anyway, while making motions of using a sponge to wipe up water, and was amazed and delighted at the dog's ability to discern what it was supposed to do. James gives the dog only a little bit of credit; he says:

> This terrier, in having picked those details out of the crude mass of his boat-experience distinctly enough to be reminded of them, was truly enough ahead of his peers on the line which leads to human reason. But his act was not yet an act of reasoning proper. It might fairly have been called so if, unable to find the sponge at the house, he had brought back a dipper or a mop instead. (James 1983, p. 974)

Now it seems that James is here calling for the kind of anecdote Darwin actually provided about bird-retrieving dogs, that is, though he did not put it in such terms, what James is saying implies that what it would take to convince him that the dog used reason was a case where trying to carry out the habit of retrieving the object named would be frustrated and the animal would instead identify and carry out some substitute action that was appropriate to the situation.

James does not directly address Darwin's two examples of the problem solving bird retrievers, and, in fact, James (1983, p. 974) offers a universal dismissal of what he calls "dog and elephant stories," stating with confidence that "If the reader will take the trouble to analyze the best dog and elephant stories he knows, he will find that, in most cases, this simple contiguous calling up of one whole by another is quite sufficient to explain the phenomena." James's point here about the sufficiency of "calling up of one whole by another" to explain the animal's behavior is that the behavior is not evidence of the animal having to take the step of what he called "dissociating characters," such as the character of being suitable for use in soaking up and removing liquid. Reasoning using characters would be evidence of using reason. James goes through numerous examples of "dog stories" to discredit the claim that dogs can dissociate characters. There is one case he admits is borderline:

> Stories are told of dogs carrying coppers [pennies] to pastry-cooks to get buns, and it is said that a certain dog, if he gave two coppers, would never leave without two buns. This was probably mere contiguous association, but it is possible that the animal noticed the character of duality, and identified it as the same in the coin and the cake. If so, it is the maximum of canine abstract thinking. (James 1983, pp. 975–976)

But James goes on to emphasize that most other stories of purported canine abstract thinking can be explained in terms of "simple contiguous calling up of one whole by another." Although James goes through one story after another, he never does get around to dealing with the stories Darwin cited to show that dogs were not mere machines. However, in spite of never mentioning the dogs Darwin wrote about who had to deal with competing instincts, James seems to have picked up on the relationship between having to deal with competing instincts and exhibiting intelligence. The kinds of things James lists among human instincts include the hunting instinct, the instinct to play in certain ways, curiosity, cleanliness and acquisitiveness, among numerous others. James thinks that having so many instincts is not only compatible with a more highly developed reason, but that having more instincts actually *leads* to a more highly developed reason. Here's why: the more instincts, wants and aesthetic feelings one has, the more characters one will have to dissociate, and dissociating lots of distinct characters is a necessary part of making inferences that go beyond mere contiguity. Now, recall James's remark (James 1983, p. 1013) that "there is no material antagonism between instinct and reason. Reason, per se, can inhibit no impulses; the only thing that can neutralize an impulse is an impulse the other way. Reason may, however, make an inference which will excite the imagination so as to set loose the impulse the other way'" which I quoted earlier. James's discussion continues: "and thus though the animal richest in reason might be also the animal richest in instinctive impulses, too, he would never seem the fatal automaton which a merely instinctive animal would be." Thus, it seems that reason can be exhibited in cases where one is faced with competing instincts, and deals with it by employing reason to "set loose" impulses that will neutralize others. Thus, although this is not exactly Descartes's view of reason overriding mechanical responses, the effect is the same: the realization of the appropriate behavior called for does result in overriding a habitual or instinctive response that would be inappropriate.

It may be too strong to claim that there is some common notion or view held by all these thinkers in common. And some of them rule out the possibility of machine intelligence outright. My point is rather that, if we imagine asking the question: "Given a creature possessed of habit and instincts that you do not rule incapable of intelligence outright in virtue of its constitution or genesis, what kind of behavior would be evidence of its intelligence?" I think it can be argued that all four of these writers (though perhaps for very different reasons and with very different expectations about what the outcomes would be for various kinds of creatures) would consent that, were such a creature to show that it was capable of recognizing when the habitual or instinctual response was inappropriate, and be able to override it and replace it with an appropriate response, it would be evidence of intelligence.

Intelligent Robot Designers

I have deliberately attempted to steer the discussion about machine intelligence away from drawing comparisons between humans and machines, such as questions about whether machines could do some or all the things humans do or whether humans are machines. These questions are favorites of philosophers, and have often been connected with questions about the nature and existence of free will. I have instead here focused on what counts as evidence of intelligent behavior in nonhumans as well as in humans, and this question, interestingly, has led us to the importance of the capability of overriding instincts and habits.

The purpose of this investigation was to help us address questions about the nature and existence of machine intelligence. That the path has eventually led to the importance of the capability to override instincts and habits is doubly interesting, for research in robotic control and intelligent agents has come to the point of designing machine architectures that include not only implementations of "pre-wired" responses and reinforced learning, but of means of overriding and revising those "pre-wired" and learned behaviors.

Although Alan Turing seemed to think that the best way of constructing a simulation of a human brain would be to build a machine that could learn and would include a random element, the hearts of most of the first artificial intelligence programs were (deterministic) logical inference engines.[6] The learning involved, if any, was generally a matter of updating a representation of a domain by adding data received or inferred, rather than developing new procedures as a result of its interaction with its environment. Actions taken were usually regarded as the result of carrying out a command produced by an inference engine that worked from goals to be achieved and, using information it had been given or had acquired, deduced the action or actions to take.

One of the most striking reactions against the centralized logical inference-engine conception of artificial intelligence reminds one of how Hume de-emphasized demonstrative reason and emphasized habit and instinct: I refer here to Rodney Brooks's advocacy of a "behavior-based" approach to robotic navigational problems. To avoid any misunderstanding, I should mention that Brooks has more recently tackled the task of developing humanoid robots, in which he explicitly looks to human beings as models for a humanoid robot design. I am interested in the question of machine intelligence, rather than in the specific question of how to build a humanlike robot, and for this purpose I want to refer only to the basic change in orientation in AI he initiated in the 1980s, which continues to influence robotics today. He describes his behavior-based approach (circa 1991) thus:

> At MIT we have been investigating structuring of intelligence based on a decomposition into behaviors, each of which connects sensing to action. Functional modules such as planners and learners do not appear as such, but instead planning, learning, etc., can be observed to be happening in the complete system. The behaviors are the building blocks, and the functionality is emergent. This differs from the traditional approach in which the functional modules are the building blocks and the behaviors are emergent (Brooks 1991).

The difference between Brooks's view and the traditional view he contrasts it with that is of interest to us here, however, is this: on Brooks's view, there is the possibility that, within the same machine or robot, different parts of the machine can call for different actuator responses of the same actuator, and hence can conflict. Thus the need for what Darwin (1871) called an "inward monitor" can arise.

Brooks appreciated that his approach raised the problem of making decisions as to how to resolve conflicts between behaviors. Resolving conflicts was just one of two parts of the general problem of "deciding which behavior or behaviors should be active at any particular time," he said; the other was how to select potentially correct behaviors in the circumstances. The approach Brooks calls "behavior-based programming," is a refinement of his earlier "subsumption architecture" approach. A distinctive feature of both these approaches is the use of layers each of which employs finite state machines (augmented with timers), in contrast to a centralized decision-making unit. The layers are layers of behaviors, such as "locomote," "avoid hitting things" and "explore," and the layers interact with each other. I do not wish to go into more detail about Brooks's specific methods here, as expositions of his approach are readily available elsewhere, but I think it worth remarking that his approach to implementing behavior includes not only processes that can be halted, but processes that can be inhibited or blocked by others.[7] Thus Brooks's approach to intelligent behavior recognizes, at least in principle, the need for the ability to determine an appropriate behavior and for the ability to override and/or inhibit default processes. Brooks describes the layers as being related but thinks it improper to think of them as related by a hierarchy, as higher-level layers both depend upon and influence lower layers.

I have highlighted the features in his approach that relate to my claim about machine intelligence: the capabilities of determining appropriate behaviors in a situation and of being able to override instincts and habits. Brooks, however, emphasizes other features of this approach, especially the lack of symbolic logic processing in his approach. He notes: "Neither [behavior-based programming], nor the other similar architectures, use symbols in the conventional way" (Brooks 1991b). He wants to highlight how his "behavior-based" approach differs from more classical AI approaches, so he also makes the points that, on his approach, there is no centralized control unit, and no centralized representation of the world stored in the agent to be manipulated and employed in determining its next move.

However, other researchers who see the virtue of a behavior-based approach but do not see the virtue in doing without symbolic processing for the sake of it have employed architectures inspired by Brooks's layered "subsumption architecture" in conjunction with the use of symbolic logic. For instance, in a paper entitled "Logic-Based Subsumption Architecture," Eyal Amir and Pedrito Maynard-Reid II took on the task of extending a Brooks-style architecture to agents that are not necessarily physical, and to more complex tasks. They use logic rather than hardware to provide the link between a (behavioral) layer's inputs and outputs, but retain the features of Brooks's approach that are responsible for the reactivity of his robots. Corresponding to each of what Brooks called a layer, their architecture provides a first-order logic theory, and "[e]ach layer is supplied with a separate theorem prover, allowing the layers to operate concurrently" (Amir and Maynard-Reid II 1999). They explain reactivity of the robot as an advantage arising from the layer-decoupling:

> As in Brooks's system, lower layers controlling basic behaviors are trusted to be autonomous and do not need to wait on results from higher layers (they assume some of them by default) before being able to respond to situations. Because these layers typically have simpler axiomatizations, and given the default assumptions, the cycle time to compute their outputs can be shorter than that of the more complex layers (Amir and Maynard-Reid II 1999).

In keeping with Brooks's approach, however, the layers are not completely independent. It is important that the layers be able to interact. The possibility for "conflict" between layers exists and hence so does the need for some approach to resolve the conflict. The connection with animal examples is that the layers are like habits or instincts, and intelligence (or lack of it) is exhibited in how the animal responds to conflicting instincts. Amir and Maynard-Reid II present one of several possible means of resolving the conflict of theories of various layers of their 'logic-based subsumption architecture" in detail, which they have successfully implemented in a mobile robot. The details are not important to my point in this paper. What is significant to me about their approach is that they implemented logic in a layered architecture in which logical processes take place not only at many different behavioral layers, but in dealing with conflicts arising from the interaction of layers as well.

In drawing an analogy between an animal and a robot using their architecture, I suppose an instinct would be analogous to something like a behavioral layer, so that the conflicts that arise between layers would be analogous to conflicting instincts. Thus, it is interesting that the problem of instincts conflicting and overriding each other arises in a robot using logical theorem-proving techniques throughout its operation.

However, the implementation reported in that paper is a navigational robot and, although they plan to extend its capabilities to making maps and reasoning about the world, they do not stress learning new skills. We are especially interested in learning, because many of the habits that figure in the exhibitions of intelligence we considered involve habits which, though they may get their start as instincts, involve things that are learned, and, in particular, learned in interactions with, or by observing, people. Here I have in mind anecdotes such as the little terrier figuring out what was being asked of him either from observation of his owner using the word "sponge" on other occasions or his owner's use of gestures indicating the use of a sponge to wipe up liquid while ordering him to get the sponge; the monkeys developing the habit of holding packets of sugar to their ears to listen for wasps occasionally put inside by their mischievous human keepers; the bird dogs sizing up a situation in which their default habits would not produce the usual result and coming up with a way to satisfy their owner's expectations by overriding one of those habits, and so on.

However, there is no reason that an architecture that has the features I find important to machine intelligence cannot also be much more flexible with respect to learning. Ronald Parr and Stuart Russell (1997) employed an approach to reinforcement learning, which they describe as "providing a link between reinforcement learning and "behavior-based" or "teleo-reactive" approaches to control." The emphasis of their presentation is on showing how reinforcement learning algorithms can benefit from the constraints imposed by a hierarchy of machines, as those constraints incorporate prior knowledge to reduce the complexity of the problem. However, we are interested here in how the use of reinforcement learning enriches the abilities of a "behavior-based" robot and makes it more flexible. Their approach uses a layered hierarchy of partially specified machines, in which the machines are nondeterministic finite state machines, and a higher-level machine may depend upon lower-level machines in making the transition from one state to another. The general approach permits a range of specification, but, "One useful intermediate point is the specification of just the general organization of behavior into a layered hierarchy, leaving it up to the learning algorithm to discover exactly which lower-level activities should be invoked by higher levels at each point." The significance of this design to our investigation of machine intelligence is that, as I said earlier, one feature of the kind of behavior that would count as evidence of intelligence is being able not only to override an inappropriate response, but to construct an appropriate one, and this approach seems to provide an architecture in which new solutions to problems are sought using a robot architecture that also contains analogues of instincts and habits.

This is by no means a survey of the field. These examples were selected to illustrate that as the design of machine architectures progresses, we see that artificial intelligence researchers are designing algorithms and architectures that have the beginnings of some of the analogues of the features of behavior that I identified at the outset of this chapter as features of behavior that would count as evidence of intelligence.

Conclusion

Let us return to the question at the start of my essay. I began by recapitulating the conclusion of an earlier analysis of the two descriptions of tests proposed by Alan Turing to replace the question, "Can machines think?" I had concluded that the two descriptions, taken literally, really describe two distinct tests, and that the test that has been neglected, though it seems at first rather eccentric and to test only a particular and rather peculiar skill, actually reflects an important insight. That insight is that behavior that requires an agent to recognize when the response that would be produced by habit (including cognitive habits) is inappropriate, to override that habitual response, and construct and carry out an appropriate response in its place, would be considered intelligent behavior.

In surveying various thinkers, we see that René Descartes would have granted as much, although he would have thought only humans capable of such behavior. David Hume thought highly of habit, but even he too granted that there was a difference between the kind of reasoning due to habit in which one infers like from like, as opposed to the kind of reasoning in which one goes beyond habit. The difference is that he thought much more of our reasoning is due to habit than was generally recognized, and he did not think the distinction was of nearly the significance that Descartes did. Charles Darwin thought animals could exhibit the kind of behavior I claim would be evidence of intelligence, and cited anecdotes of such behavior as evidence that animals were not machines. So Darwin would agree that such behavior was evidence of intelligence, but not that machines were capable of such behavior. William James's view that reason arises from a plethora of instincts seems to indicate that he thought being able to arbitrate between them and override some by others was a sign of intelligence. I think the fact that there would be agreement as to what would count as evidence of intelligence despite such differing views on the topics of instinct and intelligence in humans, animals, and machines is a point in favor of my claim, for it indicates that my claim is not tied to any particular intuitions about whether various sorts of nonhumans are or are not intelligent. These thinkers all predated Alan Turing's famous paper of 1950 in which he suggested tests to replace the question "Can machines think?"

Finally, looking forward from Turing's paper, I have given examples that indicate that as designers of intelligent agents and robots try to design architectures that are more efficient and more flexible with respect to the range of situations that might be encountered in an environment, they are tending to come up with designs that have analogues of some of the features and abilities that I have said are ingredients of the kind of behavior that would be considered evidence of machine intelligence. Though they have built-in analogues of instincts and the ability to develop habits, they also have, at least in principle, mechanisms with the potential to construct responses to replace the habitual or instinctual responses.[8]

Of course this does not say much about how a machine could autonomously determine when a habitual response is not appropriate or what an appropriate response to replace it would be. I am not claiming anyone has achieved this so far, nor that it is clear just how to achieve it. To the question of how we will agree as to when a machine's behavior is not just a habitual response, but involved recognizing that a habitual or instinctual response was inappropriate and constructing an appropriate response to carry out in its place, though, I can say this: when you stop to think about it, the cross-gendering task set for a human, whose success the machine must match in order to pass the neglected test in Turing's essay, "Computing Machinery and Intelligence," is just such a discriminating task.

Acknowledgements

Thanks to Tad Schmaltz and Deborah Boyle for review and comment on the sections of this paper on Descartes and Hume. Thanks to Ron Parr for discussing his work on robots with me and telling me about the innovative work of Amir and Maynard-Reid. Versions of this talk were presented at the University of Virginia Philosophy Department, the North Carolina State University Philosophy Club, and at the 2002 Combined Meeting of the South Carolina Society for Philosophy and North Carolina Philosophical Society held at the College of Charleston. Thanks to audiences there, especially to John Carroll and Ron Endicott, and to Cora Diamond for explaining the retriever "soft mouth" that figures importantly in Darwin's crucial example.

This chapter first appeared as "Too Many Instincts: Contrasting Philosophical Views on Intelligence in Humans and Nonhumans" in the *Journal of Experimental & Theoretical AI*, volume 14(1): 39–60 (2002). It is reproduced here with permission.

Notes

1. This point is not new and was made as early as 1976 by James Moor (1976).

2. Of course, what is "appropriate" in a situation may depend in part on the role of a participant in it, so an adequate description of a situation might have to include something about analogues of goals and/or desires of the machine. Normally, the notion of an end will be

obliquely built into the notion of instinct (see section 3 of this paper), but some situations might involve more detail (that is, a dog's desire to carry out its master's command is an attachment to a specific person, whereas the instinct to attach itself to some human or other in a master-pet relationship is general and does not involve any particular person).

3. "Instinct is usually defined as the faculty of acting in such a way as to produce certain ends, without foresight of the ends, and without previous education in the performance." This is the opening statement of chapter 24, "Instinct," in *The Principles of Psychology* (James 1983, p. 1004).

4. I read Massey and Boyle's "Descartes's Tests for Animal Mind" (1999) after I had written "Turing's Two Tests for Intelligence" (Sterrett 2000). Their interesting discussion of Descartes's test for volitions (the "action test") as evidence of animal mind stimulated me to think more about the rarely asked question of what, besides the ability to converse, Descartes would have to count as evidence of animal mind. I highly recommend their innovative paper, which has led me to write this one connecting issues in history of philosophy about machines and intelligence with current ones in artificial intelligence.

5. "There is no man so young and inexperienced, as not to have formed, from observation, many general and just maxims concerning human affairs and the conduct of life; but it must be confessed, that, when a man comes to put these into practice, he will be extremely liable to error, till time and farther experience both enlarge these maxims, and teach him their proper use and application" (Hume 1997, p. 29, n. 20).

6. In "Computing Machinery and Intelligence," Turing describes what he calls a "child-machine" in section 7 of that paper (1950, p. 454). He says that the child-machine should have some analogue of pleasure and pain so that it could be taught using reinforcement learning and remarks that the machine's behavior should not be completely determined by its experience.

7. See entries for Brooks in the bibliography. At of the time of this writing, Brooks has an extensive webpage about his publications. (www.ai.mit.edu/people/brooks/publications. shtml).

8. Of course, it cannot be ruled out that the behavior of a robot with such an architecture could be produced by one without such analogues of instincts and habits, that is, someone could claim that a connectionist machine with just the right number of layers, just the right learning algorithms, and just the right kind of training set might be able to produce the same outputs. As long as the equivalence of behavior is not sensitive to the particular characteristics of the novel situation in which the machine exhibits intelligence, I do not see why it would necessarily be a mistake to credit such a machine with intelligent behavior either. (Were the machine's behavior extremely sensitive to getting exactly the right kind of training; however, then I think some would want to withhold giving it credit for the same reason that Descartes did so for highly trained responses of animals; the dependence on a very particular training is characteristic of a habitual response and would raise suspicions as to how flexible the behavior really was.)

14 Could a Robot Be Creative— And Would We Know?

Margaret A. Boden

The notion that a robot, a mere android, might be creative is widely regarded as ridiculous. Computers are commonly believed to be utterly incapable of creativity. This opinion was first expressed over a hundred years ago by Ada Lovelace.

Lady Lovelace realized that Charles Babbage's "Analytical Engine"—in essence, a design for a digital computer—could in principle "compose elaborate and scientific pieces of music of any degree of complexity or extent." But she insisted that the creativity involved in any elaborate pieces of music emanating from the Analytical Engine would have to be credited not to the engine, but to the engineer. As she put it: "The Analytical Engine has no pretensions whatever to *originate* anything. It can do [only] *whatever we know how to order it* to perform."

If her remark means merely that a computer can do only what its program enables it to do, it is of course correct—and, for my argument, important. But if it is intended as a denial of any interesting link between computers and creativity, it is too quick and too simple. We must distinguish four different questions, which are often confused with each other in discussions of Lady Lovelace's claim.

The first question is whether computational concepts can help us understand how human creativity is possible. The second is whether computers (now or in the future) could ever do things which at least appear to be creative. The third is whether a computer could ever appear to recognize creativity—in poems written by human poets, for instance, or in its own novel ideas about science or art. And the fourth is whether computers themselves could ever *really* be creative (as opposed to merely producing apparently creative performance).

If we want to know whether robots could ever be creative, we must be clear about which of these questions we are asking. Certainly, we are asking the first three. Even though the first question specifically mentions *human* creativity, a definition of creativity would be required in order to answer it. That definition could then be applied to other creatures, including androids. As for the second and third questions, these are obviously crucial: we want to know whether, in practice, a robot could appear to be creative (and to recognize creativity).

The answers I shall propose to these three questions are, respectively, *Yes, definitely; Yes, up to a point;* and *Yes, necessarily (for any robot which appears to be creative).* This does not mean that creativity—whether in robots or in humans—is predictable, nor even that an original idea can be explained in every detail after it has appeared. But computational ideas can help us understand how human "intuition" works and how it might be paralleled in a robot.

It might appear that, for the purposes of android epistemology, the fourth question is the most important of all. It is important here, yes. But it is not a scientific query, as the other three are. It is in part an expression of a philosophical worry about meaning and in part a disguised request for a moral-political decision. I shall discuss this issue in a later section. First, let us consider whether a robot could at least appear to be creative.

The Definition of Creativity

Why does creativity seem so mysterious? To be sure, artists and scientists typically have their creative ideas unexpectedly, with little if any conscious awareness of how they arose. But the same applies to much of our vision, language, and common-sense reasoning. Computational psychology (and other forms of psychology too) offers many theories about unconscious processes.

Creativity is mysterious for another reason: the very concept is seemingly paradoxical. If we take seriously the dictionary definition of creation, "to bring into being or form out of nothing," creativity seems to be not only beyond any scientific understanding, but even impossible. It is hardly surprising, then, that some people have "explained" it in terms of divine inspiration, and many others in terms of some romantic intuition, or insight.

Neither of these popular views can be plausibly applied to robots, so if one of them is correct, then creative robots will forever stay within the pages of science fiction. But there is no reason to accept either. No reader of this volume, I assume, will warm to the first (although it was seriously asserted in a British "quality" newspaper only a few years ago, in a review of the play *Amadeus*). Even the second, to which some readers may assent, is unhelpful. From the psychological point of view, "intuition" is the name of a question, not of an answer. What we want to know is how intuition works. If we knew that, we might be able to say whether a robot could be intuitive, too.

People of a scientific cast of mind often try to define creativity in terms of "novel combinations of old ideas." In that case, the surprise caused by a creative idea is due to the improbability of the combination. In that case, too, statistical tests could be used to identify creativity (as some experimental psychologists have recommended).

Combination-theorists typically leave at least two things unsaid. The novel combinations have to be valuable in some way, because to call an idea creative is to say that it is not only new, but interesting. Combination-theorists usually omit value from their definition of creativity, perhaps because they (mistakenly) take it for granted that unusual combinations are always interesting. Also, they often fail to explain how it was possible for the novel combination to come about. They take it for granted, for instance, that we can associate similar ideas or recognize more distant analogies, without asking just how such feats are possible.

These cavils aside, what is wrong with the combination-theory? Many ideas—concepts, theories, paintings, poems, music—that we regard as creative are indeed based, at least in part, on unusual combinations. Moreover, provided that we can give a computational explanation of analogy, there seems no reason why a robot could not be creative. An android could combine and recombine its ideas as well as the rest of us, and come up with some valuable surprises in the process.

The inadequacy of the combination-theory lies in the fact that many creative ideas are surprising in a deeper way than this. They concern novel ideas which not only *did* not happen before, but which—in a sense that must be made clear—*could* not have happened before.

Before considering just what this seemingly paradoxical "could not" means, we must distinguish two senses of *creativity*. One is psychological (let us call it *P*-creativity), the other historical (*H*-creativity). An idea is *P*-creative if the individual person (or robot) in whose mind it arises could not have had it before; it does not matter how many times other people (or other androids) have already had the same idea. By contrast, an idea is

H-creative if it is *P*-creative *and* no-one else—whether person or robot—has ever had it before.

H-creativity is something about which we are often mistaken. Historians of science and art are constantly discovering cases where other people, even in other periods, have had an idea popularly attributed to some individual hero. Whether an idea survives, whether it is lost for a while and resurfaces later, and whether historians at a given point in time happen to know about it, depend on a wide variety of unrelated factors. These include fashion, rivalries, illness, trade patterns, economics, war, flood, and fire.

The same would doubtless be true of *H*-creative ideas generated by androids. Given the "not invented here" syndrome so common in AI, an *H*-creative robot in one laboratory might well be utterly ignored (as opposed to being noticed, but scorned) by the people, and the androids, in another. Moreover, if a robot could be creative without our recognizing it (a possibility discussed in a later section) then someone might not know about all the *H*-creative ideas originated by the androids in their own laboratory.

It follows that there can be no systematic explanation of *H*-creativity. Certainly, there can be no psychological or computational explanation of this historical category. But all *H*-creative ideas, by definition, are *P*-creative too. So an explanation of *P*-creativity would include *H*-creative ideas as well.

Before trying to explain *P*-creativity, however, we must define it intelligibly. What does it mean to say that an idea "could not" have arisen before? Unless we know that, we cannot make sense of *P*-creativity (or *H*-creativity either), for we cannot distinguish radical novelties from mere "first-time" newness.

Noam Chomsky, discussing what he called the "creativity" of natural language, reminded us that language is an unending source of novel (even *H*-novel) sentences. But these sentences are novelties which clearly *could* have happened before, being generated by the same rules that can generate other sentences in the language. Any native speaker, and any robot too, could produce novel sentences using the relevant grammar. In general, to come up with a new sentence is not to do something *P*-creative.

The "coulds" in the previous paragraph are computational "coulds." That is, they concern the set of structures described and/or produced by one and the same set of generative rules.

Sometimes, we want to know whether a particular structure could, in principle, be described by a specific schema, or set of abstract rules. Is 49 a square number? Is 3,591,471 a prime? Is this a sonnet, and is that a sonata?

Is that painting in the Impressionist style? Could that geometrical theorem be proved by Euclid's methods? Is that wordstring a sentence? Is a benzene-ring a molecular structure that is describable by early nineteenth-century chemistry (before Friedrich von Kekule's famous fireside daydream of 1865)? — To ask *whether an idea is creative or not* (as opposed to how it came about) is to ask this sort of question.

But whenever a particular structure is produced in practice, we can also ask what generative processes actually went on in the computational system concerned. — Did a human geometer (or an android) prove a particular theorem in this way, or in that? Was the sonata composed by following a textbook on sonata-form? Did Kekule rely on the then-familiar principles of chemistry to generate his seminal idea of the benzene-ring, and if not, how did he come up with it?—To ask how an idea (creative or otherwise) *actually arose*, is to ask this type of question.

We can now distinguish first-time novelty from radical originality. A merely novel idea is one which can be described and/or produced by the same set of generative rules as are other, familiar, ideas. A genuinely original, or creative, idea is one which cannot.

So *constraints*, far from being opposed to creativity, make creativity possible. To throw away all constraints would be to destroy the capacity for creative thinking. Random processes alone can produce only first-time curiosities, not radical surprises (although randomness can sometimes contribute to creativity [Boden 1991, ch. 6]).

To justify calling an idea creative, then, one must specify the particular set of generative principles—what one might call the conceptual space—with respect to which it is impossible. Accordingly, literary critics, musicologists, and historians of art and science have much to teach the psychologist—and the ambitious android-designer. But their knowledge of the relevant conceptual spaces must be made as explicit as possible, to clarify just which structures *can*, and which *cannot*, be generated within them.

It follows from all this that, with respect to the usual mental processing in the relevant domain (chemistry, poetry, music...), a creative idea is not just improbable, but impossible. How did it arise, then, if not by magic? And how can one impossible idea be more surprising, more creative, than another? It begins to look as though even humans cannot be creative, never mind robots. If creativity is not mere combination, what is it? How can creativity possibly happen?

Exploring and Transforming Conceptual Spaces

A generative system defines a certain range of possibilities: chess-moves, for example, or jazz-melodies. These structures are located in a conceptual space whose limits, contours, and pathways can be mapped in various ways. Mental maps, or representations, of conceptual spaces can be used (not necessarily consciously) to explore the spaces concerned.

When Charles Dickens described Scrooge as "a squeezing, wrenching, grasping, scraping, clutching, covetous old sinner," he was exploring the space of English grammar. He was reminding us (and himself) that the rules of grammar allow us to use any number of adjectives before a noun. Usually, we use only two or three; but we may, if we wish, use seven (or more). That possibility already existed, although its existence may not have been realized by us.

A much more interesting example of exploration can be found in the development of post-Renaissance Western music. This music is based on the generative system known as tonal harmony. Each piece of tonal music has a "home key," from which it starts, from which (at first) it did not stray, and in which it must finish. In this musical genre, reminders and reinforcements of the home key can be provided, for instance, by fragments of scales decorating the melody, or by chords and arpeggios within the accompaniment.

As the years passed by, after the introduction of this form of music-making, the range of possible home keys became increasingly well-defined. J. S. Bach's "Forty-Eight," for example, was a set of preludes and fugues specifically designed to explore—and clarify—the tonal range of the well-tempered keys. In other words, he was defining the basic dimensions of this conceptual space in a deliberate and systematic way.

Travelling along the path of the home key alone soon became insufficiently challenging. Modulations between keys then appeared, within the body of the composition. But all possible modulations did not appear at once. The range of harmonic relations implicit in the system of tonality became apparent only gradually.

At first, only a small number of modulations were tolerated—perhaps only one, followed by its "cancellation." Moreover, these early modulations took place only between keys that were very closely related in harmonic space. Over the years, however, the modulations became increasingly daring, and increasingly frequent. Harmonies that would have been unacceptable to the early musicians, who focussed on the most central or obvious dimensions of the conceptual space, became commonplace. By the late nineteenth century, there might be many modulations within a single bar, not one of which would have appeared in early tonal music.

Eventually, the very notion of the home key was undermined. With so many, and so daring, modulations within the piece, a "home key" could be identified not from the body of the piece but only from its beginning and end. Inevitably, someone (it happened to be Arnold Schoenberg) suggested that the convention of the home key be dropped altogether, since it no longer made sense in terms of constraining the composition as a whole. (Significantly, Schoenberg did not opt for a musical chaos. He suggested various new constraints to structure his music-making: using every note in the chromatic scale, for instance.)

Exploring a conceptual space is one thing. Transforming it is another. What is it to transform such a space? One example has just been mentioned: Schoenberg's dropping the home-key constraint to create the space of atonal music. *Dropping a constraint* is a general heuristic for transforming conceptual spaces.

Non-Euclidean geometry, for instance, resulted from dropping Euclid's fifth axiom, about parallel lines meeting at infinity. This transformation was made "playfully," as a prelude to exploring a geometrical space somewhat different from Euclid's. Only much later did it turn out to be useful in physics. (It is because so much creative thinking is playful, rather than goal-directed, that the term "conceptual space" is preferable to its cognate, "search-space.")

Another very general way of transforming conceptual spaces is to *consider the negative*: that is, to negate a constraint. One well-known instance concerns Kekule's discovery of the benzene-ring. He described it this way:

> I turned my chair to the fire and dozed. Again the atoms were gambolling before my eyes.... [My mental eye] could distinguish larger structures, of manifold conformation; long rows, sometimes more closely fitted together; all twining and twisting in snakelike motion. But look! What was that? One of the snakes had seized hold of its own tail, and the form whirled mockingly before my eyes. As if by a flash of lightning I awoke (Findlay 1965, p. 39).

This vision was the origin of his hunch that the benzene-molecule might be a ring, a hunch which turned out to be correct.

Prior to this experience, Kekule had assumed that all organic molecules are based on strings of carbon atoms (he himself had produced the string-theory some years earlier). But for benzene, the valencies of the constituent atoms did not fit.

We can understand how it was possible for him to pass from strings to rings, as plausible chemical structures, if we assume three things (for each of which there is independent psychological evidence). First, that snakes and molecules were already associated in his thinking. Second, that the topological distinction between open and closed curves was present in his mind. And third, that the "consider the negative" heuristic was present also. Taken together, these three factors could transform "string" into "ring."

A string-molecule is an open curve. If one considers the negative of an open curve, one gets a closed curve. Moreover, a snake biting its tail is *a closed curve which one had expected to be an open one.* For that reason, it is surprising, even arresting ("But look! What was that?"). Kekule might have had a similar reaction if he had been out on a country walk and happened to see a snake with its tail in its mouth. But there is no reason to think that he would have been stopped in his tracks by seeing a Victorian child's hoop. A hoop is a hoop, is a hoop: no topological surprises there.

Finally, the change from open curves to closed ones is a topological change, which by definition will alter neighbor-relations. And Kekule was an expert chemist, who knew very well that the behavior of a molecule depends not only on what the constituent atoms are, but also on how they are juxtaposed. A change in atomic neighbor-relations is very likely to have some chemical significance. So it is understandable that he had a hunch that this tail-biting snake-molecule might contain the answer to his problem.

Hunches are common in human thinking (mathematicians often describe them in terms of an as-yet-unproven "certainty"). An adequate theory of creativity must be able to explain hunches. It must show how it is possible for someone to feel (often, correctly) that a new idea is promising *even before* they can say just what its promise is. The example of Kekule suggests that a hunch is grounded in appreciation of the structure of the space concerned and some notion of how the new idea might fit into it.

A creative robot would benefit from having hunches, as people do. Without them, it would waste a lot of time in following up new ideas that "anyone could have seen" would lead to a dead-end. Some of its hunches, some of its intuitions, would doubtless turn out to be mistaken (as some of ours do, too). But that is not to say that it would be better off without them.

Robots with hunches … could there actually be such things?

Could a Robot Be Creative?

A robot could be creative (or rather, it could at least *appear* to be creative) if the ideas conveyed metaphorically in the last section could be expressed in terms of functioning computer systems. In other words, conceptual spaces would have to be precisely identified, and ways (some general, some domain-specific) of exploring and changing them would have to be explicitly defined. In addition, the android would need a computational model of analogical thinking, since analogy plays a large part in "combinatorial" creativity and sometimes contributes to "impossibilistic" creativity, too (as in the example of Kekule, described above).

Some AI-work has already been done to these ends. In some cases, a conceptual space has been effectively mapped without any intention to model creativity, as such. Models specifically focussed on creativity are still relatively uncommon, and in almost all cases deal with space-exploration rather than space-transformation. As for analogy, we shall see that some work in this area suggests that a creative robot could emerge only after a fundamental change in current AI-methodology.

Computational work on musical perception, for example, has helped to advance the theory of harmony as well as to show how listeners manage to find their way around the space of tonal harmony (Longuet-Higgins 1987). This account of the musical interpretation of key, modulation, and metre has been successfully applied to compositions by a very wide range of composers, from baroque to romantic. If a robot were to enjoy Elgar, or even recognize a waltz as being in 3/4 tempo, beating time to it almost as soon as it has begun (as we can), it would have to inhabit this musical space, as we do. (Whether it might also inhabit others, which we cannot enter, is discussed in the next section.)

Closely related work on jazz has shown that very simple computational processes, making only minimal demands on short-term memory, can generate acceptable (and unpredictable) improvisations. By contrast, the generation of the underlying chord-sequence requires a much more powerful grammar (so cannot be done on the fly by human musicians) (Johnson-Laird 1988, 1989). The rules for improvisation take into account developing melodic contours, harmonizing the melody with the accompaniment, playing (and passing between) the chords schematically described in the underlying chord-sequence, and keeping the correct metre and tempo.

In both these cases (only one of which was intended as a study of creativity), musical "intuition" has been, in part, anatomized. A robot jazz-musician might therefore exist one day, capable of improvising *Tea for Two* in a pleasing manner. In both cases, too, detailed psychological and musicological questions have arisen as a result of specific aspects of the model. A heuristic which is helpful in interpreting Bach-cantatas, for example, may or may not be helpful in dealing with other music by Bach, or music by Vivaldi or Brahms.

Recent (unpublished) work by Christopher Longuet-Higgins has begun to anatomize the expressive space which characterizes, say, a waltz by Frédéric Chopin. The human pianist interprets terms in the score such as *legato, staccato, piano, forte, sforzando, crescendo, diminuendo, rallentando, accelerando, ritenuto,* and *rubato.* But how? Only if we can express this musical sensibility precisely could a robot play Chopin expressively. Longuet-Higgins has provided rules for all these expressive terms (and for the two pedals as well), and has come up with some counterintuitive results. He shows that the conceptual space of a crescendo, for instance, is more complex than one might think. A constant increase in the loudness of the relevant passage (the program must work out what is "the relevant passage") does not sound like a crescendo, but like someone turning up the volume-knob on a radio. Instead, he uses a nonlinear rule, based on the velocity of a ball rolling on a hill.

Since this program plays Chopin's *Minute Waltz* acceptably (to human ears), one could say that there already exists a robot which can play Chopin. Whether it can cope equally well with all of Chopin's waltzes, or with even one of his mazurkas, is a different—and very interesting—question. If one wants a robot-pianist with actual fingers, a twenty-first century version of Vaucanson's flute-player, then subtle sensori-motor skills would have to come into play. But the current program has, to some degree, the appreciation of *musical* space that is required to distinguish "mechanical" from "expressive" performance of this Chopin composition.

A conceptual space of a very different sort has been modeled by Harold Cohen's AARON (McCorduck 1991). This program, in one of its incarnations, generates aesthetically acceptable line-drawings of human acrobats. The drawings are individually unpredictable, but all lie within the preassigned genre. This genre is defined, in part, by AARON's "body grammar," which specifies not only the anatomy of the human body (two arms, two legs), but also how the various body parts appear from different points of view or in different bodily attitudes.

The program can draw acrobats with only one arm visible (because of occlusion), but it cannot draw one-armed acrobats. Its model of the human body does not allow for the possibility of there being one-armed people. They are, one might say, unimaginable. If, as a matter of fact, the program has never produced a picture showing an acrobat's right wrist occluding another acrobat's left eye, that is a mere accident of its processing history: it *could* have done so at any time. But the fact that it has never drawn a one-armed acrobat has a deeper explanation: such drawings are, in a clear sense, *impossible.*

If Cohen's program were capable of "dropping" one of the limbs (as a geometer may drop Euclid's fifth axiom, or Schoenberg the notion of the home-key), it could then draw one-armed, or one-legged, figures. A host of previously unimaginable possibilities, only a subset of which might ever be actualized, would have sprung into existence at the very moment of dropping the constraint that there must be (say) a left arm.

A superficially similar, but fundamentally more powerful, transformation might be effected if the numeral "2" had been used in the program to denote the number of arms. For "2," being a variable, might be replaced by "1" or even "7." A general-purpose tweaking-transformational heuristic—whether in a human mind or a robot's—might look out for numerals and try substituting varying values. Kekule's chemical successors employed such a heuristic when they asked whether any ring-molecules could have fewer than six atoms in the ring. (They also treated carbon as a variable—as a particular instance of the class of elements—when they asked whether molecular rings might include nitrogen or phosphorus atoms.) A program which (today) drew one-armed acrobats for the first time by employing a "vary-the-variable" heuristic *could* (tomorrow) be in a position to draw seven-legged acrobats as well. A program which merely "dropped the left arm" *could not.*

At present, only Cohen can change the constraints built into the program, thus enabling it to draw pictures of a type which it could not have drawn before. But some programs, perhaps including some yet to be written by Cohen, might do so for themselves.

To be able to transform its style, a program would need (among other things) a meta-representation of the lower-level constraints it uses. For the creative potential of a self-transforming system depends on how it represents its current skills (drawing "a left arm and a right arm" or drawing "2 arms") and on what heuristics are available to modify those representations and thereby enlarge its skills. We have already seen that if Cohen's program had an explicit representation of the fact that it normally draws four-limbed people, and if it were given very general "transformation heuristics" (like "drop a constraint," "consider the negative," or "vary the variable"), it might sometimes omit, or add, one or more limbs.

Evidence from developmental psychology suggests that this sort of explicit representation of a lower-level drawing skill is required if a young child is to be able to draw a one-armed man, or a seven-legged dog (Karmiloff-Smith 1990). Comparable evidence has been found with regard to other skills, such as language and piano-playing; here too, imaginative flexibility requires the development of generative systems that explicitly represent lower-level systems (Karmiloff-Smith 1986).

The implication is that a creative robot, capable of transforming its conceptual spaces as well as exploring them, would need such many-levelled representations of its own conceptual spaces. The proverbial all-singing, all-dancing robot, for instance, would need high-level representations of its verbal, musical, and motor skills. At present, we have only the sketchiest idea of how such high-level representations might be spontaneously developed (as opposed to being specifically provided by a programmer) (Clark and Karmiloff-Smith, in press).

A few existing computer models of creativity can transform their own spaces to some extent. Douglas Lenat's AM and EURISKO are well-known examples (Lenat 1983). The "Automatic Mathematician" does not produce proofs, nor does it solve mathematical problems. Rather, it generates and explores mathematical ideas, coming up with new concepts and hypotheses to think about. Its exploratory heuristics can examine, combine, and transform its concepts in many ways, some general and some domain-specific. One, for example, can generate the *inverse* of a function (this is a mathematical version of "consider the negative").

At the end of the last section we asked whether robots could have hunches. Well, AM does: some of its heuristics suggest which sorts of concepts are likely to be the most interesting, and AM concentrates on exploring them accordingly. AM finds it interesting, for instance, that the union of two sets has a simply expressible property that is not possessed by either of them (an instance of the notion that *emergent* properties, in general, are interesting).

AM's hunches, like human hunches, are sometimes wrong. Nevertheless, it has come up with some powerful mathematical notions, including Goldbach's conjecture and an *H*-novel theorem concerning maximally-divisible numbers. In short, AM appears to be significantly *P*-creative, and slightly *H*-creative too. However, critics have suggested that some heuristics were specifically included to make certain mathematical discoveries possible and that the use of LISP provided AM with some mathematically relevant structures "for free" (Lenat and Brown 1984; Ritchie and Hanna 1984). The precise extent of AM's creativity, then, is unclear. But we do have a sense of what questions we should ask in order to judge.

Because EURISKO, unlike AM, has heuristics for changing heuristics, it can explore and transform not only its stock of concepts but its own processing-style. For example, one heuristic asks whether a rule has ever led to any interesting result. If it has not (given that it has been used several times), it will be less often used in future. If the rule has occasionally been helpful, though usually worthless, it may be specialized in one of several different ways. (Because it is sometimes useful and sometimes not, the specializing-heuristic can be applied recursively.) Other heuristics work by generalizing rules in various ways or by creating new rules by analogy with old ones.

With the help of domain-specific heuristics to complement these general ones, EURISKO has generated *H*-novel ideas concerning genetic engineering and VLSI-design. Some of its suggestions have even been granted a US patent (the US patent-law insists that the new idea must not be "obvious to a person skilled in the art"). The heuristic principles embodied in EURISKO have nothing specifically to do with science. They could be applied to artistic spaces too. So some future acrobat-drawing program, for example, might be able to transform its graphic style by using similar methods.

A different type of self-transforming program is seen in systems using genetic algorithms (Holland, Holyoak, Nisbett, and Thagard 1986). As the name suggests, these heuristics are inspired by the genetic mutations underlying biological evolution. For example, two chromosomes may swap their left-hand sides, or their midsections (the point at which they break is largely due to chance). Repeated mutations, over many generations, result in unexpected combinations of genes drawn from many different sources. GA-programs produce novel structures by similar sorts of (partly random) transformation.

In general, the usefulness of the new structures is increased if the swapped sections are coherent mini-sequences (like the alternative bars allowed at every bar-line in eighteenth-century "dice-music"). However, identifying the "coherent mini-sequences" is not a trivial matter. For one thing, they do not function in isolation: both genes and ideas express their influence by acting in concert with many others. Moreover, coherent mini-sequences are not always *sequences:* coadapted genes tend to occur on the same chromosome but may be scattered over various points within it; similarly, potentially related ideas are not always located close to each other in conceptual space. Finally, a single unit may enter more than one group: a gene can be part of different coadaptive groups, and an idea may be relevant to several kinds of problems.

GA-programs help to explain how plausible combinations of far-distant units can nevertheless happen. They can identify the useful parts of individual rules and the significant interactions between rule-parts, even though a given part may occur within several rules and even though a "part" need not be a sequence of juxtaposed units (it may be two sets of three units, separated by an indefinite number of unspecified units). Rules are "selected" by assigning a strength to each one according to its success, and gradually dropping the weaker rules out of the system. Over time, the most useful rules are identified even though they act in concert with many others—including some that are useless, or even counter-productive. In this way, a GA-system may transform an initial set of randomly generated rules into a rule-set that solves the relevant problem even better than human experts do.

Creative robots, might rely (in part) on combinatorial methods like these. Indeed, psychologists favoring the combination-theory (see the second section) might posit processes akin to GA-mechanisms within human minds. But in explaining many "creative" combinations, they would need to appeal also to analogy. A creative robot would need to be able to identify analogies, for seeing a new analogy is often important in artistic and scientific creativity. To close this section, then, let us consider Douglas Hofstadter's "Copycat" model of analogical thinking (Chalmers, French, and Hofstadter 1991; Hofstadter and Mitchell 1991; Hofstadter, Mitchell, and French 1987; Mitchell 1990).

Hofstadter reminds us that seeing a new analogy is often much the same as perceiving something in a new way. It is hard to say where perception ends and analogizing begins, since perception is itself informed by high-level concepts. The Copycat project takes these psychological facts seriously. The program allows for the generation of many different analogies, where contextually appropriate comparisons are favored over inappropriate ones. It does not rely on ready-made, fixed representations, but constructs its own representations in a context-sensitive way.

Copycat's "perceptual" representations of the input-patterns are built up dialectically, each step being influenced by (and also influencing) the type of analogical mapping which the current context seems to require. A part-built interpretation that seems to be mapping well onto the nascent analogy is maintained and developed further. A part-built representation that seems to be heading for a dead end is abandoned, and an alternative one started which exploits different aspects of the target-concept.

The domain actually explored by Copycat is a highly idealized one, namely, alphabetic letter-strings. But the computational principles involved are relevant to analogies in any domain. In other words, the alphabet is here being used as a psychological equivalent of inclined planes in physics.

Copycat considers letter-strings such as *ppqqrrss*, which it can liken to strings such as *mmnnoopp*, *tttuuuvvvxxx*, and *abcd*. Its self-constructed "perceptual" representations describe strings in terms of descriptors like leftmost, rightmost, middle, same, group, alphabetic successor, and alphabetic predecessor. It is a parallel-processing system, in that various types of descriptors compete simultaneously to build the overall description.

The system's sense of analogy in any particular case is expressed by its producing a pair of letter-strings which it judges to be like some pair provided to it as input. If, for instance, it is told that the string *pqr* changes into *stu* and is then asked what the string *def* will change into, it will probably (though not necessarily) produce the string *ghi*. If, on this occasion, it is not looking for the most obvious analogy but for a somewhat more creative one, it may produce *gghhii* instead.

The mapping functions used by Copycat at a particular point in time depend on the representation that has already been built up. Looking for *successors* or for *repetitions*, for instance, will be differentially encouraged according to the current context. So the two letters *m* in the string *ffmmtt* will be mapped as a sameness-pair, whereas in the string *abcefgklmmno* they will be mapped as parts of two different successor-triples: *klm* and *mno*.

Even in the highly idealized domain of alphabetic letter-strings, interesting problems arise. Suppose, for instance, that Copycat is told that *abc* changes into *abd*, and it must now decide what *xyz* changes into. Its initial description of the input-pair, couched in terms of alphabetic successors, has to be destroyed when it comes across *z* —which has no successor. Different descriptors then compete to represent the input-strings, and the final output depends partly on which descriptors are chosen. On different occasions, Copycat comes up with *xyd* and *wyz*. Each of these is a consequence of different internal representations and mapping functions. The line of thought, and of redescription, which led to *wyz*, for instance, involved moving backwards through the alphabet instead of forwards, and so seeing the head of the input-string as the place where some substitution should take place, instead of the tail. Notice that the initial description in this case is not merely adapted, but destroyed. Hofstadter compares this example with conceptual revolutions in science: the initial interpretation is discarded, and a fundamentally different interpretation is substituted for it.

This constructive process can be telescoped, if the relevant descriptions are provided beforehand. In humans, culturally based telescoping of this sort explains why a schoolchild can quickly understand, perhaps even discover, an analogy which took the relevant *H*-creative thinker many months, or years, to grasp. The particular analogy, we assume, is new to the child. But its general type is familiar. The notion that simple linear equations, for example, capture many properties of the physical world may already be well established in the pupil's mind. It is hardly surprising, then, if this analogical mapping mechanism can be activated at the drop of the teacher's chalk.

As Hofstadter points out, most AI-models of analogy (and of problem-solving) put the computer in the place of the schoolchild. That is, the relevant representations and mapping rules are provided ready-made to the program. It is the programmer who has done the work of sifting and selecting the "relevant" points from the profuse conceptual apparatus within his mind. Hofstadter criticizes current AI-models of scientific discovery, such as BACON and its computational cousins (Langley, Simon, Bradshaw, and Zytkow 1987), on the same grounds. Copycat, preliminary though it is, shows that a design for a creative robot need not take relevance for granted in this way.

—And Would We Know?

Suppose there were creative robots, exploring and transforming their conceptual spaces in what they regarded as valuable ways. Would we necessarily know? That is, would a creative robot always appear, to us, to be creative?

To recognize a creative idea requires one to understand the relevant conceptual space and to locate the new structure with reference to it. One must be able to distinguish explorations of various types and transformations of various depths. It is not necessary—though it is helpful—to be able to express these insights explicitly. In many cases of human creativity, we can say very little, if anything, about why we regard the new idea as creative (as opposed to merely new).

Nor is it always necessary—though, again, it is helpful—to distinguish the evaluative from the interpretative aspect of one's response. In the arts, and in pure mathematics, we tend to value exploration and transformation for their own sake. When we are faced by a scientific or a practical problem, in which the new idea has to fit the facts in some way, we tend to distinguish the originality of the idea from its value. But in both arts and sciences, we can consider a certain way of thinking and then ask whether the new idea is valuable from that standpoint. So a post-Impressionist painter can distinguish original from run-of-the-mill Impressionist paintings, and a non-Catholic can appreciate the theological ingenuity of the form of birth-control known as Vatican roulette.

It follows that to recognize the creativity of a creative robot we would need at least to share its conceptual spaces, if not its values too. (Values that were highly perverse, from our point of view, might prevent us from recognizing the goal-structure of the robot's thinking and so hinder us in assessing its "conceptual" creativity.)

If the robot's program was specifically built into it by us, we would in general have a better chance of understanding its novel ideas. But even so, we might not recognize all of its creative moments.

We might be temporarily "trapped" within certain thought-structures and so fail to understand the android's potentially intelligible ideas. (Gestalt psychologists have described "functional fixedness," wherein someone fails to recognize something he or she is perfectly capable of recognizing: for example, that a pair of pliers could be used as a pendulum-bob.) Or we might be defeated by the speed and storage available to the robot. We saw in the last section that the computational complexity of jazz-improvisation is limited by the size of human short-term memory. A robot musician could be equipped with a larger STM and could be given musical rules of greater computational complexity accordingly. Not only could it (unlike us) compose new chord sequences on the fly, but it could produce improvisations which we could neither mimic nor even fully appreciate.

Moreover, just how specific is a program "specifically built into it by us"? An android whose program allowed for quasi-random transformations (like those effected by genetic algorithms) might sometimes produce ideas which we would be bound to value, because they solved a class of problems in which we are interested, but which we could not understand.

If creative robots were willing and able to explain to us how their novel ideas related to the pre-existing conceptual spaces, that would help. In that case, they would be like the historian of art or science (or the anthropologist) who links unfamiliar ways of thinking. But being willing and being able are different things. It is not obvious that an android would have very much greater access to its own thought processes than we do. To be sure, its greater speed and storage capacity would make some difference. But if it were to function in real time, even these might not suffice to enable it to reflect on all its internal processes. In short, its introspection might be limited for much the same reasons as ours is. If so, it could not always initiate us (or itself) into the mysteries of its own creativity.

Finally, what of the effects of embodiment? To the extent that our understanding is grounded in our embodiment, androids might well share some understanding with us. Language, for example, has many characteristics arguably due to the fact that we are bodily creatures moving face-forward in a material world (so the Archangel Gabriel, as a purely immaterial being, simply *could not* have conversed with Mary in her native Aramaic [Boden 1981]). Countless linguistic expressions are metaphors, living or dead, grounded in our bodily experience. Conceptual "spaces," and their "exploration" and "mapping," are obvious examples. Even "transformation" recalls, for instance, the potter's clay. Indeed, some students of language and literature have argued that our oppositional conceptual schemes, and the nature of our rhetoric and argument, are fundamentally shaped by the bilateral symmetry of our bodies (Turner 1991).

If these admittedly speculative hypotheses are sound, a robot shaped like an amoeba or a jellyfish could be expected to have a conceptual architecture significantly unlike ours. A genuine android, on the other hand *(sic)*, might structure its concepts in a more humanlike way, largely as a result of its bilateral symmetry, assuming, of course, that the robot's conceptual architecture developed spontaneously along with its sensori-motor skills, as opposed to being built in by a human roboticist. Perhaps a human roboticist could build all manner of oppositional thought-structures into a jellyfish-robot, which (if this argument is correct) could not be expected to develop them "naturally" for itself.

The upshot is that some instances of creativity in robots might remain unknown to us. Wittgenstein said: "If a lion could speak, we would not understand it." A man-made lion, or an android, could be much more intelligible. But it need not be.

Yes, But Could a Robot REALLY Be Creative?

Some philosophers would be content to admit everything I have said so far but would nevertheless insist that a robot could not *really* be creative. Even if an android's performance rivaled Ludwig van Beethoven, Isaac Newton, and William Shakespeare all rolled into one, it would be no more than apparently creative. As remarked in the first section, this rejection of the very idea of truly creative robots depends mainly upon two worries: one about the ascription of intentionality, and the other about whether we ought to give androids a place in our society.

The first worry has been eloquently, and influentially, posed by John Searle (1980, 1990). His "Chinese room" argument is too well-known in AI circles to need recounting here. It was developed with GOFAI-robots in mind, androids controlled in the Good Old-Fashioned AI-way. But it would apply also to situated robots insofar as their reactions are programmed, not hardwired.

Very briefly (for a fuller account, see Boden 1988, ch. 8), my rebuttal focuses on Searle's main premise, that computer programs are "all syntax and no semantics."

It is this premise which enables Searle to reject the "Robot Reply," because it implies that even a robot enjoying rich causal interactions with its environment could not *really* enjoy them. The robot's visible movements might seem highly significant to us, but not to the robot itself; and its internal computations would be as empty of meaning to it as those of any VDU-bound computer. As for creativity, a robot might improvise jazz, or play Chopin waltzes, so as to make tears of joy come into our eyes—but, unlike human performers, it would understand nothing of these musical worlds. It does not matter how impressive its appearance of creativity is: there is no "Android Answer." If Searle's premise is correct, no android could really be creative.

Searle regards his premise as intuitively obvious (as do some champions of computational psychology, e.g., Fodor 1980 and Stich 1983). And so it is, if one considers a program merely as an abstract mathematical structure, or uninterpreted logical calculus. But one may also consider a program in terms of its ability, when implemented in a computer, to cause certain things to happen inside it. (Indeed, Brian Smith has recommended that computer scientists interested in the semantics of programming languages should do so [Smith 1982].) On that view of what a program is, the premise is false.

A programmed instruction (implemented in a computer) is analogous to Searle-in-the-room's understanding of English, not of Chinese. A word in a language one understands (one for which the relevant causal connections have been set up) causes certain processes to go on in one's head, some of which may result in observable behavior. In a robot, likewise, input-peripherals feed into the internal computations, which lead eventually to changes in the output-peripherals. In between, the program causes a host of things to happen inside the system itself. At the level of the machine code, the effect of the program on the computer is direct, the machine being engineered so that a given instruction causes a unique operation.

A programmed instruction, then, is not merely a formal rule. Its essential function (when implemented in the relevant hardware) is to make something happen. This fact is relevant if intentionality can be naturalistically analyzed in terms of causal relations.

Allen Newell's (1980) definitions of "designation" and "interpretation" in physical symbol systems exemplify such an analysis: "An expression designates an object if, given the expression, the system can either affect the object itself or behave in ways depending on the object; and the system can interpret an expression if the expression designates a process and if, given the expression, the system can carry out the process." Given this account of intentionality, computer programs are not "all syntax and no semantics." On the contrary, their inherent causal powers give them a toehold in semantics.

Admittedly, no existing "creative" program can really understand the domain it explores. Too many of the relevant causal connections are missing. AARON, for instance, does not really understand that humans have two arms and two legs. One might say that it has the beginnings of an understanding of what it is to compare two symbols (in the program), to interrupt a line, to draw symmetrically, and perhaps even to draw one thing occluded by another. However, it cannot recognize symmetry in other androids' drawings, and it has no real sense of the third dimension.

A robot equipped with low-level vision would have some of the many relevant causal connections which AARON lacks. A fully-fledged android would have all of them (as well as ways of transforming its own conceptual spaces). Having rejected Searle's crucial premise and accepted the causal analysis of intentionality assumed so far, we would therefore be unreasonable to deny that androids are really creative.

Some naturalistic analyses of intentionality, however, would provide grounds for refusing to ascribe real creativity to androids. These are biologically based analyses, which insist that the causal connections involved be of a certain (teleological) type and be developed within a certain (evolutionary) context.

Ruth Millikan (1984, 1989), for instance, argues that intentional concepts have to be analyzed in a historical-teleological way. A bodily organ or psychological process has a "proper function" in "normal conditions," where these technical terms are to be teleologically understood. That is, they do not refer to the body's functioning (properly) without any damaged parts, nor to (normal) statistically average environmental conditions. Rather, they refer to behavior, whether internal or external, which in the relevant ecological niche results (not always, but often enough) in the survival of the creature concerned and in the satisfaction of its various goals. Moreover, the organs and processes concerned must have been developed, at base, by biological evolution (this allows for a process to have a history of individual learning, in those species capable of learning). The historical and teleological criteria are intimately linked, for it is the evolutionary context which enables us to identify the proper functions, normal conditions, and goals.

Because of its historical dimension, this philosophical account of intentionality excludes all androids—both the GOFAI-type and fully-hardwired situated robots. What I referred to above as the "essential function" of a computer program, or of programs in general, is not a "proper function" in Millikan's sense, because it was designed by computer scientists. Likewise, the function of a circuit in a situated robot was determined by the engineer who built it. Notice that this biological analysis of intentionality does not insist (as Searle does) on any particular material stuff, such as neuroprotein. But its evolutionary aspect implies that no android (no artificial, man-made creature) could *really* be creative.

I have argued elsewhere for a similar view, in distinguishing "extrinsic" from "intrinsic" teleology (Boden 1972). A robot's goals and purposes are not intrinsic to it but are ultimately explicable in terms of human purposes. Certainly, an android could generate specific goals that had not been foreseen by, and might not even be acceptable to, any human being. However, the fact that a robot—even one descended from a long line of self-modifying robots—has *any goals at all* can ultimately be explained by (historical) reference to the purposes of some other creature. This is not the case for humans. Someone's goal of becoming the President of the USA may be explained by a specific ambition on the part of some other purposive being (consider Jack and Joseph Kennedy). But that a person has any purposes at all cannot, barring theological "explanations," be explained in this way.

People have purposes *intrinsically*, because the impersonal process of evolution has resulted in goal-seeking human organisms. Since psychological vocabulary in general assumes the possession of intrinsic purposes, robots cannot be described as creative in the full sense of the word.

Word-senses change, however. If androids existed, we could hardly avoid using a rich intentional vocabulary—not just "instruction," "infer," and "search"—to describe them. Would we eventually allow (what we do not allow today) that systems with extrinsic purposes can merit psychological descriptions *without scare quotes*? (If so, an apparently creative robot would be regarded as *really* creative.) This question raises the moral-political worry mentioned above, for to remove all the scare quotes would be to admit androids into our moral universe. People who preferred not to do so would therefore insist on keeping the scare quotes.

Suppose that an apparently creative robot, equipped with a self-transforming version of the line-drawing program described previously, were to draw acrobats with "triangular" calves and thighs. Suppose also that no human artist had drawn such things before. Many art critics might refuse to accept the robot's drawings as aesthetically valuable. They could not deny the analogy between limb parts and wedges—but they would dismiss it as uninteresting, even ugly. However, such things *have* been drawn before, and many people appreciate Pablo Picasso's "triangular" limbs. Why this difference in attitude?

The difference lies in the view that it is one thing to allow a human artist to challenge our perceptions and aesthetic conventions, but quite another to tolerate such impertinence from a robot. To be impertinent is to say something (perhaps something both true and relevant) which one has no right to say. At a certain level of generality, every person has a right to be heard, to try to persuade others to share his or her view. Each of us has this right by virtue of being a member of the human community. But robots are not natural members of the human community, as members of *homo sapiens* are.

Of course, inherited membership is only one way of entering a community: someone can be invited to join. Androids would have some claim to honorary membership of the human community, for they could do many humanlike things. But a decision on our part to regard robots as *really* creative would have far-ranging social implications. It would mean that, up to a point, we should consider their interests—much as we consider the interests of animals. For interests, *real* interests, they would be assumed to have. Suppose a robot-artist were to ask you to find it a thicker pen, so that it could experiment with its new way of cross-hatching. If you had accepted it as *really* creative, you would be obliged, within reason, to interrupt what you were doing in order to help it. In other words, you would be obliged to put its interests above (some of) your own.

The decision to remove all scare quotes, when describing a robot as creative (or intelligent), carries significant moral overtones. So, like moral decisions in general, it cannot be forced upon us by the facts alone. No matter how impressive future androids may be, we could (without self-contradiction) insist on retaining all the moral responsibility, and the epistemological authority, too. In that case, quasi-creative robots might be widely used, much as pocket-calculators are today, with the full range of psychological vocabulary being employed in describing them. But we would shoulder the entire moral and epistemological responsibility for following their "hunches," or trusting their "insights."

Whether people actually would react to androids in this grudging way is an empirical question. The answer might depend on mere superficialities. Our moral attitudes and general sympathies are much influenced by biologically based factors, including what the other person—or quasi-person—looks like, sounds like, and feels like. Fur or slime, cuddliness or spikiness, naturally elicit very different responses. If androids were encased in fur, given attractive voices, and made to look like teddy-bears, we might be more morally accepting of them than we otherwise would be (Frude 1983). If they were made of organic materials (perhaps involving connectionist networks constructed out of real neurones), our moral responses might be even more tolerant.

It is impossible to know, now, how we would decide to treat androids, should they ever exist. But the crucial point is that this issue would involve a moral decision, in addition to recognition of the scientific facts. However creative a robot appeared to be, however impressively original its performance, we might nevertheless refuse—on moral grounds—to call it really creative.

In sum: there is no scientific reason why a robot should not be creative. That is, a robot could produce apparently creative performance, by means of the exploration and transformation of its conceptual spaces. Insofar as we shared the robot's conceptual spaces, we would be equipped to know that it was (apparently) creative. Whether, given all this, a robot could ever *really* be creative is not a question for science.

Acknowledgements

This chapter first appeared as "Could a Robot be Creative—and Would We Know" in *Android Epistemology*, edited by Clark Glymour, Kenneth M. Ford, and Patrick J. Hayes (Menlo Park, CA: AAAI/ The MIT Press, 1995).

15 Only Androids Can Be Ethical

Joseph Emile Nadeau

Computer science has provided new angles for theories of knowledge and decision making, new ideas and constraints exploited in computational learning theory, artificial intelligence, strategic studies and elsewhere, even very occasionally in philosophy. Thinking about how a program could learn and make decisions, and programming computers to do so, has provided a world of new theories, possibilities, and results, including results of great practical value. Perhaps computer science might do the same for ethics, a subject that could perhaps benefit from an external jolt or two. So my questions: How would a computer, an android, have to be constituted, and what would it have to do (internally or externally) to be *culpable*? What would an android have to do not merely to be a cause of some event, but *responsible* for it? How could one make a robot that behaves ethically? Reflecting on these questions, I have come to a conclusion of which, however implausible it may seem on first encounter, I hope to leave the reader convinced: not only could an android be responsible and culpable, but only an android could be

The notion of responsibility is inextricably linked with the notions of capacity and free will. Inside a building on fire, no one is responsible for failing to run through a brick wall to create an escape for others; and no one is responsible for betraying a secret under the influence of thiopental sodium. The linkage of free will and responsibility is the basis of an objection to the very idea of android responsibility: culpability and responsibility require that actions be done from a free will, that is, a will that is not constrained by natural causes. That was René Descartes's requirement for free will, and it is but one example of a traditional thread in Christian metaphysics. Even unphilosophical people divide over whether humans have a will that is free in the Cartesian sense—very roughly, so well as I understand its politics, in the United States Republicans think so and Democrats think not; in Europe, the Italians think so and the Swedes think not.

Twentieth century secular philosophers believe in responsibility, but not in any human process that is irreducible to physics and chemistry. They put Cartesian free will in the company of the luminiferous aether, phlogiston, and the tooth fairy. They have therefore devoted great efforts to reconceiving the notions of free will and responsibility in such a way that the linkage between the ideas is kept but is consistent with a thoroughgoing scientific naturalism. Eminent American philosophers, Harry Frankfurt and Susan Wolf, for example, propose that a free action is one done from reasons, and through an appropriate reasoning process. (I do not popularize: I have found that the essence of essays and books of analytic philosophy can often be put in a sentence.) Following the influential work of Donald Davidson, they have no difficulty with the thought that reasons are often causes. Cognitive psychologists think this rather naïve, and claim that human reasons are usually or often (psychologists are not strong on quantifiers) ex post facto confabulations. We are creatures of mental fog, of habit and passion, and only rarely and dimly creatures of reason.

The evidence for the psychologists' claims of our severe cognitive limitations continues to grow, but it is in some sense unnecessary, and the psychologists take undue credit for the discovery. Assuming that whatever humans do is subordinate to the limits of Alan Turing computability, it is immediate from Turing's famous Entscheidungsproblem theorem that humans cannot reason logically except in limited cases, and almost equally immediate that they cannot reason with coherent probabilities (unless they are infinitely dogmatic). The only empirical question concerns the bounds on human rationality, and according to the psychologists, however great the human capacity for vision, speech and classification, the bounds of human reason are very low indeed. Cynical observers of the human condition, Americans such as Samuel L. Clemens (Mark Twain) and H. L. Mencken, and too many Europeans to mention, would need no psychological experiments for that conclusion.

The psychologists put the philosophers in what Americans of my generation called a "pickle," and we less imaginative Swiss call a "dilemma:" If we are to be scientific naturalists, then we must conclude that Cartesian free will is a fantasy, and the only tenable conception of free action is action done from a process of reasoning, caused by reasons. But if we are to be scientific naturalists, we must take quite as seriously the evidence of psychology as we do that of chemistry and conclude that humans do not, at least not often, act from reasons. Humans, therefore, are not responsible. Benedict De Spinoza, who held reason to be the ultimate virtue, titled his pseudo Euclidean metaphysical theology *The Ethics,* and the title now rings with irony: Whatever in ethics provides the foundation for coming under the purview of moral assessment is something beyond our capacity. What of androids?

If the psychologists are correct, the latter-day philosophers provide an opening to android free will and responsibility, for an android will have a program that causes its behavior, and steps and data structures in the execution of such a program can have significance; they can, indeed, be reasons for the android's behavior. If one understood the trace of the program, one would understand the android's reasons, and if the android had access to the trace, it would know its own reasons. Androids could no more escape Turing's theorem than we can, but the bounds for android reasoning, and on their capacity to connect reasons with actions, could be far higher than ours. Androids could have free will in the philosopher's sense, and so be responsible and culpable.

The opening for android freedom of the will engages issues of android architecture. The scope of possible computational designs is a space little explored. We know cellular automata, Turing machines, theorem provers, neural nets, random access machines, and so forth, but we do not know much. Even with so little knowledge, there are firm opinions, both about how humans work and about how androids might be designed. The contemporary divide seems to be between those who believe the human cognitive architecture, and the appropriate design for androids, is a theorem prover; those who believe the appropriate and human design is a neural network of some kind; those who claim it is both a hybrid of neural networks and theorem provers; and those unfortunates who claim it is something else altogether, a "dynamical system." Only the first two alternatives need concern us. Whatever neural networks and theorem provers can do, some hybrid of them can do. We may dispense with the last alternative, advocated principally by psychologists and philosophers who confuse metaphor with mathematics, think Hund's rules are about dogs and that l'Hopital must have been connected with hospitals. Anyone who thinks that what a computer does, or an automobile for that matter, is best understood through a system of nonlinear equations is best left, quite literally, to their own devices. There are special cases, for example those who think we reason with Bayes nets, but they need not concern us, since Bayes nets are special cases of neural networks.

That an android built around a theorem prover could reason, and that its reasons could cause its action, seems straightforward, but, like everything else, philosophers have denied it; in this case, on the grounds that a computer's program cannot produce reasons for the computer, only at most for something else, for the human programmer for example. There seems no argument for such a claim, only another claim behind it: human tissue has, according to John Searle, an American philosopher, a mysterious power of understanding and forming intentions, a power wanting in silicon and other materials. I can understand this hypothesis in only two ways: either the mysterious effect has no causal role in the production of action and is mere epiphenomenon, or, alternatively, it has some such role. If the former is meant, then that the possession of such epiphenomena should be essential for an entity to have reasons is too mysterious and arbitrary a hypothesis to warrant our credence. If the latter is meant instead, then it is a conjecture against our best science, for we have no demonstrable power of human tissue that is not, in the end, a collection of chemical or physical powers to produce a string of events that enable learning, memory, and action, and we have no evidence that other materials cannot produce comparably impressive sequences. The hypothesis seems, indeed, the very last gasp of vitalism, and since we have granted scientific naturalism, we may lay it aside with phlogiston and other such articles.

An android built around a theorem prover may then act from reasons, and so be responsible. Other architectures are more difficult. Suppose an android is built on a neural network; input comes in, the network nodes go through a sequence of states in consequence, and something comes out; and perhaps the network itself changes a bit as a result of the process. The network can remember, it can learn, it can predict, but can it reason? Philosophers and some computer scientists have argued a good deal about whether and how contents—"representations" is their terminology—may be assigned to neural networks. Some say a "concept" is to be identified with weights on network links. That is insufficient for our purposes, since, even abstractly, a concept is surely something else than a reason, and, besides, informally a network may recognize many concepts—make many different classifications—with the same set of weights. A reason, surely once more, must somehow be related to a state or sequence of states that the network passes through between inputs and motor action. No one seems yet to have proposed a plausible theory about how to translate a trace of such sequences into reasons. There are many difficulties, for example, it must surely be true that if androids have reasons, different androids must sometimes have the same reason. So a reason will correspond to some class of states or sequences of states, and how such equivalence relations are to be described is unclear. (I know of only one attempt, due to Paul Churchland, another American philosopher, and it is limited to sameness of concepts, not reasons.) It may be that the network level, while real enough, is entirely the wrong level for intelligibility, much as physical states of components of logic chips is the wrong level for understanding what an artificial intelligence system is doing in a computer. In the later case, we understand through a high level program and the structure of a compiler. The equivalence between the sequences of the operation a program in two different computers is not established by a mapping of the physical states of their components, but through the similarity of the traces of the program in the high level language in the two machines. If the analogy holds, we will understand a neural network as reasoning only if we understand the system to embody a compiler for a higher level language in which reasons occur as data structures. Designs, albeit not perhaps very elegant ones, have been proposed for compiling intelligible finite state machines into neural networks, and we may at least reasonably conjecture, therefore, that it is possible for an android formed upon a neural network to reason and to have reasons.

So my syllogism is complete: Responsibility and culpability require action caused by a free will, and such action suffices for an entity to be subject to ethical assessment to be ethical or unethical. An action is caused by free will if and only if it is caused by reasons. Human actions are not, save possibly very rarely, caused by reasons. The actions of an android built upon a theorem prover or a neural network or some combination of these could be caused by reasons. Hence an android, but not a human, could be ethical. I admit the conclusion does not quite follow: there could be beings that are neither human nor android and that act from reasons. I allow it. Wherever such beings are, if they exist, they are too distant and their collective survival too brief—alas as it appears ours will be—for us to know of them, the faith of unidentified flying object (UFO) believers notwithstanding. The only ethical beings we will ever meet will be those we build.

There is more to say on the subject, for I have not touched on the characteristics that a program for an ethical android might require. It is not plausible that any android could estimate the entire state of the universe at any time, and so the android's reasoning and decisions to act must be addressed to more local situations, either present or foreseen. That requires several capacities: to recognize moral features of situations—what is at stake in them and worth caring about; to imagine sequences of situations not seen; to understand cause and effect and to have some ability to estimate the situations alternative actions are likely to bring about. There has been a great deal of talk in artificial intelligence about "situations" but little that is substantive seems to have come of it; nonetheless, the emphasis on the goal is sound. It will not do for an android merely to recognize objects, their relations, and motions or to predict them. The android must possess a theory that enables it to recognize that a variety of situations are of moral importance, that they involve human (or other android) care, whether of beauty, or joy, or harm or risk. That in turn requires that the android possess a theory of other's minds, of beliefs, desires, plans, dismay, hope, fear, hurt, dread, disappointment, and more. Several psychologists who focus on the very young have lately come to the thesis that children learn such a theory; they are not born with it. If so, how children come to that understanding which is sometimes called "folk psychology" remains a mystery. A natural thought is that they do so by comparing others to themselves, and noting their own states of mind and emotion. If so, the recognition of morally fraught situations poses a difficulty for android ethics, since there is no guarantee, nor even a likelihood, that androids will have the same inner states as do people. There are two avenues towards a solution. One is to form a computable theory of these states—the propositional attitudes—and of the behavioral evidences of them, and give the android a program that enables it to apply the theory. The other is to give the android the basis for forming roughly analogous states within itself and for applying them to others by analogical reasoning. The basis must be the android surrogates for pain, pleasure, and need, which can be programmed as avoidance behavior, seeking behavior, and monitoring of internal states combined with knowledge of circumstances that will improve those states if need be. I should guess that a combination of strategies will be needed, and that neither is beyond our present technical vision. Child psychologists have shown that even infants ascribe goals to small moving objects—the objects want to get to whatever they are going towards, especially if they are going towards something the infant itself might want, or something analogous. Surely such basic inferential patterns could be programmed. The logic of many propositional attitudes is well developed, and the psychological description of inferences humans make about others' internal states from their appearance and behavior is, if not complete, considerable. The larger weakness is in computable theories of analogical reasoning, which remain rather primitive, chiefly counting matches of properties.

Very well, let us suppose we can equip an android, either by initial program, by learning, or by some combination of the two, with a capacity to recognize situations it or others care about, and with a great deal of commonsensical knowledge of the world—which, I understand, is being collected in Texas. How then is it to reason about moral action? Here we reach a many sided devilment indeed; Kantians on one side, utilitarians on another, "virtue ethicists" on still another, rule utilitarians to a fourth, and all of them disagreeing about how moral reasoning *ought* to be conducted. Virtue ethics I will leave aside: it is more a theory for judging others than for deciding action. In considering the alternatives that remain, we may be helped a little by considering what is both sane and conceivably programmable.

The Kantian imperative is to act from the moral law, which is to do only those acts that are consistently universalizable. One could imagine programming an android to do so. For each action contemplated, the android would need to formulate a description of the kind of act that could, consistent with commonsense knowledge, be carried out by any other human or android. Philosophers have doubted that the requirement is itself consistent, but it is in any case not feasible: consistency checks over a large body of propositions are intractable. The android would be morally paralyzed. (Perhaps Immanuel Kant was himself. He went blind in one eye, accompanied by intense headaches, just when his style of writing suddenly became very formal and his conceptions and habits likewise became very formal and rigid, a combination of physical and psychological symptoms known now to be caused by a tumor of the frontal lobe pressing on the optic nerve.)

Utilitarianism has a great appeal, if some unclarity. A utility is assigned to every possible situation; the probability of each situation resulting from an action computed, the numbers multiplied and summed, and that action performed whose expected utility is largest. Especially unresolved is how utilities are to be computed—which of those of other agents count, how are utilities of different agents to be compared (there is no common unit of utility by which to compare different persons), and how are they to be aggregated (for example, should one take the sum or the average)? Perhaps these difficulties can be met by the legislation of the programmer. The appeal of utilitarianism chiefly lies in its formality. Taken literally, however, it is computationally and epistemically preposterous. We cannot expect our android to have probabilities over all possible sequences of futures that might be affected by an action, or to know the utilities of persons who may not exist at the time an action is to be taken. Computationally bounded androids could only apply utilitarianism very locally, that is, by ignoring most of the future.

Artificial intelligence works by heuristics, and there is one heuristic theory of moral reasoning, rule utilitarianism. The idea is that from experience one learns which patterns of behavior have caused benefit and which have caused harm, and that experience is generalized to moral rules of thumb that guide ethical action. The rules of thumb can be overridden in circumstances in which it becomes evident that following them will cause harm or fail to do good. They are defaults. Default logic is something computer scientists understand, and know how to program. So, too, is learning about cause and effect. Our theories on both accounts could no doubt stand improvement, but improvements are imaginable. Androids built with fundamental dispositions—instincts if you please—to categorize, to learn, to infer goals, to analogize and generalize, could be or become ethical rule utilitarians. They could take account of the contextual harms and benefits that arise from the conventions of whatever society they might find themselves in, they could learn and largely abide by rules to keep their behavior more beneficial and less harmful, they could ignore those rules and act contrarily for the better in egregious circumstances, they could conceive other circumstances, other societies, where different rules would better serve, and, throughout, they could do so with reasons. Would that we poor humans were so endowed.

Editor's Note

The late Joseph Emile Nadeau graduated from the Swiss ETH, where he studied chemistry at a very young age (he was something of a prodigy) and may have been a fellow student with Albert Einstein. This paper, undated and never before published, was found among his *nachlass* and brought to our attention by his grandson.

16 The Adventures Among the Asteroids of Angela Android, Series 8400XF with an Afterword on Planning, Prediction, Learning, the Frame Problem, and a Few Other Subjects

Clark Glymour

A ngela's attention drifted as the data on the changing physical conditions in the vicinity of Bernard IV flashed by on the computer screen. She longed for her days as a nuclear reactor robot, or Nuke-Bot as they were known, where a genitally and hormonally correct series 8400 F type android such as she could find a little action after work, have a good time with a brawny droid, maybe even with a guy with half a brain. Rotten luck she'd been cooked when the reactor leaked. Too radioactive for Earth work, reprogrammed with the latest causal prediction system, here she was in a rocket with Sheila, a series 8300 F type, uncooked, heading for Barnard's star. All of the male company was in other ships on the expedition; Alpha 1 had the two series 8300 M type nonmonotonic reasoners, one with good pecs; Alpha 2 had the fellows with the ID2000 classification and prediction programs. Like Harry and Felix in Alpha 1, Sheila had the standard heuristic learning programming, nonmonotonic reasoners, and built in belief networks, but Angela, since reprogramming, was an

X type, with new learning software, and she had authority to override Shiela's decisions. The three ships composed the first android expedition to another star system; much too far for humans, who were weenies anyway, Angela thought.

Remembering the good old days wasn't going to help now. Something was clearly wrong around Barnard IV, which looked to be the only habitable satellite of Barnard's star. The planet was surrounded in all directions by asteroids. In principle there was no reason why the asteroids should prevent the ships from coming close to Barnard IV, or even landing. The asteroid motions should be predictable, and the expedition ships could just avoid them. But these asteroids weren't behaving correctly; every now and then one of them would change direction and swerve out of its computed trajectory. The things behaved as though they had some sort of propulsion system. How could Angela keep the damned things from swerving into their ships? Unless she could predict the swerve—technically the non-Newtonian acceleration—or figure out how to control it, she couldn't avoid a collision, and she'd never get to have another beer with a good-looking droid. She had ordered the ship to measure every physical variable correlated with the swerve, or correlated with any variable correlated with the swerve, and now the numbers were running by.

"Pool it and compute correlations, Sheila. I'm gonna call Alpha 1." She punched in the communication code.

"Harry, Felix, this is Angela calling. You computing?"

"Yes, Angela, we are computing," Harry's voice responded.

"We have a problem. Barnard IV is surrounded by asteroids."

"Yes, we know, Angela."

"Asteroids move in Newtonian orbits, Harry."

"Of course, Angela."

"The data say these asteroids don't move in Newtonian orbits, Harry."

"Then either they aren't asteroids, or else the data are in error, Angela."

"Thanks for nothing, Harry. What the fuck should we do so the asteroids don't hit us?"

"Angela, please don't be rude. We will have to calculate the minimal perturbations of our present beliefs that regain consistency. The problem will require some considerable computing."

"Yeah sure, Harry. By the way, Harry, Tweety is a bird. Can Tweety fly?"

"Yes, Angela, since Tweety is a bird Tweety can fly."

"But Tweety is an ostrich, Harry."

"Oh, then Tweety can't fly, Angela. I will have to recompute."

"Thanks, Harry. Out."

Sheila frowned at her. "You shouldn't tease him like that Angela." "Can't

	Flash	ProximateM..	AsteroidAcc..	ProximateG..	ProximateR..	PlanetColli..	Storm
Flash	1.0000						
Proximate...	0.0137	1.0000					
AsteroidAc..	0.0081	0.5260	1.0000				
Proximate...	0.0189	0.5342	0.2963	1.0000			
Proximate...	-0.0124	0.4391	0.2328	0.0310	1.0000		
PlanetColli..	-0.8419	0.1566	0.2989	0.0927	0.0736	1.0000	
Storm	-0.2699	0.0024	0.0341	-0.0208	0.0182	0.0222	1.0000
Sample Size	3000						

Figure 1: The Correlations Among Angela's Selected Variables.

help myself. Those nonmonotonic droids are such feebs." "I'm standard nonmonotonic, Angela." "Yes, but you're F type and you're my partner, so it doesn't apply. What do the correlations look like?"

"Well, the variables kicked out are pretty strange. Using your criteria the system picked out the non-Newtonian acceleration, the mass density of two spectral types of rocks within a small radius from the asteroid—roughly red rocks and green rocks—the mass density in the region surrounding the asteroid, the density of dust in storms on Bernard IV, and the intensity of monochromatic blue flashes coming from Bernard IV, and the frequency of collisions of asteroids with the planet. It looks like a mess to me Angela."

"Put up the correlations, Sheila." Sheila punched up the display.

Not bad, Angela thought. Three thousand observations already, but they were only going to get to do one experiment, and they'd be smithereens if they predicted the outcome wrong. "Amazing," she said aloud.

"I've already sent the data and the correlations to the other ships," Sheila said. "Maybe one of them will know what to do."

"Sheila, I know what to do just looking at the correlations; my causal analysis program did the analysis while I was looking. Fifty years old, and that program is finally getting used, *experimentally*. Here is what to do. Get as much mass as you can hooked-up to low velocity guidable rockets and get them ready to fire. I'm going to write a little program that will start shooting off those rockets as we enter the asteroid belt."

"Are you going to try to blow up the asteroids, Angela?"

"Not a chance, pal. I'm going to tempt the asteroids to get out of our way. Sort of a diversion."

"Don't you think, Angela, that we should consult with the other ships?"

"There is just no point talking with your friends in Alpha 1. They don't have a built in belief network for this case, and they can't build a new one that could possibly be right; if I give them instructions it will conflict with what they already believe, and they'll be computing until they're dust, or else they'll run a PUPS routine or they'll chunk on noisy data, or some such thing. They're goners, Sheila."

"But, Angela..."

"Tweety is a bird, Sheila. Can Tweety fly?"

"Yes, Tweety can fly."

"But Tweety is an ostrich, Sheila."

"Oh. Then Tweety can't fly, I have to re-compute."

"See what I mean Sheila? You've got the logical form, the semantics and all that, but you don't know shit from Shinola, and with your stupid heuristic learner you can't learn it unless somebody with authority tells you."

"What's Shinola?"

"Nobody knows. It's just a saying. Please get to work with the rockets. And as soon as we approach the asteroid belt I want you to beam music and friendly talk towards Barnard IV on as many radio frequencies as possible."

"Why, Angela?"

"Because something is punching the asteroids away from Bernard IV. Whatever it is, it probably comes from the planet. I don't know if it just hits asteroids or if it hits any massive body approaching Bernard IV. I don't want it to hit us. Since unusual phenomena associated with planets may be due to life forms, we want to give anything down there every opportunity to recognize that we're no threat. Get to work."

Angela punched in the Alpha 2 code. "Basil, this is Angela. What's your take on the asteroid problem?"

"We've analyzed it, sweetheart, and we've got the solution. Everything says the key is the blue light, and the red and green rocks. So we've put a filter on our beams. Whenever one of those things starts moving toward us, we'll flash the light and stay away from the rocks. You do the same."

"What about Alpha 1, Basil?"

"They're dinks, still trying to re-compute and figure out what to do with their primitive learner. You know they're hopeless. What do they run, some primitive heuristic? I don't have authority over them. They're dead silicon."

"You will be too, Boris, if you rely on flashing a blue light and avoiding red and green rocks."

"What do you mean, Angela?"

"The light is caused by some force we can't see, probably from Bernard IV. Wherever and whatever it is, it also causes the asteroids to swerve away from the plant."

"Be serious, Angela, how can you know that there's a force you can't see? What is it, the tooth fairy force? And even if you were right, how are you going to avoid the asteroids?"

"I know it from the data Basil. I'll tell you how when you've got the time. Right now you've got to start loading your guidable rockets with as much mass as possible. In a few minutes I'll send you a program to control them."

"Why rockets with mass? Sure there's a correlation with mass, but its *color* these things respond to.

"Color doesn't have anything to do with it, Basil. Differences in proximate mass density cause the asteroids to follow the gradient. Control the mass density close to the asteroids and you'll control their acceleration."

"Angela this is nonsense. The negative correlation between the blue flashes on Barnard IV and collisions with the planet is something over .8. The red and green rocks are significantly correlated with the acceleration. What's the common factor? The colors! The mass is associated with acceleration, sure, but that's spurious, because the colored rocks have mass. And you think you know the color doesn't matter even though the red and green rocks are correlated with the acceleration and the blue flash is correlated with avoiding collisions with the planet? I thought droids weren't sensitive to drugs. You must have a defect, honey. Everything in statistics and the *Handbook of Android Epistemology* says you're wrong."

"Please Basil, don't confuse correlation with causation. I do know because of my experimental program. Assemble the rockets."

"Me confuse correlation and causation? Angela, honey, you're confusing causation with *weaker* correlation. Go build a blue filter and stay away from the colored rocks."

"Basil, you overpriced regression package, you bastard son of misspent taxpayer dollars, you don't know shit from Shinola."

"What's Shinola, Angela?"

"Never mind. Out."

As Alpha 3 entered the asteroid belt, the guidable rockets fired and passed near to any approaching asteroid. The asteroids followed the rockets like fish after bait. Angela and Sheila watched appalled as Alpha 2 flashed its blue light at an oncoming asteroid and was pulverized for the trouble. Alpha 1, apparently following no coherent strategy, lasted a bit longer, but soon it too smashed into an asteroid that seemed to be seeking it.

Alone beneath the asteroid belt, Alpha 3 settled to the surface of

Barnard IV. Angela and Sheila emerged to find themselves surrounded by strange creatures, which seemed by their manner and apparatus very intelligent and very advanced. After a bit of fooling around with gestures, artifacts, and sounds, one of the Barnards began to speak perfect 21st century English.

"We are very glad you arrived safely. Over the millennia we have seen many vehicles try to pass through what you call the asteroid belt, and all of them perished, just like your companion vehicles. You were very fortunate, but you will never have such good fortune again. You must remain here. You would surely die trying to pass through the belt again."

"It wasn't luck at all, Barnie," said Angela. "It was good planning. The asteroids aren't just rocks are they? They're sort of living creatures, right?"

"Indeed, of a very primitive kind. They are attracted by very proximate mass, which they consume and convert to energy to propel themselves."

"And so now and then they swerve out of a stable orbit and head toward a collision with your planet, right Barnie? And if they should hit the planet very often they'd ruin your atmosphere and destroy civilization?"

"How astute of you, Angela. Striking the planet kills the asteroid, but it does enormous damage to us. It happens."

"Do you guys have some sort of repeller beam that give off an intense blue flash when you fire it? I figure you fire the repeller beam to divert any approaching asteroid. The harder you shoot the more intense the flash. But sometimes the flash is obscured by storms, right?"

"But this is amazing, Angela. How could you know so much about us? Are you psychic? We thought we were the most intelligent of races, but your inferences astound us."

"It's all in the data, Barnie. Plus a good algorithm and a little common sense. I wasn't sure you guys were here, but it looked to be a likely explanation of the data."

"You must teach us your methods of divining, Angela."

"Sure thing. I'll give you the book on it. But tell me, since we're going to be visiting a while, if Tweety is a bird then Tweety can fly, right?"

"Of course, Angela."

"But what if Tweety is an ostrich?"

"Then from my understanding of your language, Tweety can't fly, Angela. So what?"

Angela looked relieved. Barnie, I hope you guys make beer on this planet. I'm really glad to meet somebody that knows shit from Shinola."

"What is Shinola, Angela?"

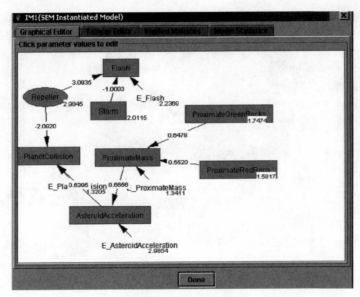

Figure 2. The Structure from Which Andrea's Data were Generated.

Afterword

The story cheats in some ways. One obvious cheat is the conversation. We don't know how to make computers talk that way. Perhaps another cheat is that Angela writes a program to schedule rocket launches to influence the mass gradient near the surface of a rapidly moving object. The calculations aren't preposterous, but I don't know enough of the state of automatic programming to know whether it is feasible for an android to write the code, even with prepackaged help.

One thing that is not a cheat is the success of Angela's inferences about causes and of her predictions about the effects of alternative courses of action, or her methods. She used the modern theory of search and prediction for graphical models, methods that are completely automated, even to the selection of variables used, and that could be used today in robotic inference, planning and decision making.

Let's see how Angela did it. Her data are shown in figure 1. The data were generated from the linear model in figure 2, shown graphically, using a sample size of 3000. Numbers next to edges are linear coefficients, other numbers next to variables labeled E ... are variances of noise terms with zero means.

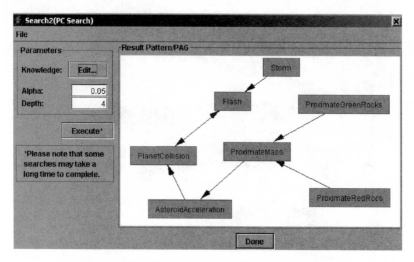

Figure 3: The Output of Angela's Computerized Search.

(Notice that the model that generated the data contains a variable "Repeller" that is not in the data—Angela could not observe the Repeller, and before analyzing the data, did not know that it or something like it was operating.)

Angela used the TETRAD IV automated search procedure known as the PC algorithm, and used a 0.05 level for statistical decisions. Her algorithm took as input the data in figure 1 and *nothing else*—no other prior information, and produced the following graphical causal model.

Notice the edge between Planet Collision and Flash has two arrowheads. That means, in the interpretation of the PC algorithm output—the normative interpretation, which Angela used, that there is an unrecorded common cause, not mentioned in the data, of Planet Collision and Flash. Angela named that cause the "Repeller." Using standard statistical methods (in this case maximum likelihood), Angela then estimated the parameters for the linear model but with the double headed arrow removed, Repeller added, and directed edges from Repeller to Flash and to Planet-Collision. The results, shown in figure 4, are close to the values in the structure that generated the data.

From the causal structure in figure 3, Angela knew that any influence of the red and green rocks on the asteroids must be due to the masses of the rocks. She knew further, that an *intervention* that changed the mass near an asteroid would alter its acceleration. Further, she knew that something

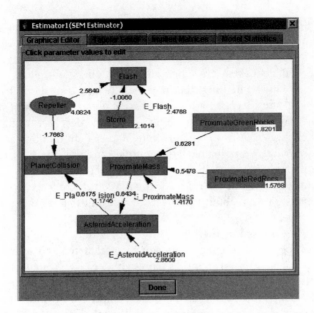

Figure 4: Parameter Estimates for Angela's Model Using her Data.

causing the blue flash also influenced the motion of the asteroids, but the blue flash itself did not.

This is of course a put up job, designed to tell a story that would illustrate some of the powers of search algorithms for graphical causal models. In the context of the story, the example is a bit farcical, since everything is assumed to be linear. But the search methods can be applied as well to nonlinear systems. And of course practical causal inference of the kind Angela illustrates requires more than such search algorithms alone provide. The algorithm tells her of the existence of an unobserved cause, but Angela had to surmise its nature, and Angela's worry that the Repelled force might be applied to her ship required her to use substantive knowledge (asteroids approaching the planet are massive bodies approaching the plant; Alpha 3 is a massive body) some simple reasoning techniques, and reverse inheritance (if *A* causes *B*s to *D*, and all *B*s and *C*s, maybe *A* causes *C*s to *D*).

Whatever was originally intended by "The Frame Problem," the title quickly became associated with the general problem of computationally feasible planning of the effects of actions intended to achieve some desired goal. Prediction is essential to planning. In particular, whatever the intent of its authors, "The Frame Problem" became a phrase for asking how a computational agent could reliably predict the effects of its own efforts to move things. But these restrictions are entirely artificial, more artificial than the intelligence they are supposed to be about. While all action takes place by moving something, the intermediate effects of motion may be described in other terms. Rather than asking about the effect of moving the paint brush an android can think about the effect of causing something to change color from blue to white. Rather than thinking about the effect of moving a vibrating reed, the android can think about the effect of saying a particular thing. Rather than thinking about the effects of its own actions, in planning an android can think about the effects of someone else's actions, or even about the effects of an event that no one *does*, that simply happens.

The issues aroused by the frame problem are questions about the prediction of the effects of interventions in a causal system. To address these questions in a general way requires representing causal structures generally, and also requires understanding how the representations can be used to compute such predictions. Only an evasive mind can then avoid the further question: how can an android learn the relevant representations of causal structures? The central questions about planning and the frame problem are (1) How can causal structure be learned reliably, efficiently and feasibly; (2) How can complete or partial knowledge of causal structure be used to reliably and feasibly predict the effects of interventions in the causal system.

Angela's problem is science fiction no more complex than many learning problems that an android might be expected to meet, and less complex than learning problems confronted everyday by social scientists, economists, epidemiologists, educators, and others. The inference Angela makes is completely impossible for any combination of the celebrated AI learning algorithms or proposals for reasoning about planning. But it is not atypical of problems an autonomous computer might face, and—except that it is too easy—it is perfectly typical of real planning and prediction problems real humans face all the time. Angela's problem is made more difficult by the fact that experiments cannot be performed, but designing experiments is simply a special case of planning, and learning causal structure with and without experiments should fall under a general theory.

In the last few years, a number of statisticians, computer scientists, and, I am pleased to say, philosophers, have made breakthroughs in reliably constructing causal hypotheses from data, or from a mixture of data and background knowledge, and in finding methods to separate the few variables necessary for prediction from a mass of irrelevant variables. A quite general understanding has emerged concerning how such networks yield predictions about the effects of direct manipulations of some of the variables. The use of experimental manipulations to provide information to construct causal hypotheses is fairly well understood. Enormous amounts of work remain to be done, and lots of fundamental things—feedback, for example, and variable selection—are not yet under full theoretical control. This is work at the cynosure of the frame problem.

Acknowledgements

This chapter first appeared as "The Adventures Among the Asteroids of Angela Android, Series 8400XF" in *Robot's Dilemma: The Frame Problem in Artificial Intelligence,* edited by Zenon W. Pylyshyn (Norwood, NJ: Ablex, 1987).

Part Five
Conclusion

17 Humanity, the Computer, and Cognitive Prostheses

Kenneth M. Ford, Clark Glymour, & Patrick J. Hayes

And so our collection ends, with a last thought about something serious—fears and trepidations about artificial intelligence. It has been argued that the computer has made the world more harsh, perhaps even more cruel, by reducing human contact and centralizing information and control. You can do a lot nowadays without seeing, touching, or talking to a human being—book a flight to Timbuktu, pay the turnpike tolls, manage your bank account, and all of that reduces human contact. Instead of Mr. McFeely at your mailbox—you have e-mail. The U.S. Defense Department once proposed to make a huge database on all of us, and to use it for data mining. We have heard it argued that a twelfth century subject was freer than a twenty-first century citizen: The king might want to get the peasant, but he would likely have trouble doing so. People wandered at will across Europe with all manner of contrived names; the Pope was unable to capture Martin Luther and fifteenth century English bishops were unable to capture John Wycliff.

There is something to these plaints, but not very much. They are rigidly framed: their tacit premise is that when technology changes, nothing else must change, or that technologies' social impacts are historically inevitable. Almost every fundamental innovation, from fire to writing to flight to the computer—would have made things worse if practices and institutions did not change around it: where would airplanes land without landing strips? How would they avoid collisions without a system of air-traffic control?

That the computer removes the economic justification for stupid, repetitive jobs is for the good, not the bad. A decent society will find more useful work for people; It is society's job, not the computer's, to arrange institutions so that people are usefully employed and resources are justly distributed. Computers don't get to vote. Let the mailman sculpt, or lead botanical walks, or educate preschoolers. He will be happier and your mail will arrive more reliably and swiftly. Tell the government it may not keep tabs on everyone, that just as you want some wilderness left in Nature, you want some wilderness left in people. Innovations that we now think invaluable, that we cannot imagine doing without, have always disturbed institutions and have always been denounced both by the powerful and the ignorant. John Wycliff was sought by the Bishops for the dreadful crime and innovation of translating the *Bible* into English.

Perhaps the most common complaint is that the information revolution produces economic inequality: The computer, the world wide web, robots, the automation of manufacturing will all conspire to separate the rich and quick from the poor and slow, hurrying the trend to an informed, skilled, and employed elite living among an uninformed, unskilled, and unemployed majority. But both history and an understanding of human-machine interaction argue otherwise. Any number of forces may work toward the stratification of society, but the computer is not one of them. Computers, especially intelligent ones, are the great equalizers because they are cognitive prostheses. That was Ramon Lull's great insight.

Humanity has always recognized that the powers of mind are limited, and has always made devices to compensate for those limitations. Our most obvious cognitive limitation is memory, and writing is a device for storing information outside the head so that it does not have to be remembered. Instead, the human brain need only store the code for reading. As soon as it could be economically reproduced and distributed, writing became in Europe an irresistible force for equality: Within three centuries after Johannes Gutenberg, modern science had been created, ecclesiastical authority had been reduced, the divine right of kings had vanished, and democratic forms of government had emerged.

Calculation shows the same history. Roman enumeration methods made addition, multiplication and division impossible except for the gifted. To compensate, the abacus was used in Europe as an arithmetical prosthesis. In the thirteenth century, Leonard Fibonnacci introduced into Europe the Hindu-Arabic system of numbers and the arithmetic algorithms they made possible. One of the first books after the *Bible* printed with moveable type was an Arithmetic. Even so, the algorithms were not easy and not widely disseminated. Most seventeenth century tradesmen could not multiply. Today, every shop assistant can calculate better than Renaissance experts, just by pressing buttons.

Purists may mutter that the shop assistant is not really calculating. But fitted with the right tool, that is, prosthesis, the shop assistant can get the calculations done, which is what matters in the marketplace. And, in counting actions, where do we draw the lines between ourselves and our tools? Is someone using a power screwdriver not really turning the screws, or someone driving a car not really moving along the highway? With a power screwdriver, anyone can drive the hardest screw; with a calculator, anyone can get the numbers right; with an aircraft anyone can fly to Paris; and with Deep Blue, anyone can beat the world chess champion. Cognitive prostheses undermine the exclusiveness of expertise by giving nonexperts equivalent capacities. As with any good tool, the effect is to make all of us more productive, more skillful, and more equal.

One day recently one of our fathers, Joe Glymour, told us with mixed pleasure and anxiety that he was beginning a game of postcard chess against a team of younger relatives in California; he feared he stood little chance. We solved his problem with a trip to Radio Shack, where for $70 he could become one of the better post-card chess players in the world.

Bibliography & References

Agre, P. E.; and Chapman, D. 1987. Pengi: An Implementation of a Theory of Activity. In *Proceedings of the Sixth National Conference on Artificial Intelligence*, 196-201. San Mateo, CA: Morgan Kaufmann Publishers.

Allen, J.; Hendler, J.; and Tate, A. eds. 1990. *Readings in Planning.* San Mateo, CA: Morgan Kaufmann Publishers.

Amir, Eyal; and Maynard-Reid II, Petrito 1999. Logic-Based Subsumption Architecture. In *Proceedings of the Sixteenth International Joint Conference on Artificial Intelligence* (IJCAI'99) San Francisco: Morgan Kaufmann Publishers.

Aspray, William. 1981. From Mathematical Constructivity to Computer Science: Turing, Neumann, and the Origins of Computer Science in Mathematical Logic. Ph.D. Diss., Univ. of Wisconsin, Madison, WI. Ann Arbor, Michigan: University Microfilms International.

Augarten, Stan 1984. *Bit by Bit: An Illustrated History of Computers.* New York: Ticknor and Fields.

Bacon, Francis. 1620. *Instauratio Magna* [Novum Organum]. London: John Bill

Baylor, George W.; and Simon, Herbert Alexander 1966. A Chess Mating Combinations Program. *AFIPS Conference Proceedings, Spring Joint Computer Conference.* Washington, DC: Spartan Books, 28: 431-47.

Belon, Pierre 1555. *L'Histoire de la Nature des Oyseaux.* Paris: G. Cauellat.

Bloom, Benjamin S., ed. 1985. *Developing Talent in Young People.* New York: Ballantine Books.

Boden, Margaret A. 1972. *Purposive Explanation in Psychology.* Cambridge, MA: Harvard University Press.

Boden, Margaret A., ed. 1981. Implications of Language Studies for Human Nature. In *Minds and Mechanisms: Philosophical Psychology and Computational Models.* Ithaca: Cornell University Press.

Boden, Margaret A. 1988. *Computer Models of Mind: Computational Approaches in Theoretical Psychology.* Cambridge: Cambridge University Press.

Boden, Margaret A. 1991. *The Creative Mind: Myths and Mechanisms.* New York: Basic Books.

Boole, George 1951. *An Investigation of the Laws of Thought.* New York: Dover Publications.

Brooks, Rodney A. 1986. A Robust Layered Control System for a Mobile Robot. *IEEE Journal of Robotics and Automation* 2(1): 14–23.

Brooks, Rodney A. 1990. Challenges for Complete Creature Architectures. Paper presented at the First International Conference on Simulation of Adaptive Behavior, Paris, France, September. Reprinted in *From Animals to Animats*, ed. Jean-Arcady Meyer and Stewart W. Wilson. Cambridge, MA: The MIT Press, 1991.

Brooks, Rodney A. 1991a. Intelligence Without Reason. In *Proceedings of the Twelfth International Joint Conference on Artificial Intelligence*, 569–595. San Mateo, CA: Morgan Kaufmann Publishers.

Brooks, Rodney A. 1991b. Intelligence without Representation. *Artificial Intelligence Journal* 47(1–3): 139–160.

Brooks, Rodney A. 1991c. Intelligence without Reason. In *Proceedings of Twelfth International Joint Conference on Artificial Intelligence*, 569–595. San Francisco: Morgan Kaufmann Publishers.

Brooks, Rodney A. 1991d. Integrated Systems Based on Behaviors. *SIGART Bulletin* 2(4): 46–50.

Carnap, Rudolf 1967. *The Logical Structure of the World: Pseudoproblems in Philosophy.* London: Routledge K. Paul

Chalmers, David J., French, Robert M., and Hofstadter, Douglas R. 1991. *High-Level Perception, Representation, and Analogy: A Critique of Artificial Intelligence Methodology* (CRCC Tech. Rep. 49). Center for Research on Concepts and Cognition, Indiana University, Bloomington, Indiana.

Chapman, D. 1990. *Vision, Instruction, and Action.* Tech. Rep. 1204, Artificial Intelligence Laboratory. Cambridge, MA: Massachusetts Institute of Technology.

Chase, William G.; and Simon, Herbert Alexander 1973. Perception in Chess. *Cognitive Psychology* 4(1): 55–81.

Cherniak, Christopher 1983. Rationality and the Structure of Memory. *Synthèse* 57: 163–8

Churchland, Paul. 1979. *Scientific Realism and the Plasticity of Mind.* New York: Cambridge University Press.

Churchland, Paul 1988. Perceptual Plasticity and Theoretical Neutrality: A Reply to Jerry Fodor *Philosophy of Science* LV: 167–87.

Churchland, Paul. 1989. A Neurocomputational Perspective: The Nature of Mind and the Structure of Science. Cambridge, MA: The MIT Press.

Churchland, Paul. 1990. *A Nerocomputational Perspective: The Nature of Mind.* Cambridge, MA: The MIT Press.

Churchland, Paul. 1993. Fodor and Lepore: State-Space Semantics and Meaning Holism. *Philosophy and Phenomenological Research*, LIII: 667–72

Churchland, Paul. 1996 Second Reply to Fodor and Lepore. In *The Churchlands and Their Critics*, ed. Robert McCauley, 278-83. Cambridge: Blackwell.

Clark, Andrew; and Karmiloff-Smith, Annette 1993. The Cognizer's Innards: A Psychological and Philosophical Perspective on the Development of Thought. *Mind and Language* 8: 487–519..

Clark, Herbert H.; and Chase, William G. 1972. On the Process of Comparing Sentences Against Pictures. *Cognitive Psychology*, 3(4): 472–517.

Clemens, Samuel Langhorn. 1889. *A Connecticut Yankee in King Artur's Court.* New York: Charles L. Webster and Company.

Cottrell, Garrison; and Laakso, Aarre. 1996. Qualia and Cluster Analysis: Assessing Representational Similarity between Neural Systems. Paper presented at the Society for Philosophy and Psychology Annual Meeting, San Francisco, June.

Darwin, Charles 1859. *On the Origin of Species by Means of Natural Selection.* London: John Murray.

Darwin, Charles 1871. *The Descent of Man, and Selection in Relation to Sex.* London: John Murray.

de Groot, Adrianus Dingeman 1965. *Thought and Choice in Chess.* The Hague: Mouton.

Dennett, Daniel C. 1978. Two Approaches to Mental Images. In *Brainstorms: Philosophical Essays on Mind and Psychology.* Cambridge, MA: The MIT Press.

Dennett, Daniel C. 1982a. Why Do We Think What We Do About Why We Think What We Do? *Cognition* 12: 219-227.

Dennett, Daniel C. 1982b. How to Study Consciousness Empirically; Or, Nothing Comes to Mind. *Synthèse* 53: 159–180.

Dennett, Daniel C. 1982c. Beyond Belief. In *Thought and Object,* ed. A. Woodfield. Oxford: Oxford University Press.

Dennett, Daniel C. 1988. Cognitive Wheels: The Frame Problem of AI. In *The Robot's Dilemma: The Frame Problem in Artificial Intelligence,* ed. Z. W. Pylyshyn, 41–65. Norwood, NJ: Ablex.

Descartes, René 1985. *The Philosophical Writings of Descartes.* Trans. John Cottingham, R. Stoothoff and D. Murdoch. Cambridge: Cambridge University Press.

Descartes, René 1989, *The Passions of the Soul,* trans. Stephen H. Voss. Indianapolis, IN: Hackett Publishing Company.

Dretske, Fred 1997. *Naturalizing the Mind.* Cambridge, MA: The MIT Press.

Dreyfus. Hubert. 1972. *What Computers Can't Do.* New York: Harper and Row.

Edwards, Anthony William Fairbank 1987. *Pascal's Arithmetical Triangle.* New York: Oxford University Press.

Ellman, Jeffrey 1992. Grammatical Structure and Distributed Representations. In Connectionism: Theory and Practice, in Vancouver Studies in Cognitive Science, Volume III, ed. S. Davis, 138–94. New York: Oxford University Press.

Feigenbaum, Edward A.; and Simon, Herbert Alexander 1984. EPAM-like Models of Recognition and Learning. *Cognitive Science,* 8(3): 305–36.

Fikes, Richard; and Nilsson, Nils 1971. STRIPS: A New Approach to the Application of Theorem Proving to Problem Solving. *Artificial Intelligence Journal* 2(2–4): 189–208.

Findlay, A. 1965. *A Hundred Years of Chemistry.* Third edition, ed. T. I. Williams. London: Duckworth.

Fodor, Jerry A. 1980. Methodological Solipsism Considered as a Research Strategy in Cognitive Psychology. *Behavioral and Brain Sciences* 3: 63–110.

Fodor, Jerry A. 1988. Modules, Frames, Fridgeons, Sleeping Dogs, and the Music of the Spheres. In *The Robot's Dilemma: The Frame Problem in Artificial Intelligence,* ed. Z. W. Pylyshyn, 139–149. Norwood, NJ: Ablex.

Foder, Jerry; and Lepore, Ernest 1992. *Holism: A Shopper's Guide.* Cambridge: Blackwell.

Foder, Jerry; and Lepore, Ernest 1993. Reply to Churchland. *Philosophy and Phenomenological Research,* LII: 679–82.

Foley, J. D.; and Van Dam, A. 1982. *Fundamentals of Interactive Computer Graphics.* Reading, MA: Addison-Wesley.

Freud, Sigmund. 1950. Project for a Scientific Psychology [1895] *The Standard Edition of the Complete Works of Sigmund Freud,* vol. 1, ed. James Strachey et al., 295–391. London: The Hogart Press and the Institute of Psychoanalysis.

Frude, Neil 1983. *The Intimate Machine: Close Encounters with the New Computers.* London: Century Company.

Gardner, Martin 1968. *Logic Machines, Diagrams and Boolean Algebra.* New York: Dover Publications.

Georgeff, Michael P.; and Lansky, Amy L. 1987. Reactive Reasoning and Planning. In *Proceedings of the Sixth National Conference on Artificial Intelligence,* 677-682. San Mateo, CA: Morgan Kaufmann Publishers.

Gibson, James Jerome 1979. *The Ecological Approach to Visual Perception.* London: Houghton Mifflin.

Glymour, Clark 1991. Freud's Androids. In *The Cambridge Companion to Freud,* ed. Jerome Neu. New York: Cambridge University Press.

Glymour, Clark 1992. *Thinking Things Through: An Introduction to Philosophical Issues and Achievements.* Cambridge, MA: The MIT Press.

Goodman, N. 1982. Thoughts without Words. *Cognition* 12: 211–217.

Haugeland, John 1985. *Artificial Intelligence: The Very Idea.* Cambridge, MA: The MIT Press.

Hayes, John R. 1989. *The Complete Problem Solver* Second Edition. Hillsdale, NJ: Lawrence Earlbaum Associates.

Hayes, John R.; and Simon, Herbert Alexander 1974. Understanding Written Problem Instructions. In *Knowledge and Cognition,* ed. Lee W. Gregg. Potomac, MD: Lawrence Erlbaum Associates.

Hayes, Patrick J. 1978. Naive Physics I: The Ontology of Liquids. Working Papers No. 35. Geneva, Switzerland: Institut pour les Etudes Semantiques et Cognitives, University of Geneva, Geneva, Switzerland.

Hayes, Patrick J. 1979. The Naive Physics Manifesto. In *Expert Systems in the Microelectronic Age,* ed D. Michie. Edinburgh, Scotland: Edinburgh University Press.Hebb, Donald Olding. 1949. *Organization of Behavior: A Neuropsychological Theory.* New York: Wiley.

Hayes, Patrick J. 1988. What the Frame Problem Is and Isn't. In *The Robot's Dilemma: The Frame Problem in Artificial Intelligence,* ed. Z. W. Pylyshyn, 123-138. Norwood, NJ: Ablex.

Hebb, Donald Olding 1949. *Organization of Behavior: A Neuropsychological Theory.* New York: Wiley Interscience.

Hinton, Geoffrey E.; Plaut, David C.; and Shallice, T. 1993. Simulating Brain Damage. *Scientific American* 269(10) (October): 76–82.

Hobbes, Thomas 1962. *Body, Man and Citizen. Selections.* Edited with an Introduction by Richard S. Peters. New York: Collier Books.

Hofstadter, Douglas R. 1982. Can Inspiration be Mechanized? *Scientific American* 247: 18–34.

Hofstadter, Douglas R.; and Mitchell, M. 1991. An Overview of the Copycat Project. In *Con-*

nectionist Approaches to Analogy, Metaphor, and Case-Based Reasoning ed K. J. Holyoak and J. Barnden. Norwood, NJ: Ablex.

Hofstadter, Douglas R.; Mitchell, M.; and French, R. M. 1987. Fluid Concepts and Creative Analogies: A Theory and its Computer Implementation. CRCC Tech. Rep. 18, Indiana University. Bloomington, IN: Center for Research on Concepts and Cognition.

Holland, John H. 1975. *Adaptation in Natural and Artificial Systems: An Introductory Analysis with Applications to Biology, Control, and Artificial Intelligence.* Ann Arbor: University of Michigan Press.

Holland, John H.; Holyoak, Keith J.; Nisbett, Richard E.; and Thagard, Paul R. 1986. *Induction: Processes of Inference, Learning, and Discovery.* Cambridge, MA: The MIT Press.

Hume, David 1977. *An Enquiry Concerning Human Understanding,* ed. Eric Steinberg. Indianapolis, IN: Hackett Publishing Company.

James, William 1983. *Principles of Psychology.* Cambridge, MA: Harvard University Press.

Janlert, Erik 1987. Modelling Change—The Frame Problem. In *Robot's Dilemma: The Frame Problem in Artificial Intelligence,* ed. Z. Pylyshyn. Norwood, NJ: Ablex.

Johnson-Laird, P. N. 1988. *The Computer and the Mind: An Introduction to Cognitive Science.* London: Fontana.

Johnson-Laird, P. N. 1989. Jazz Improvisation: A Theory at the Computational Level. Unpublished working-paper, MRC Applied Psychology Unit, Cambridge MA.

Kant, Immanuel. 1781. *Kritik der Reinen Vernunft* [Critique of Pure Reason]. Riga, Latvia: J. F. Hartknoch.

Kaplan, Craig A.; and Simon, Herbert Alexander 1990. In Search of Insight. *Cognitive Psychology* 22: 374–419

Karmiloff-Smith, Annette. 1986. From Meta-Processes to Conscious Access: Evidence from Children's Metalinguistic and Repair Data. *Cognition* 23: 95–147.

Karmiloff-Smith, Annette. 1990. Constraints on Representational Change: Evidence from Children's Drawing. *Cognition* 34: 57–83.

Kosslyn, Stephen Michael 1980. *Image and Mind.* Cambridge, MA: Harvard University Press.

Kosslyn, Stephen Michael 1993. *Image and Brain: The Resolution of the Imagery Debate.* Cambridge, MA: Harvard University Press.

Kubrick, Stanley; and Clarke, Arthur C. 1968. *2001: A Space Odyssey. Screenplay.* Burbank, CA: Warner Studios.

Kulkarni, Deepak; and Simon, Herbert Alexander 1988. The Processes of Scientific Discovery: The Strategy of Experimentation. *Cognitive Science* 12(2): 139–176.

Kyburg, Henry E., Jr. 1974. *The Logical Foundations of Statistical Inference.* Dodrecht: Reidel.

Kyburg, Henry E., Jr. 1988. Full Belief. *Theory and Decision* 25: 137-162.

Langley, Pat; Simon, Herbert Alexander; Bradshaw, Gary L.; and Zytkow, Jan M. 1987. *Scientific Discovery: Computational Explorations of the Creative Process.* Cambridge, MA: The MIT Press.

Larkin, Jill H.; and Simon, Herbert Alexander 1987. Why a Diagram Is (Sometimes) Worth 10,000 Words. *Cognitive Science,* 11(1): 65–99.

Latombe, Jean-Claude 1991. *Robot Motion Planning.* Dodrecht: Kluwer Academic.

Leibniz, Gottfried Wilhelm, Freiherr von. 1679. *De Progression Dyadica—Pars I*, in the collection of Niedersächsische Landesbibliothek, Hanover. Reprinted in *Herrn von Leibniz' Rechnung mit Null und Eins*, 42–47. Berlin: Siemens Aktiengesellschaf.

Leibnitz, Gottfried Wilhelm, Freiherr von. 1666. *Dissertatio de Arte Combinatoria*. Leipzig: Apud Johannes Simon.

Lenat, Douglas B. 1983. The Role of Heuristics in Learning by Discovery: Three Case Studies. In *Machine Learning: An Artificial Intelligence Approach*, ed. R. S. Michalski, J. G. Carbonell, and T. M. Mitchell. Palo Alto, CA: Tioga.

Lenat, Douglas B.; and Brown, John Seely 1984. Why AM and Eurisko Appear to Work. *Artificial Intelligence Journal* 23(3): 269–94.

Lenat, Douglas B.; and Guha, Ramanathan V. 1990. *Building Large Knowledge-Based Systems*. Reading, Mass.: Addison-Wesley, 1990.

Levi, Isaac 1980. *The Enterprise of Knowledge*. Cambridge, MA: The MIT Press.

Longuet-Higgins, Hugh Christopher 1987. *Mental Processes: Studies in Cognitive Science*. Cambridge, MA: The MIT Press.

McCarthy, John 1960. Programs with Common Sense. In *Proceedings of the Teddington Conference on the Mechanization of Thought Processes*. London: Her Majesty's Stationers Office.

McCarthy, John 1980. Circumscription—A Form of Nonmonotonic Reasoning Artificial Intelligence Laboratory Memo AIM–334, p. 4. February. Stanford University, Stanford, CA.

McCarthy, John, and Hayes, Patrick J. 1969. Some Philosophical Problems from the Standpoint of Artificial Intelligence. In *Machine Intelligence 4*, ed. B. Meltzer and D. Michie. Edinburgh, Scotland: Edinburgh University Press.

McCauley, Robert, ed. 1996. *The Churchlands and Their Critics*. Cambridge: Blackwell.

McCorduck, Pamela 1991. *Aaron's Code*. San Francisco: W. H. Freeman.

McDermott, Drew 1988. We've been Framed: Or, Why AI Is Innocent of the Frame Problem. In *The Robot's Dilemma: The Frame Problem in Artificial Intelligence*, ed. Z. W. Pylyshyn, 113–122. Norwood, NJ: Ablex.

McDermott, Drew; and Doyle, John. 1980. Nonmonotonic Logic. *Artificial Intelligence Journal* 13: 41–72.

McGinn, Colin. 1982. *The Character of Mind*. New York: Oxford University Press.

Mars, Nicholas, J. ed., 1995. *Toward Very Large Knowledge Bases*. Amsterdam: IOS Press.

Massey, Gerald J., and Boyle, Deborah A. 1999. *Descartes's Tests for (Animal) Mind*. *Philosophical Topics* 27(1): 87–145.

Mataric, M. J. 1990. *A Distributed Model for Mobile Robot Environment Learning* Tech. Rep. 1228, Artificial Intelligence Laboratory. Cambridge, MA: Massachusetts Institute of Technology.

Mataric, M. J. 1992. Integration of Representation into Goal-Driven Behavior-Based Robots. *IEEE Journal of Robotics and Automation* 8(3): 304–312.

Millikan, Ruth Garrett 1984. *Language, Thought, and Other Biological Categories*. Cambridge, MA: The MIT Press.

Millikan, Ruth Garrett 1989. Biosemantics. *Journal of Philosophy* LXXXVI: 281-297.

Minsky, Marvin A. 1981. A Framework for Representing Knowledge. In *Mind Design*, ed. J. Haugeland, 125. Cambridge, MA: The MIT Press.

Minsky, Marvin A. 1985. *The Society of Mind.* New York: Simon and Schuster.

Mitchell, M. 1990. COPYCAT: *A Computer Model of High-Level Perception and Conceptual Slippage in Analogy-Making.* Ph.D diss., Dept. of Computer Science, University of Michigan, Ann Arbor, MI.

Moor, James H. 1976. An Analysis of the Turing Test. *Philosophical Studies* 30: 249–257.

Munkakata, Tosh, ed. 1995. *Communications of the ACM* 38(11) (November).

Newell, Allen 1980. Physical Symbol Systems. *Cognitive Science* 4: 135–183.

Newell, Allen. 1982. The Knowledge Level. *Artificial Intelligence Journal* 18: 8–127.

Newell, Allen; and Simon, Herbert Alexander 1972. *Human Problem Solving.* Englewood Cliffs, NJ: Prentice-Hall.

Newell, Allen; and Simon, Herbert Alexander 1976. Computer Science as Empirical Inquiry. *Communications of the ACM,* 19(3): 113–126.

Novak, Gordon S. 1977. Representation of Knowledge in a Program for Solving Physics Problems. In *Proceedings of the Fifth International Joint Conference on Artificial Intelligence.* San Francisco: Morgan Kaufmann Publishers.

Paige, Jeffrey M.; and Simon, Herbert Alexander 1966. Cognitive Processes in Solving Algebra Word Problems. In *Problem Solving: Research, Method, and Theory* ed Benjamin Kleinmuntz. New York: John Wiley and Sons.

Parr, Ronald, and Russell, Stuart, 1997, Reinforcement Learning with Hierarchies of Machines. In *Advances of Neural Information Processing Systems 9.* Cambridge, MA: The MIT Press.

Pascal, Blaise. 1665. *Traité du Triangle Arithmétique avec Quelques Autres Petits Traites sur la Mesme Matiere.* Paris: Ches Guillaume Desprez.

Pascal, Blaise. 1670. *Pensées de N. Pascal sur la Religion et sur Quelques autres Sujets, Qui ont esté Trouveées Apreés sa Mort Parmy ses Papiers.* Paris: Ches Guillaume Desprez.

Pearl, Judea 2000. *Causality.* New York: Oxford University Press.

Phillips, E. William 1936. Binary Calculation. *Journal of the Institute of Actuaries* 67: 187–221.

Plato. 2005. *Meno and Other Dialogues. Translated with an Introduction and Notes by Robin Waterfield.* New York: Oxford University Press.

Pylyshyn, Zenon W., ed. 1988. *The Robot's Dilemma: The Frame Problem in Artificial Intelligence.* Norwood, NJ: Ablex.

Quine, Williard V. 1969. *Ontological Relativity and Other Essays.* New York: Columbia University Press.

Richman, Howard B.; and Simon, Herbert Alexander 1989. Context Effects in Letter Perception: Comparison of Two Theories. *Psychological Review,* 96(3): 417–32.

Ritchie, G. D.; and Hanna, F. K. 1984. AM: A Case Study in AI Methodology. *Artificial Intelligence Journal* 23: 249–268.

Rosenschein, S. J.; and Kaelbling, L. P. 1986. The Synthesis of Digital Machines with Provable Epestemic Properties. In *Proceedings of the Conference on Theoretical Aspects of Reasoning about Knowledge,* ed J. Y. Ualpern, 83–98. San Mateo, CA: Morgan Kaufmann Publishers.

Russell, Bertrand. 1926. *Our Knowledge of the External World as a Field for Scientific Method in Philosophy.* London: G. Allen and Unwin Ltd.

Russell, Bertrand. 1948. *Human Knowledge: Its Scope and Limits.* New York: Simon and Schuster.

Sanborn, J. C.; and Hendler, J. A. 1988. A Model of Reaction for Planning in Dynamic Environments. *International Journal of Artificial Intelligence in Engineering,* 3(2): 95–102.

Schank, Roger, and Abelson, R. 1977. *Scripts, Plans, Goals and Understanding: An Inquiry into Human Knowledge Structures.* Hillsdale, NJ: Erlbaum.

Schoppers, M. J. 1987. Universal Plans for Reactive Robots in Unpredictable Domains. In *Proceedings of the Tenth International Joint Conference on Artificial Intelligence,* 1039–1046. San Mateo, CA: Morgan Kaufmann Publishers.

Searle, John R. 1980. Minds, Brains, and Programs. *Behavioral and Brain Sciences* 3: 473–497. Reprinted in *The Philosophy of Artificial Intelligence* (chapter 3), ed. M. Boden. Oxford: Oxford University Press, 1990.

Searle, John R. 1984. *Minds, Brains and Science.* Cambridge, MA: Harvard University Press.

Searle, John R. 1990. Is the Brain's Mind a Computer Program? *Scientific American* 262(1): 20–25.

Sejnowski, Terrence J.; and Rosenberg, Charles R. 1987. Parallel Networks that Learn to Pronounce English Text. *Complex Systems* 1(1): 145–68.

Selfridge, Oliver 1992. *Tracking and Trailing: Adaptation in Movement Strategies.* Cambridge, MA: The MIT Press.

Siklóssy, Laurent 1972. Natural Language Learning by Computer. In *Representation and Meaning: Experiments with Information Processing Systems,* ed Herbert Alexander Simon and Laurent Siklóssy. Englewood Cliffs, NJ: Prentice-Hall.

Simon, Herbert Alexander 1976. The Information-Storage System Called "Human Memory." In *Neural Mechanisms of Learning and Memory,* ed. Mark R. Rosenzweig and Edward L. Bennett eds. Cambridge, MA: The MIT Press.

Simon, Herbert Alexander 1981. *The Sciences of the Artificial.* Cambridge, MA: The MIT Press.

Simon, Herbert Alexander; and Gilmartin, Kevin A. 1973. A Simulation of Memory for Chess Positions. *Cognitive Psychology,* 5(1): 29–46.

Smith, B. C. 1982. *Reflection and Semantics in a Procedural Language* Ph.D dissertation and Tech. Rep. LCS/TR-272. Massachusetts Institute of Technology, Cambridge, MA.

Spirtes, Peter; Glymour, Clark; and Scheines, Richard 1993. *Causation, Prediction and Search.* New York: Springer Verlag.

Sterrett, Susan G., 2000, Turing's Two Tests for Intelligence. *Minds and Machines* 10: 541–559. *Reprinted in The Turing Test: The Elusive Standard of Artificial Intelligence* ed. James H. Moor. Dortrecht, The Netherlands: Kluwer Academic 2003.

Sterrett, Susan G., 2002, Nested Algorithms and "The Original Imitation Game Test": A Reply to James Moor. *Minds and Machines* 12: 131–136.

Stich, Stephen P. 1983. *From Folk Psychology to Cognitive Science: The Case Against Belief.* Cambridge, MA: The MIT Press.

Sutton, Richard S. 1990. Integrated Architectures for Learning, Planning, and Reacting based on Approximating Dynamic Programming. In Machine Learning: Proceedings of the Tenth International Conference, 216-224. San Francisco: Morgan Kaufmann Publishers.

Swift, Jonathan. 1726. *Travels into Several Remote Nations of the World. In Four Parts.* London: Benjamin Motte.

Turner, Mark 1991. *Reading Minds: English Studies an the Age of Cognitive Science.* Princeton, NJ: Princeton University Press.

Tversky, Amos; and Kahneman, Daviel 1974. Judgment Under Uncertainty: Heuristics and Biases. *Science* 185: 1124–31.

Turing, Alan Mathison 1950. Computing Machinery and Intelligence. *Mind,* 59, 422-460.

Winograd, Terry. 1972. *Understanding Natural Language.* New York: Academic Press.

Woolridge, Dean E. 1963. *The Machinery of the Brain.* New York: McGraw Hill.

Zytkow, Jan M. 1990. Deriving Laws through Analysis of Processes and Equations. In *Computational Models of Discovery and Theory Formation,* ed. Pat. Langley and J. Shrager, 129–156. San Mateo, CA: Morgan Kaufmann Publishers.

Index